the tucci cookbook

also by stanley tucci

The Tucci Table

the tucci cookbook

stanley tucci

with joan and stan tucci,
gianni scappin, and mimi taft

recipes previously published in *Cucina & Famiglia*

GALLERY BOOKS

new york • *london* • *toronto* • *sydney* • *new delhi*

The author is donating 10 percent of his advance and 25 percent of any of his subsequent earnings from this book (in each case net of agency fees) to the Food Bank for New York City. To learn more, please visit foodbanknyc.org.

Gallery Books
A Division of Simon & Schuster, Inc.
1230 Avenue of the Americas
New York, NY 10020

First Gallery Books hardcover edition October 2012

Recipes previously published in *Cucina & Famiglia*

GALLERY BOOKS and colophon are registered trademarks of Simon & Schuster, Inc.

For information about special discounts for bulk purchases, please contact Simon & Schuster Special Sales at 1-866-506-1949 or business@simonandschuster.com.

The Simon & Schuster Speakers Bureau can bring authors to your live event. For more information or to book an event contact the Simon & Schuster Speakers Bureau at 1-866-248-3049 or visit our website at www.simonspeakers.com.

Designed by Jaime Putorti
Photographer and Food Stylist: Francesco Tonelli
Prop Stylist: Deborah Williams

Manufactured in the United States of America

10 9 8 7 6 5 4 3

Library of Congress Cataloging-in-Publication Data
Tucci, Stanley.
  The Tucci cookbook : family, friends, and food / Stanley Tucci.
     p. cm.—(Gallery original nonfiction hardcover)
1. Cooking, Italian. I. Title.
  TX723.T83 2012
  641.5945—dc23
                          2012011322
  ISBN 978-1-4516-6125-5
  ISBN 978-1-4516-6128-6 (ebook)

We dedicate this book to our respective families and to yours

contents

Stanley at the age of three in Depew Park, Peekskill, New York

preface

by stanley tucci

Throughout my childhood, almost every night in the middle of dinner, my father would shake his head and ask, "What does the rest of the world eat?" That's how good my mother's cooking has always been—to my dad, it was inconceivable that anyone could possibly eat as well as we did. And I agreed with him every time.

Today, as an adult who has traveled enough to have experienced a number of cultures and cuisines, I still agree with my father. Not that I haven't discovered incredibly delicious dishes outside the old homestead, but for consistent ingenuity and excellence, my mother's cooking is hard to beat. I am all too aware of the cliché at work here: the eldest son of an Italian American family saying, in essence, that no one cooks as well as his mother. But in this case it is not mere sentiment that leads me to this conclusion, but a sensitive and discerning palate.

Whether this palate is a God-given gift or something that has been honed over the years, I cannot say. I would think it is a little bit of both. Having grown up in a household that was "food obsessed," I cannot help but put a more-than-ordinary emphasis on what goes into my mouth and how it tastes. My family spends hours deciding what to make for a certain meal and days preparing it, and while the food is being eaten, discusses not only its merits and its faults, but what it tasted like when prepared at such and such a restaurant, or by this and that family member or friend, and what it really should be served with, which inevitably leads to a discussion of where it was first eaten and with what, and how *that* dish was prepared and how one day wouldn't it really be nice to make that dish, which really is one of the best dishes ever eaten, though it could never compare to a dish once eaten in . . . and so on and so on.

Food, above politics, art, or personal matters, is the subject to which we return over and over again. Possibly because we derive nourishment from it not only physically but spiritually, and to us, the creation of a great meal is perhaps the ultimate artistic endeavor. Edible art.

There is some truth to the old adage "Most of the world eats to live, but Italians live to eat." My parents instilled in my sisters and me a great respect for our heritage and its traditions. Consequently, in my work I feel it is necessary to explore and celebrate from whom and where I come. The film *Big Night* was born partly from this need. In writing it with my cousin Joseph Tropiano, I hoped to offer not only a positive view of Italians (i.e., no gangsters) but a more humanistic view, one that would show the complexity of this extraordinary people.

During the final stages of writing the script, Isabella Rossellini was kind enough to enable me to visit any of her friend Pino Luongo's six restaurants so I might continue my research. I chose Le Madri, where I was introduced to the head chef, Gianni Scappin. For the next year and a half I would visit him and he would teach me whatever I asked to be taught. We would also spend hours just talking about food, restaurants, Italy versus America, my hopes for the film, and his hopes for his own restaurant.

Little did Gianni know that in so many ways he influenced my creation of the character that I played in the film. I ended up using many of his inflections, intonations, and gestures as Secondo. This, coupled with his knowledge of Italian cuisine and the machinations of running a restaurant, was invaluable.

The fact that Gianni is from northern Italy was also of great value to me. I learned a great deal about the similarities and vast differences between northern and southern Italian cuisine from him, which is fascinating to me and a big part of the inspiration for this book. I am the grandson of Calabrian immigrants, and most of the food both sides of my family cooked was primarily from that region. After I had introduced Gianni to my parents and saw that they were fast becoming friends, it occurred to me that a cookbook combining the recipes of two northern and southern Italian families would be a wonderful opportunity for them to share their personal and culinary histories with anyone who loves a good story and good food.

Also, for selfish reasons, I did not want the recipes that I had grown up with to disappear with the passing of my parents in years to come. The influence of these dishes has been so significant in shaping who I am that I felt it would be foolish if they were not documented for me, my children, and future generations. I knew Gianni felt the same way about his family's recipes as well.

As I got to know Gianni better, I realized that not only was he an intelligent, witty, and generous person, but he was also an artist. To watch him create a meal is fascinating. He is a whirlwind of passion and professionalism, and if you are ever fortunate enough to taste the results of his culinary expertise, you will understand what I mean when I use the word "artist."

While working side by side with Gianni in the ensuing years, I have learned quite a bit about him, his family, and the history that inspired him to become a chef. He was raised in the tiny village of Mason Vicentino, which is located halfway between Venice and Verona in the area of Italy known as the Veneto. This region is very close to the Austrian border, and over the centuries, due to war and politics, the Veneto has alternated between Austrian and Italian rule. This has greatly influenced the local culture and cuisine—which I think is evident in some of Gianni's recipes.

Gianni grew up in a modest, frugal home with a brother and three sisters. His parents worked hard running the family restaurant, Trattoria alla Pesa, and at age fourteen, Gianni began his own pursuit of a culinary career. He attended Recoaro Terme Culinary Institute, which offers an extensive externship program, and as a result, he worked in the kitchens of luxury hotels all over Italy—in Piedmont, Emilia-Romagna, Liguria, Lombardy, Trentino Alto Adige, and Sardinia. With each assignment he became familiar with the variety of ingredients and methods of preparation for which these different regions of Italy are known.

Gianni arrived in New York in 1983, after having worked in England, where he learned English, and at the Excelsior Hotel on the Lido in Venice, where he learned to work with large teams of other cooks. When he became the executive chef of Castellano, a highly successful restaurant in New York, Gianni began adding home-style dishes to the menu—focaccia, tiramisu, and risotto, all of which were practically unknown in the United States at the time—and the popularity of Castellano skyrocketed, suddenly drawing celebrities such as Mick Jagger and Clint Eastwood.

Nine years later, after a stint in Washington, D.C., where his restaurant Bice was awarded three and a half stars by the *Washington Post,* Gianni became the head chef at Pino Luongo's Le Madri, where we met. It was during his years at Le Madri that Gianni developed the balance between sophistication and simplicity that you will find in his recipes.

It was a real treat to bring together my parents and Gianni to create this book, to listen to them talk about the preparation of food in great detail, comparing and contrasting their methods and watching them learn from each other. Since Gianni is a classically French-trained professional chef, and my mother is a self-taught, just plain great cook, one might assume their working methods and approaches would be very different. But as it turns out, this was not necessarily true. Just like anyone who is very good at what he or she does, both Joan and Gianni are very specific about certain aspects of preparing a dish, such as dough-kneading techniques, the exact size to dice a carrot, what type of frying pan to use. But when it came to measurements during the testing process, the answer from both of them was often, "it depends." Needless to say, this drove our collaborator Mimi a bit mad, as she was the one who had to document with as much exactitude as possible the proper measurements for each recipe. However, as you will see, it all worked out in the end.

There is a strong connection between *Big Night* and this book. I've always felt that film was partly about respect for one's heritage and the pursuit of truth in one's art. To me this cookbook embodies those themes. It is a collection of recipes by people I love, who love to cook because they love their past and want to pass its truths on to the next generation.

In each recipe, we have worked hard to document those often elusive touches and techniques that result in a great meal as opposed to an ordinary one. By worrying over each detail—for the first time in either the Tucci or the Scappin family history—we have committed to paper the ingredients needed to create a collection of extraordinary meals that reflect the land and the people we came from and that give us so much joy day after day. We hope this cookbook becomes a source for as many of your own unforgettable meals as its recipes have for ours.

Buon appetito!

Gianni Scappin and Stanley at Le Madri in the mid-1990s

Stanley in front of the brick oven in his backyard

February 13, 1960, Joan and Stan Sr.'s wedding day. From left, Pop Tropiano, Mom Concetta, Stan, Joan, Mom Teresa, and Pop Stanislao

Italian stone carvers and their families at a three-day picnic in Northfield, Vermont, circa 1910

an introduction
to the tropiano and tucci families

JOAN TROPIANO TUCCI

Over the years as our children established homes of their own, I found that I was regularly receiving calls from them asking how one or another of their favorite dishes was made. When Stan and I retired, we had the time to compile a list of our combined family favorites using a software program that formatted recipes—even giving you the breakdown of calories for each ingredient. At first we shared these recipes with just our children, but after *Big Night,* we received requests for recipes from far and wide.

Fortunately, when we had the opportunity to create a cookbook, we already had many of the Tucci and Tropiano recipes written up. To personalize the book further, we decided to tell the stories of our two families and how their individual histories came together in the meals we share, whether at special occasions or as simple weekday dinners. I relied on my memories of stories that I had been told and, when in doubt, consulted my siblings as I wove together this family chronology.

My father, Vincenzo Tropiano, was born in 1896 in Cittanova, Italy. After serving as a battlefield medic during World War I, he emigrated to the United States in 1917 in search of work. He wound up living in Verplanck, New York, near Peekskill, leaving behind his parents, four sisters, two brothers, and fiancée, all of whom he hoped would join him in America once he got settled. But only his sister, Anna, ended up coming to New York. His other three sisters—Carmela, Giovanna (for whom I was named), and Concetta—stayed in Calabria and married local boys, while his brothers found work in France. Throughout his forty years working at the Trap Rock Corporation, Pop, as we called him, was the breadwinner for both the family he was raising and the one he left behind, regularly mailing money, clothing, and other items back to Italy.

Concetta Trimarchi, my mom, was born in 1908 and came to the United States with her family when she was six years old. Her family opened a boardinghouse in Verplanck, where my mom worked—she worked so hard as a young girl that she only completed school through the sixth grade. But she continued to teach herself at home, writing in Italian and English, reading avidly, and eventually taking care of all the household finances.

Even after she married, Mom continued to work hard—both at raising her five children and at her job on the assembly line at Standard Brands. Yet somehow, in addition to her eight-hour workday, she still found time to pickle green tomatoes, can pears and peaches, bottle eggplants, peppers, and tomatoes, make beer and root beer, bake her own bread, and, in her spare time, do the laundry, sewing, cooking, and baking.

My parents met through mutual friends—Verplanck had a large Italian population—and in 1926 decided to marry, but first Pop had to send a letter to his fiancée in Italy to let her know. Needless to say, she wasn't happy about the news, and when she wrote him back she enclosed a pair of scissors to symbolize the severing of their relationship. I don't know if it's an Italian tradition or not, but in my family whenever we give someone a knife or scissors as a gift, we always put a shiny new penny in with it to show that it is given with good intentions.

Vincenzo and Concetta had a long and happy marriage, celebrating more than sixty wedding anniversaries together and raising five children: Grace, Joseph, Angelina, Giovanna (me), and Vincent. Our first home was a two-family house set on a large piece of property on Verplanck's Point—my family lived downstairs, my cousin Katherine lived with her family upstairs, and my grandmother lived with us and helped raise us while my parents were at work.

The house on the Point was basically a mini-farm. Fruit trees were in abundance—cherry, mulberry, peach, plum, pear, fig—and Pop cultivated a wonderful grape arbor. We raised rabbits, pigs, turkeys, a cow, goats, and chickens. Everyone helped in the garden, tilling the soil and planting in the spring, harvesting and canning in the fall. Pop worked a full day at Trap Rock and then, during the long days of the warmer months, he worked another half day in the garden. That was his health club.

We were surrounded by relatives and neighbors and shared each other's happiness and grief through good times and bad. As children we felt safe and secure in this environment.

Around 1958, my parents moved into another two-family house on Broadway, closer to town, where I lived for two years before I married Stan. I thought Pop was very brave to undertake building a house at the age of sixty. The garden was smaller but large enough for the two of them, and there was always extra if any of us needed vegetables. Pop planted several fruit trees, including wonderful fig trees. All the animals were gone, except for a few rabbits, which he enjoyed raising. He built a big outdoor fireplace for grilling and for boiling the large vat of water they used to bottle tomatoes every fall. We have photographs of our son, Stanley, around age three, helping Pop to build this fireplace.

Pop brought cuttings from the original grape arbor on the Point to the new house, building a new arbor that expanded as our family grew. Tables were arranged beneath the grapes and the makeshift awning that Pop fashioned out of a tarp to protect us from the hot sun or rain when we gathered to celebrate occasions at my parents' house. Everyone brought food, and in most of the photographs of these gatherings you can see coolers lined up against the side of the house, filled with each family's contribution to the meal. Those coolers hardly ever went home empty. They were usually refilled with loads of freshly picked fruits and vegetables from my parents' garden.

One of our most important family gatherings was held every July for the Feast of Our Lady of Mount Carmel. Pop was a charter member of the Our Lady of Mount Carmel Society, and my brothers, Joe and Vinnie, are still members. The feast began on Thursday night and ended on a Sunday evening with a tremendous fireworks display, attracting people from all over the area.

On Sunday there was a special mass—my sister Angie, who has a beautiful operatic voice, sang at it—followed by a procession, where members of the society, accompanied by visiting marching bands, carried a statue of Our Lady of Mount Carmel through the village. Every year my sisters and I got new dresses for the occasion; we would always march behind Pop, carrying our flags and following the band. For many years, he had the honor of carrying the statue. It was draped with a sash that people would pin money to as the parade passed by. This always brought tears to the eyes of my family members, although I'm not sure why—emotional Italians, I guess!

What I looked forward to was the celebration after the parade. My parents would invite friends, neighbors, and visiting band members to share in the feast and help us celebrate this wonderful saint's day. Forty people were nothing to feed! We all helped with the cooking and cleaning and were happy to do it.

In addition to the feast, we had our traditional family bocce game. The competition was fierce—my sister Grace especially hated to lose. The family game always ended with cries of "Wait until next year" and hugs all around. Then the game was turned over to the children and non–family members.

When Stan and I were first married, we lived in Peekskill, New York; shortly after Stanley was born, we moved to an apartment in Mount Kisco, which was close to Stan's new job at Horace Greeley High School. We got to know our landlords, Mary and Angelo Cascioli, very well. Angelo enjoyed fishing in the nearby reservoirs. When he caught perch, Mary would flour and pan-fry the fillets. She always sent some upstairs for Stanley, who, at age two, greatly enjoyed them.

Occasionally Mary and Angelo would invite us downstairs to join them, their granddaughters, Pam and Maria, their son, Vincent, and daughter-in-law, Mary, for dinner. Mary would place a huge oval board in the center of the table, onto which she would pour cooked polenta. The polenta was then topped with a ragù sauce of stewed meat and meatballs. Each person was given a fork and we ate toward the center, incorporating a little polenta in the sauce for each bite. At the beginning of the meal one of the children would ask for a meatball, but Angelo would tell them they had to eat their way in before they could have one. Young Stanley and I enjoyed this fun and delicious meal, but Stan had a hard time sharing at the communal board and usually opted to eat something else.

Our daughter Gina was born in 1964, and the following year we bought a house in Katonah, New York, where Christine was born in 1967 and where we still live today. Our lives were busy and full of family activities. As often as possible we got together with my family and Stan's, so this generation of children got to know one another very well.

In 1973, Stan had an opportunity to take a year's sabbatical in Florence, Italy. Little did we know what a lasting influence it would have on us as well as on our three small children. Stan studied sculpture, the children attended school, becoming fluent in Italian, and I went to bookstores to learn about the wonderful northern Italian food. Although my Italian was limited, I knew enough to read recipes. Tortellini, *lasagne verde,* rice salad—I wanted to eat like a Florentine and taught myself to cook like one. Today I still enjoy making those recipes.

My parents came to visit, and we all traveled to Calabria together. My mom had returned to Italy only a few times before, but Pop had gone back as often as he could, traveling by boat on a round-trip journey that took four weeks to complete. It was not easy for him to leave his wife and five children for such a long stretch; I always thought he was very brave.

Our visit to Calabria to see Pop's sisters and their families was quite an adventure. We slept on straw mattresses and were awakened by a donkey braying early in the morning, and Stan shaved looking into a broken mirror hanging in the chicken coop. I recall the children being mesmerized by the photographs of relatives in their coffins that lined the bedroom dresser. And of course, we ate really well—grilled rabbit, goat, homemade crepes, bruschetta made with home-pressed olive oil as green as spring trees—and we laughed a lot. I would not have missed it for the world.

When Pop retired after forty years of working for the Trap Rock Corporation, the company honored him for all his hard work by naming a barge after him, the *Vincenzo Tropiano.* For several years we saw it on the Hudson River; now my nephew Joseph sees it in Long Island Sound, near his home in Greenwich. Pop enjoyed his retirement and continued to work hard in his garden. He loved to experiment with grafting different fruit trees—always trying new things, like splicing a branch of a peach tree onto a pear tree in an attempt to come up with some exotic fruit!

After Pop died in 1987 at the age of ninety-one, Mom continued to garden, along with my brothers, and she continued to cook, but she complained about being lonely. This usually meant that only five people had come to visit instead of eight or ten. Her neighbors teased her, claiming Mom had so much company she needed valet parking!

Mom had always been very independent. She had tried to teach Pop to drive, but he almost hit the garage and that ended it. She continued to drive until her early eighties although her eyesight was failing, and eventually my brother Vince had to take her keys away. This cramped her style because when she baked something she wanted it to be delivered right away. My brothers and their wives lived nearby, and they helped Mom out during the week. On the weekends she would go to stay with her daughters. I always knew we would be cooking a lot when Mom came to visit.

Mom was a great storyteller. All the children came around when she was visiting, and my daughter Gina especially enjoyed spending time with her just to listen to her stories about growing up. Mom was proud of all her grandchildren and was anxious to share her words of wisdom with them. She never understood how we ended up with two actors in our family, and she often suggested to Stanley and Christine that they get regular office jobs. They laughed and told her not to worry. But how Mom bragged when Chris was on a soap opera or Stanley was in a movie—especially when they were on TV and all her friends could watch. She had to sit very close to the television, but just hearing their voices made her happy. It was especially thrilling for her to see her grandsons Stanley and Joseph sharing the limelight at a special viewing of the movie *Big Night* that was held in the Paramount Center for the Arts in Peekskill. The performance was sold out and the audience was full of family, friends, and neighbors from the community where we had all grown up.

When Mom died in 1997, at age eighty-eight, she had twenty-three grandchildren and twenty great-grandchildren. She and Pop taught us the significance of family and we all understood that preparing and sharing food together would continue to be a central part of our family life.

In 1997, Stan and I had the opportunity to return to Italy with his sister Rosalinda and her husband, Lee. We again traveled to Calabria to visit many of the same family members we had seen with Mom and Pop in 1973. Pop's sisters Carmella and Concetta are still alive, maintaining the family traditions. Fig trees and homemade soppressata, salami, pasta, and wine are still a big part of their lives, and our family still figures in the stories they tell. Carmella, Concetta, and their families were like drapes around us, smothering us with their love.

Now that Stanley, Gina, and Christine have grown up, it seems that we never have enough time together—but we do still get together for holidays and dinners on most weekends. Our extended family has grown to such an extent that it is difficult to find a home where we all fit.

My sister Grace and her husband, Tony, have a large enclosed, heated patio, reminiscent of the tarp-covered arbor my father built on the Point, where we have held many a great Easter egg hunt. The entertainment at these events was often provided by Stanley on drums, my nephew Joe (who cowrote the *Big Night* screenplay with Stanley) on keyboard, and occasionally my daughter Christine, who would sing for us—followed by tears and applause from all the adults as usual. But when they wanted to form a union and get paid, we fired them! I still keep a collection of instruments in the house so that during festive dinners we can take a break between courses, improvising while working up an appetite.

The Tucci and Tropiano children love to cook, and several of them are very inventive chefs. Food remains central in their lives as they establish their own families and households. The telephone calls requesting recipes continue to this day. For this book we selected recipes from our families, others we picked up during our year in Italy, some grew out of Stanley's friendship with Gianni Scappin in preparation for *Big Night,* and many recipes we have created on our own. Part of the fun of collaborating with Gianni was the conversations we had comparing the variations between dishes both our families made. Sometimes these could be attributed to the different parts of Italy where our families came from—his from the north, and mine and Stan's from the south—and sometimes it was just personal preference. What we share is a tendency to improvise; if I am missing one ingredient, such as an herb or a type of cheese, I substitute with what I have on hand. I hope you will find the recipes gathered in this book an inspiring beginning as you create your own family traditions.

STAN TUCCI

My family's history has always fascinated me. Over the years, I have researched the Tuccis' ancestry, adding information and gradually tracing our lineage back to the 1600s. It's very satisfying for me to put together the puzzle pieces that add up to our particular story, and I enjoy sharing the information I've gathered with my children and grandchildren. In writing this, I didn't think it was necessary to go back to Greek and Roman times to trace my family's love for food, so I will begin the Tucci family history with my grandparents.

In 1905 my mother's parents, Domenico and Apollonia Pisani, left their mountain-top village of Serra San Bruno in Calabria, Italy, and traveled to Naples, where they planned to board the ship *Sicilia* that would take them to America. They were accompanied by a relative and their five children: my mother, Teresa, and her siblings, Ralph, Dominic, Henry, and Candida. When the family arrived in Naples, they discovered that something was wrong with Henry's eyes. He returned to Serra San Bruno with the relative who had accompanied them to Naples and remained in Italy with his grandparents for two years until he was finally reunited with his family in America.

The Pisani family settled in Northfield, Vermont, joining Apollonia's brother, Emilio Politi, who was already established there. Northfield was one of several Vermont hill towns around Barre where work could be found cutting granite, marble, and slate. Drawn by the promise of work, hundreds of Italians journeyed there every year. The community my grandparents joined was so heavily populated by Italians that the area was nicknamed "Spaghetti Square" because of all the fresh pasta drying on outdoor racks.

My grandfather Domenico moved to America to find work and because he wanted his sons to avoid Italy's mandatory military service. He had spent four unhappy years in the Italian cavalry and did not want his boys to suffer as he had. Ironically, time and circumstances conspired and his two oldest sons, Dominic and Ralph, served in the U.S. Army during World War I. Henry was too young for World War I and too old for World War II. However, Edwin, the youngest son, served in World War II, and three of Domenico's grandsons served in the armed forces during World War II and the Korean conflict.

My father, Stanislao, was born in 1889 in the small town of Marzi in Consenza, Italy, the second son of Francesco and Rosa Tucci. Pop had three brothers: Rosario, Angelo, and Vincenzo, and a sister, Marina. My grandfather Francesco was a stonecutter all his life. His search for work in the mid-nineteenth century took him to Egypt, India, and the United States. In 1904 Pop, at age fifteen, sailed from Italy to the United States on the *Neckar* with a cousin and joined his brother Rosario in Vermont. Upon his arrival, Pop lived for a short time in the crowded community of Little Italy in New York City. He was fond of telling us that the apartment he shared with other Italians was so crowded that there was no more sleeping space, even on the floor, so he slept on the fire escape. Pop soon left the city and headed north to Northfield, Vermont, where he had heard that he could find stonecutting work.

In advance of his moving to Northfield, Pop arranged to take a room in a boardinghouse run by Emilio and Maria Politi. The Politi boardinghouse was located next door to that of my grandparents, the Pisanis. My mom, Teresa, heard a lot of gossip about the crazy Cosentino who was coming to board next door. When she first saw Pop she thought the comments were true because he walked into the house carrying a rifle!

Pop apprenticed as a stonecutter. Within a few years he had gained a reputation and respect among his peers as a master of carving and lettering in stone. When I was a young man we would travel together to New York City and Pop would proudly point out the facades of various buildings that displayed his stone carving, including the Corinthian column capitals of the Soldier's and Sailor's Monument on Riverside Drive and some of the window tracery on the Cathedral of Saint John the Divine.

Eventually Pop and my mom began a chaperoned courtship. Mom was working in a clothing store in Northfield. Pop would visit her during his lunch break from his stonecutting job at Cross Brothers, which was located one block away. Pop tended to overextend these visits, which made him late getting back to work. He had a friend whose job it was to blow the factory horn, the signal that everyone should be back at work. He told Pop, "I'll blow the horn five minutes before the actual time and that will be a warning to you. This way you will not be late when the second and final horn blows." When I visited Northfield about thirty years later, the tradition of blowing two horns was still in practice—although no one seemed to know why.

My parents were married in February 1914. Pop recalled that it was so cold that day that the top hinge of the front door was frosted over. He used the frozen hinges as a type of thermometer. If the lowest hinge on the door was frozen, the temperature was 10 degrees below freezing; a frozen middle hinge meant 20 degrees below; a frozen top hinge indicated a temperature at least 30 degrees below freezing.

Shortly after my parents were married, they moved to Peekskill, and in 1915 my brother Frank was born. There were quarries in Peekskill where Pop found work, and a few years later, he and his brother Rosario purchased a retail monument business in nearby Van Cortlandtville, establishing the Tucci Brothers Monument Works.

In 1936, the two brothers decided to go their separate ways. Rosario named his business "Tucci Memorials" and Pop named his "Stanley Tucci and Son."

After a series of moves, the Tucci and Pisani families purchased a duplex home on Washington Street in Peekskill. This is the house I grew up in, along with my brother, Frank, and my two sisters, Dora and Rosalinda. My mom's parents lived in the other half of the house with my two unmarried uncles, Edwin and Henry, and my unmarried aunt, Emilia.

Our extended family of uncles, aunts, and cousins lived either within walking or short driving distance from this duplex. Our home served as a center for innumerable large family gatherings. Actually, most of the family stopped by every evening. I was nurtured by this intense family life throughout my elementary and high school years.

When I graduated from high school, I pursued a degree in art education at the State University of New York at Buffalo, and then went on to receive a master's in art education from Columbia University. In 1953, I volunteered for the draft, requesting an August or September induction so I could more easily apply for a teaching position after completing the two years of compulsory service in the army.

In 1955, I was living at home and began to teach art at the Drum Hill Junior High School in Peekskill. At the end of the school year, I enrolled in a two-month art study tour that was part of Columbia University's summer program. We toured the ancient art centers of eight western European countries, including Italy. This was my first trip to my parents' native land, and no city captivated me more than Florence. I knew that somehow I would return there to live. I continued to teach at the junior high for five more years. In an effort to return to Italy, I decided to apply for a teaching position at the U.S. military base in Naples.

Shortly before accepting the position, I attended a local church picnic. I was alone, and Joan was there with a date who spent most of his time playing cards. Joan and I walked together to watch another picnic group that was dancing to the rhythm of empty beer cans knocked together. From that August day on, we spent some part of every day together. When we decided to marry, I discovered that the military could not guarantee that Joan would be allowed to join me in Naples. I was not as adventurous as my Italian ancestors who had bravely left Italy and their families behind when they came to America, so I chose to stay in the United States with Joan and we were married six months after we met.

Eighteen years went by before I had another opportunity to return to Italy. In 1973, while teaching at Horace Greeley High School in Chappaqua, New York, I received a sabbatical to study figurative sculpture at the Accademia di Belle Arti in Florence. Our year in Italy was probably the most important move my family and I ever made. The effects are evident in so much of our lives today—the language, culture, art, music, family, and food, food, food!

Our trip to Italy strongly influenced Joan's cooking. When Joan and I got married she did not have any cooking experience to speak of. I don't know if this is universally true, but in the homes of the Italian American families I knew, the girls never did any cooking prior to marriage. All the cooking was done by the mother, and often the father participated in the preparation of meals. Yet all these young girls, upon marriage, became wonderful cooks. My guess is that food, family, and tradition are such an integral part of the Italian heritage that there is a subconscious obligation and a desire to cook as well as their mothers did. Joan has an endless curiosity about food paired with a willingness to test new ideas, ingredients, and techniques that has resulted in her becoming an excellent, confident home cook.

Perhaps the most important consequence of our trip to Italy was that our children had an opportunity to understand that our family traditions extended beyond ourselves and are connected to a complex, strong, and ancient culture. Stanley and Gina continue to speak Italian today. Gina majored in Italian at college, and currently teaches English as a second language in New York State's Valley Central School District. Christine, who was only six the year we lived in Florence, was somewhat less influenced by the trip, but she did have the best Italian pronunciation of the three children. However, all three of the children remember our frequent visits to museums, churches, and galleries in Florence, Venice, and Rome. When we returned to America, I suggested going to visit a museum and they ran from the room shouting "No!" But their love of art and culture is strong today and surely must be rooted in our time in Italy.

The influence of our trip is also, I believe, evident in Stanley's first directorial effort, *Big Night*. This story of two immigrant Italians running a restaurant in New Jersey in the 1950s uses food as a metaphor for the conflict between art and commerce. Stanley's preparation for *Big Night* led to our meeting Gianni Scappin, whom Stanley apprenticed with after he and his cousin Joseph finished writing the movie's screenplay. Our conversations with Gianni always came around to food, and we found that, despite the different parts of Italy that our families came from, we shared a common appreciation for the traditions that shaped the meals we prepared for our families and friends. Joan and Gianni's collaboration has resulted in a cookbook that brings together wonderful examples of northern and southern Italian family cooking. The recipes Joan has contributed to this book—at least half of which originated with my family—focus on vegetables and pasta. Their preparation always involves the use of olive oil, a reflection of the southern Italian agricultural tradition. Gianni's recipes include the use of dairy products, which are in abundance in the north of Italy.

Joan and Gianni brought together very different qualifications to the process of creating this book. Gianni is professionally trained and has had a wide range of experiences, while Joan's many years as a home cook were defined by her compulsive desire not only to learn but to create new recipes. They both have a wonderful sense of humor that is displayed when they are working together in the kitchen. Joan loves to tease Gianni about his English (which he speaks very well!) and Gianni loves to tease Joan about anything from our electric stove to the size of our frying pans. But when we are together we mostly enjoy discussing food.

While we are in the midst of cooking a meal, we talk about variations on those recipes, critique other meals we have eaten, talk about meals we are looking forward to, wonder what we should eat the next time we are together. I think it is no exaggeration to say that when two Italians get together, within five minutes they will be discussing food. It is from this environment that Joan began her cooking journey, and this book is infused with that spirit.

Tucci timpano pan

a note about wine

by tyler coleman

Is a 1971 Barolo from Giacomo Conterno the perfect wine pairing for Joan and Gianni's Risotto alla Milanese? While I would relish the opportunity to try the two together, I certainly wouldn't push back from the table in disgust if other wines were offered with the dish, such as a younger nebbiolo or an earthy red Burgundy. The fact is, when it comes to pairing food and wine, there's often no one right answer.

Unfortunately, many diners think there is only one wine that they should have with a given dish. Generally, this is because they read somewhere or heard as much from someone in passing. But if it's not available, the angst of finding a replacement wine often ends in frustration. And everyone knows that angst and fine food make for terrible dinner partners.

On the flip side of the precision of finding the perfect wine, others simply scoff at the notion of pairing wine and food. If they like only a big red Châteauneuf-du-Pape, for example, then they will have that with Maryland crab cakes or Chinese food, turning a deaf ear to the advice of oenophiles. It's hard to argue against pairing the wines you like with the foods you like—indeed, a recent survey found that most wine in America is actually consumed away from food, so it's not wrong to simply opt for the wine you like. Still, it's not exactly pushing the gustatory envelope. Moreover, some pairings do bomb and you'd like to avoid them—and you'd hate for the sommelier to come storming out to your table the way Primo did in *Big Night* when a diner ordered pasta and potato dishes together.

So I suggest a middle ground, one that avoids the frustration of looking for the one perfect wine yet is more adventuresome than the "one wine fits all" approach of simply having the same wine for every meal. There are a few classic pairings that really hit the ball out of the park, such as: oysters and Muscadet; a pale, dry sherry and Marcona almonds; roast chicken and a cru Beaujolais; port and Stilton; and on the more luxurious side, white truffles and Barolo or foie gras and Sauternes. But generally there are plenty of combinations that will work well no matter the meal.

The approach here suggests thinking about wine by style and then offers a style of wine that will work with a given dish from this cookbook. I make some specific picks for each style of wine at the end of this section. But first we need to discuss some generalities for success in pairing food and wine.

PAIRING

Pairing wine and food is both an art and a science. Here are six simple suggestions:

1. **Wines with higher acidity than the food really sing.** Squeezing a lemon with its bright acidity onto a fish filet enlivens the taste; the same is true with wines that have higher acidity. Wines with higher acidity pair magically with rich, creamy foods, fish dishes especially; they are incredibly versatile and that's why they are often on my table and will be recommended a lot with these recipes. Some examples of these wines include: sauvignon blanc, champagne, Riesling, or Muscadet for whites, and Pinot Noir, Gamay, or sangiovese for reds. Dry rosés also have great acidity.

2. **Avoid power struggles.** If the dish is spicy, such as Angry Penne (page 133), bow to its supremacy and serve a light wine; trying to outmuscle it with a 16 percent alcohol Zinfandel can only lead to unleashing the gustatory equivalent of a heavyweight title bout in your mouth. If you really want to serve a huge wine, try a lighter dish; the obverse also applies.

3. **Sweet tames spice.** Potent spices don't feature too much in the recipes here, but as a general rule of thumb, having some gentle sweetness to the wine can moderate the spice.

4. **Tannins crave meat.** Tannins give red wine a chompy, dry bitterness—think oversteeped tea—that can be off-putting when a wine is young. However, those

same tannins provide a structure for aging, as with nebbiolo or Bordeaux, and complement the fat and protein of meat.

5. **With sweet wine and dessert, one is always a loser.** Similar to avoiding a power struggle between a big wine and a rich food, pairing a sweet wine and a sweet dessert will likely result in only one winner. A sweet wine will end up tasting less sweet, just as a dessert made with berries will taste bitter by contrast. Thus, with rare exceptions, it's one or the other—either dessert or dessert wine, not both. Many ultrasweet wines actually pair well with savory foods, such as the classic pairing of port and Stilton.

6. **If it grows together, it goes together.** This saying comes from the local, seasonal food movement, but it is readily applicable to wine. Simply, regional foods pair well with regional wines. Think about mortadella and Lambrusco, both from Emilia-Romagna (the region around Bologna), which represent one of those classic pairings where the food and the wine improve each other. White truffles and Barolo certainly qualify, as do Serrano ham and Rioja and charcuterie with white wines from Alsace.

Because wine pairing can cause undue anxiety, it's good to have a wine that you can turn to in an emergency that has a high rate of versatility and success. That wine is champagne. Champagne is often saved for toasts and boat christenings, but it is actually remarkably food-friendly. If you've never had a bowl of popcorn (try popping it with coconut oil!) and a glass of champagne while watching your favorite movie, a tremendous treat awaits you. Moreover, it turns regular meals into celebratory occasions; it really is the host's ace in the hole. Of course, the budget does not always allow champagne, but there are some very serviceable options from the world of sparkling wine, including cava and prosecco, the Spanish and Italian equivalent of French champagne.

One final topic worth noting is alcohol levels in wine. The past decade or two have seen a notable rise in alcohol levels in part because of global warming and also because winemakers have chosen to make their wines that way. While the calorie-conscious may love the efficiency of faster intoxication, when it comes to food, higher alcohol content can get in the way in part because you can have fewer glasses of it while remaining good at dinner conversation and in part because higher alcohol wines tend to have lower acidity, making them less agile food partners.

WINES HAVE STYLE

Open the wine list at a restaurant with a progressive wine program and you will often see wines sorted by flavor profile, not by grape or region. Organizing a list according to how each wine tastes in the glass makes sense given the restaurant setting, where wine is expressly meant to pair with food. Also, it is often more user-friendly to choose a wine based on flavor or style as opposed to going by grapes or regions, since some grape varieties have many wine guises. Take Riesling, for example. From the Clare Valley in Australia, the wines are bone-dry with a laserlike acidity. But from the Mosel, the wines have a little (or sometimes a lot) of residual sugar to balance the acidity and make the wines a little more round, or full-bodied. The same could be said of Pinot Noir. The grape naturally has a high acidity, but various renditions run the gamut of lean, to minerally earthy, to high alcohol and woody.

So that's how I'll be making the wine pairings in this book: by style. Generally, there are six styles, a light, medium, and full-bodied style for both whites and reds. There are also the discrete categories of sparkling, rosé, and dessert wines to cover. Let's do the tour, starting with the whites.

Lighter-bodied whites: With the decline in the popularity of oaky Chardonnay, this racy category that includes sauvignon blanc, Pinot Grigio, and dry Riesling has taken off. This category also includes "patio pounders" such as vinho verde, a simple choice for outdoor dining that lets the food really shine. The wines are mostly fruit-forward, have a lean acidity that make them food-friendly, and are unburdened by oak.

Middleweight whites: These wines have a bit more structure and are more serious than simple quaffers. The structure that sets them apart is a mineral quality that's reminiscent of wet stones. To taste the structure I am describing, consider the difference between a Chardonnay from somewhere like Australia as opposed to a Chablis, which is made from the Chardonnay grape. The Chablis is likely to have a more stony quality thanks to the cooler climate and the fact that the grape vines actually are grown in soils with chalk, limestone, and fossilized seashells. Try the same experiment with a New Zealand sauvignon blanc and a French Sancerre, which grow in similar soil to Chablis. Other examples of this category include some white Burgundies, Muscadet, or Pinot Gris.

Fuller-bodied whites: The effect of fullness in a white wine can come from three things: sugar, oak, or alcohol. For the sugar, such as with Riesling or Gewürztraminer, the best examples are accompanied by an underlying acidity, which prevents the wines from feeling too heavy. Oak can be overdone if the wine sees a lot of new wood, which comes from putting the wine in new, small barrels for expensive wines or from putting the wood in the wine by way of dunking a giant bag of oak chips, as happens in lower-priced wines that want that oaky taste. More alcohol in the wine can make it seem fuller and, incidentally, sweeter. It takes a deft hand for the winemaker to pull off a fuller-bodied wine effectively. And in general, I prefer these wines with richer foods and usually in winter.

Lighter-bodied reds: With alluring fruit and palate-stimulating acidity, these lighter reds match a wide variety of dishes superbly. Lots of hugely enjoyable wines fall into this category, including some Pinot Noir, cru Beaujolais, Barbera, and Frappato to name a few. For people who prefer more full-throttle reds, they might seem like summer reds. But really their food-friendliness makes them irresistible all year-round. One summer twist is to serve them slightly chilled, as the low level of tannins can make them seem not astringent but rather refreshing that way.

Middleweight reds: This category has a bit more structure, including—you got it—more minerality as with their white counterparts. In this regard, Cabernet Franc from the Loire and Dolcetto are in line with the leaner style of reds. An unoaked Malbec lies right in the middle, while a California Merlot or oaked Malbec would be a plusher style middleweight.

Fuller-bodied reds: This is where the thunder rolls, the dark berry notes dominate, and oak or alcohol may be (overtly) present. These are the sort of "hedonistic fruit bombs" championed by some critics that can impress through a sheer show of force rather than subtlety. These include big Zinfandels, some Cabernet Sauvignons, southern Rhône wines, and many Australian shirazes. But this category isn't all over-the-top; there are northern Rhône syrahs with alluring black olive notes and some Zinfandels that have a pleasant spiciness, as do some Nero d'Avola. However, tread carefully when selecting a wine in this category, as some drink more like cocktails than companions for food.

Sparkling: Champagne is the best known sparkling wine. The cool climate and chalky soil of this region about a hundred miles to the east of Paris produce nervy, distinctive wines, often worthy of contemplation, as they are more food-friendly than commonly thought. Other sparkling wines include the more carefree prosecco from Italy, with its smaller, more gentle bubbles, or cava from Spain, as well as sparkling wine from California.

Dry rosé: Drinking the pink has become increasingly popular since the days when white Zinfandel was in vogue, but cloying, sweet wines have marred the reputation of dry rosés in the Provençal style. In the past few years, they have found a more receptive audience and have exploded in popularity. The good acidity and food-friendliness of this carefree wine also adds to the appeal.

Dessert wines: Ranging from ice wine to botrytized wines to fortified wines such as port, dessert wines still have a place at the table, even if people are drinking less of them. They go well with savory foods or in place of dessert, rather than with it. Madeira is the most exciting new dessert wine—and it's only four hundred years old. But it has become invigorated in the American market because the deliciously aromatic drink has a complexity that makes it suitable for pairing with dishes that precede the cheese course.

So herewith the style matrix:

	LIGHT	MEDIUM	FULL
White	New Zealand sauvignon blanc Pinot Grigio dry Riesling vinho verde	Sancerre Chablis Assyrtiko Pinot Gris	oaky Chardonnay Gewürztraminer Alsatian Riesling fiano
Red	Beaujolais Barbera Frappato some Pinot Noir	Loire Cabernet Franc Dolcetto Malbec Merlot	Cabernet Sauvignon shiraz Zinfandel northern Rhônes Nero d'Avola

GETTING THE MOST OUT OF WINE

Finally, here are three quick tips for getting the most out of the wine you drink, whichever style works for you.

1. **Have some good stemware.** Sure, what matters most is the wine *in* the glass, not the glass itself. And countless dinners have been merrily consumed in Italy with those squat, straight glasses for ages. But having a good crystal glass that tapers at the top can enhance the wine experience by concentrating the aromas. The glasses are not expensive; you can find a good, impact-resistant one for ten dollars. Splurge. And remember, you don't need to burden your cabinets with a different one for each grape variety from each region, as some are marketed.

2. **Find a good shop.** Bacchus delights in you having a relationship with a good local wine merchant. Go in, tell them the recipe in this book you are making and the suggested wine style, and see what they come up with. Take it home, try it. Go back and tell the same clerk what you thought of it. Or go in with a budget and ask for a few wines in various styles, keep the receipt near the corkscrew, and on it note your reactions to the wines. Take the receipt back to the store. This interpersonal feedback loop is where good local merchants excel, making them worth their weight in happily pulled corks.

3. **Chill a bottle in five minutes.** For those summer days or urgent needs for sparkling, keep a bucket on hand. Fill it with ice, then add some water, a good helping of salt (which lowers the freezing point of the water), and the wine bottle. Rotate or stir occasionally for best results.

SOME WINE PICKS

Whereas wine drinkers a generation ago suffered through limited wine selections (remember the prevalence of those straw-covered bottles of Chianti?), the amount and diversity of wines available today in America resembles a wine lover's Nirvana. Wines from obscure grapes and previously unheralded regions, both domestic and foreign, stream into wine stores and restaurants. A wine store manager may have to choose which wines to stock from literally thousands of selections. In the United States the TTB (Alcohol and Tobacco Tax and Trade Bureau), which regulates wine labels, has seen wine label applications double over the past ten years, to more than 130,000 in 2011.

While it can be hard to find specific wines, here are a few producers worth seeking out in the categories mentioned.

Champagne: Pierre Péters, Camille Savès, Roederer

Prosecco: Col Vetoraz, Nino Franco

Muscadet: Domaine de la Pépière, Jo Landron (Fief du Breil), Guy Bossard (Domaine de l'Ecu)

Chablis: Alice de Moor, William Fèvre, Vincent Dauvissat

California Chardonnay: Chateau Montelena, Ridge Vineyards, Mount Eden

Cru Beaujolais: Marcel Lapierre, Château Thivin, Jean-Paul Brun (Terres Dorées)

Loire Cabernet Franc: Domain Bernard Baudry, Catherine et Pierre Breton, Clos Rougeard

Barbera: Bera, Giacomo Conterno, De Forville

New World Pinot Noir: Copain Wine Cellars, Cristom, Rippon

Red Burgundy: Michel Lafarge, Domaine Ligier-Belair, Domaine Faiveley

Chianti: Montesecondo, Isole e Olena, Montevertine

Barolo: Giacamo Conterno, Giuseppe Mascarello, Teobaldo Cappellano

Syrah: Jean-Louis Chave, Thierry Allemand, Copain Wine Cellars

California Cabernet Sauvignon: Ridge Vineyards, Dominus, Chateau Montelena

Nero d'Avola: Arianna Occhipinti

appetizers and salads

antipasti ed insalate

My mother and I share an enthusiasm for that moment when family and friends arrive at our homes. We love the excitement of people coming through the door, embracing, talking, and greeting one another, and we take pleasure in introducing new visitors to the group. From my mother I learned the custom of always having an assortment of little dishes set out—olives, salami, cheese, and *biscotti* (twice-baked bread)—with wine or espresso at the ready so that guests feel warmly welcomed. To these little dishes I will add one of the appetizers from this section of the book. Many of them can be prepared in advance, as they store well and can generally be served at room temperature or easily reheated.

In the Veneto region of Italy, where Gianni comes from, they use the term *cicchetti* to describe these appetizers—it is a Venetian term for "little bites." Cicchetti may be as simple as half a hard-boiled egg topped with a slice of anchovy and drizzled with olive oil, or more complicated, such as sliced frittata. The appetizer recipes that follow will help whet the appetite for the following meal or make a meal in themselves when accompanied by a green salad and bread. And don't forget the wine!

bruschetta with tomato

bruschetta con pomodoro

There are endless ways of making bruschetta, but this is our favorite. You can leave the skins on the tomatoes or peel them. To make peeling easier, blanch the tomatoes in boiling water for a couple of minutes, then cool them in cold water to loosen the skins. The only rule with bruschetta is to use the best olive oil you can find, preferably a cold-pressed variety.

Bruschetta is a terrific hors d'oeuvre, but it doesn't lend itself to advance preparation—nothing is worse than soggy bruschetta. So the best way to prepare and serve it is to mix the tomatoes, garlic, and parsley in a small serving bowl, then toast the bread, rub it with garlic, and place it on a platter with the bowl of tomatoes. If you set this out along with other hors d'oeuvres—olives, soppressata, a hunk of Parmesan cheese—guests can serve themselves while you pour the wine.

4 medium-size ripe tomatoes, coarsely chopped

8 fresh basil leaves, chopped

1 tablespoon fresh Italian, flat leafed parsley, chopped

3 cloves garlic, finely chopped, plus 1 clove garlic, cut in half

¼ cup cold press or extra virgin olive oil

Kosher salt and freshly ground black pepper

4 slices Italian bread, toasted

Additional cold press or extra virgin olive oil to drizzle on top (optional)

In a medium-size bowl, mix the tomatoes, basil, parsley, chopped garlic, and olive oil, and season with salt and pepper. Rub the toasted bread with the garlic halves, then top with equal portions of the tomato mixture. Drizzle extra virgin olive oil on top if desired, and serve immediately.

— SERVES 4 —

WINE PAIRING: Sparkling, light white, and light red

recipe continued on next page

VARIATIONS: Grilled or toasted bread that has been rubbed with garlic may also be topped with:

Cauliflower: ½ head cauliflower florets boiled until tender, coarsely chopped, tossed with 3 tablespoons olive oil and 1 tablespoon red wine vinegar, and seasoned with salt and pepper.

Mushrooms: ½ pound mushrooms, coarsely chopped, 2 tablespoons chopped fresh Italian, flat leafed parsley, 2 teaspoons finely chopped garlic, and 2 tablespoons olive oil, cooked to soften over medium-high heat.

Charcuterie and cheese: A soft cheese such as Robiola, topped with a thin slice of cured sausage, prosciutto, speck, or salami

Eggplant Antipasto (page 10)

White Bean Antipasto (page 15)

Venetian Salted Cod Pâté (page 6)

marinated olives
olive marinate

This recipe is for spicy marinated olives. Serve them as part of an appetizer or to accompany a simple lunch. They also make a nice gift.

¼ cup fennel seeds

1 tablespoon cumin seeds

⅛ teaspoon ground cardamom

1 cup Picholine olives (mild, green)

1 cup Sicilian olives (small, green, oval)

1 cup kalamata olives (black)

1 cup extra virgin olive oil, plus more for covering

2 tablespoons loosely packed long thin strips orange zest (from about 1 orange)

5 cloves garlic

⅛ tablespoon red pepper flakes

1. Place the fennel seeds, cumin seeds, and ground cardamom in a small sauté pan set over low heat. Toast the spices, stirring frequently, until they begin to release their aroma, about 5 minutes. Remove from the heat.

2. Place the olives, olive oil, orange zest, garlic, and red pepper flakes in a large bowl. Add the toasted spices and stir with a large spoon to evenly coat the olives. Allow to marinate at room temperature for 24 hours. Discard the garlic and transfer the olives to a large jar. Add enough olive oil to cover, seal with a lid, and store in the refrigerator for up to 5 days. Serve at room temperature.

— SERVES 6 TO 8 —

WINE PAIRING: Sparkling, light white, and sherry

venetian salted cod pâté

baccalà mantecato

Don't be put off by the cod's aroma, because once the *baccalà* is soaked in liquid for a full day the smell disappears and its sweet taste is revived. (We selected salt cod for this recipe because it is widely available in American supermarkets.) When Gianni was old enough to drive, it was his job to go to a nearby town, Bassano del Grappa, every week to pick up a whole dried cod for Friday's fish dinner, in the Catholic tradition. The aroma was so pungent and the trips so frequent that his car smelled perpetually fishy. ("You don't know what a hard time I had trying to sell that car!" Gianni adds.) This dish is best served still warm on toasted bread that has been rubbed with garlic or on a slice of grilled polenta.

1 pound salt cod

2 cups milk or heavy cream

3 cloves garlic

1 Idaho potato (about 10 ounces), peeled, cut in half, and sliced

¾ cup extra virgin olive oil

2 tablespoons chopped fresh Italian, flat leafed parsley

2 tablespoons freshly grated Parmesan cheese

Freshly ground black pepper

1. Soak the cod in a large saucepan filled with cold water for 24 hours, changing the water three times during this period. Drain the cod and return it to the saucepan. Add the milk, which should cover the fish (add additional milk if necessary), two of the garlic cloves, and the potato. Bring to a boil, cover, and simmer until the potato is tender when pierced with a knife, 20 to 25 minutes.

2. Drain the fish, reserving ¼ cup of the soaking liquid, the potato, and the garlic. Remove and discard all bones from the cod.

3. Puree the cod in a food processor along with the reserved liquid, potato, garlic, and the remaining garlic clove. With the food processor running, add the olive oil in a steady

stream and process until smooth. Stir in the parsley and cheese, season with pepper, and serve immediately.

— SERVES 6 TO 8 —

WINE PAIRING: Sparkling, full white, and light red

VARIATIONS: Stir one of the following ingredients into the completed baccalà:

¼ cup seeded and diced red, yellow, or orange bell pepper

¼ cup pitted and diced kalamata olives

½ cup small cubes peeled all-purpose potatoes that have been cooked in boiling salted water until tender, about 8 minutes

grilled mozzarella cheese
mozzarella in carrozza

This recipe is Nonna Tucci's variation on the classic Italian sandwich, which I remember my grandmother preparing for me with fresh mozzarella on slices of round or long Italian bread—if you can't find Italian bread in your market, look for a loaf with a crisp crust and a soft, spongy inside perfect for sopping up olive oil or sauce. Following her example, my father now makes this simple but tasty sandwich for my children using the freshest hand-made mozzarella that he buys at local cheese or gourmet stores. Serve it for lunch with a light salad, or cut into squares to serve with drinks before dinner. When properly cooked and bitten into, the mozzarella in this "Italian grilled cheese" will produce long strings (the kids love competing to see who can pull the longest strings). These sandwiches may be prepared one hour in advance. Before serving, reheat in an oven at 350° F.

4 ounces fresh mozzarella cheese, cut into
   thin slices
4 slices Italian bread
1 large egg

1 tablespoon water
Kosher salt
¼ cup olive oil

1. Divide the slices of mozzarella between two slices of the bread. Cover with the remaining two slices of bread to make two sandwiches, and set aside.

2. In a shallow bowl, beat the egg, water, and a little salt. In a large sauté pan large enough to hold both sandwiches, warm the olive oil over medium-high heat. Dip the sandwiches in the egg mixture, and when the oil is hot but not smoking, add them to the pan. Cook until golden brown on both sides, about 3 minutes per side. You may also brown the edges of the bread by using tongs to hold the sandwich upright in the pan.

3. Remove from the pan, slice in half, and serve.

— SERVES 4 —

WINE PAIRING: Sparkling, light white, and light red

eggplant antipasto

c a p o n a t a

This is the dish that really launched the collaboration between Gianni and my parents on this book. I remember Gianni at my wedding to my wife, Kate, commenting over and over how delicious the *caponata* was. He kept asking me if my mother had in fact made it, and I assured him that she had. That confirmed his admiration for my mother's cooking, and I watched as he returned to the hors d'oeuvre table for another helping at least half a dozen times. As a result of the mutual admiration between Gianni and my parents, what started out as a Tucci family cookbook has grown by at least half with Gianni's input.

Caponata should taste *agro dolce,* which means slightly sweet and slightly sour. It makes a delicious accompaniment to grilled meat or fish and may be prepared up to one week in advance. Cover and store in the refrigerator, then return to room temperature or reheat before serving.

½ cup plus 2 tablespoons olive oil

1 medium-size eggplant, cut into 1-inch cubes (about 5 cups)

1½ cups onions, coarsely chopped

1 cup celery, coarsely chopped

2½ cups canned whole plum tomatoes (about one 28-ounce can)

1 tablespoon capers, drained, rinsed, and dried

1 tablespoon pine nuts

1 tablespoon sugar, plus 2 teaspoons

3 tablespoons red wine vinegar

1 teaspoon kosher salt

Freshly ground black pepper

1. Warm ½ cup of the olive oil in a large skillet set over medium-high heat. Add the cubed eggplant and cook until lightly browned but still firm, about 5 minutes. Transfer to a wide, deep saucepan or flameproof casserole and set aside.

2. Warm the remaining 2 tablespoons olive oil in the skillet. Stir in the onions and cook until wilted, about 4 minutes. Stir in the celery and then the tomatoes, crushing them

with your hands or the back of a slotted spoon as you add them to the pan. Simmer over medium-low heat until the tomatoes begin to sweeten but the celery is still crisp, about 15 minutes. Stir in the capers and pine nuts. Transfer this vegetable mixture to the casserole with the eggplant.

3. In a small saucepan set over low heat, stir the sugar and vinegar. Warm until the sugar dissolves. Stir into the eggplant mixture in the casserole. Season with salt and pepper.

4. Cover the casserole and simmer over low heat, stirring frequently, until the tomatoes are cooked and the vegetables are tender but not mushy, 15 to 20 minutes. Serve the caponata warm or at room temperature.

—SERVES 6—

WINE PAIRING: Sparkling, full white, and light red

mozzarella and tomato

mozzarella e pomodoro

Mozzarella cheese is used in a lot of the recipes in this book, but here it is the main ingredient. Fresh, handmade mozzarella—which is widely available at gourmet stores—bears no resemblance to the commercial type. It is well worth it to find the freshest mozzarella when preparing this recipe.

This simple dish heightens the flavor of ripe summer tomatoes and may be served as a first course or as part of a buffet. During the winter I use thin slices of sun-dried tomatoes packed in olive oil in place of fresh tomatoes.

1 whole fresh mozzarella cheese (about 1 pound)

2 large ripe tomatoes

5 fresh basil leaves

3 tablespoons extra virgin olive oil

Kosher salt and freshly ground black pepper

Cut the mozzarella and tomatoes into ½-inch-thick slices. Arrange on a serving platter, alternating slices of mozzarella and tomatoes. Place the basil leaves between a few of the mozzarella and tomato slices. When ready to serve, drizzle with the olive oil and season with salt and pepper.

— SERVES 6 —

WINE PAIRING: Sparkling, light white, and light red

fried pasta

pasta fritta

Most people have never heard of fried pasta, but once you've tasted it, you'll be addicted. It's usually made with leftover plain pasta, but it may be prepared with freshly boiled pasta. The Tucci side of the family traditionally fried linguine, until Stan's sister Rosalinda experimented with frying penne and ditalini and found that they were equally delicious. Now our new favorite pasta for frying is orecchiette. Fried pasta may be prepared as a lunch dish, served with a tossed green salad, or as an irresistible appetizer before dinner, accompanied by a glass of wine.

Kosher salt

1 pound linguine

¼ cup plus 1 tablespoon olive oil

1. Bring a large pot of water to a rapid boil. Add salt and the linguine. Cook according to the package instructions. Drain and toss with 1 tablespoon of the olive oil.

2. Warm the remaining ¼ cup olive oil in a large frying pan set over medium heat. When the oil is hot but not smoking, add enough pasta to form a thin layer, spreading it out to fill the pan. (When frying smaller quantities of pasta, reduce the amount of oil proportionately.) Fry the pasta until it is evenly browned and sticking together as a solid piece, approximately 6 to 8 minutes. Turn the pasta and continue cooking to evenly brown the other side, about 6 minutes. Remove from the heat and transfer to a cutting board or serving dish. Season with salt. Cut the pasta into wedges with a pizza cutter or a sharp knife. Serve immediately. Repeat with any remaining pasta.

— SERVES 6 —

WINE PAIRING: Sparkling, medium white, and light red

VARIATIONS: Smaller pastas, such as penne, ditalini, or fusilli, will not stick together but will fry nicely and may be eaten as individual pieces.

white bean antipasto

antipasto di cannellini

This dish is great served as an antipasto along with several other hors d'oeuvres—a selection of olives, roasted peppers, soppressata, and Parmesan, or goat's or sheep's milk cheese—or as a lunch dish accompanied by a tossed green salad. Our favorite variation is the shrimp, presented on a bed of lettuce with a slice of focaccia on the side.

2 cups cooked (or drained and rinsed canned) cannellini beans

½ cup extra virgin olive oil

¼ cup chopped red onions

Two 5-inch sprigs fresh rosemary

½ teaspoon balsamic vinegar

Kosher salt and freshly ground black pepper

1 tablespoon chopped fresh basil leaves

In a serving bowl, toss the beans with the olive oil and red onions. Remove the rosemary leaves from the stems and add to the beans. Toss, then add the vinegar and season with salt and pepper. Toss again before adding the basil. Just before serving, toss the beans once more and test for seasoning.

— SERVES 6 —

WINE PAIRING: Sparkling, medium white, and medium red

VARIATIONS: Add 1 tablespoon freshly squeezed lemon juice to the basic recipe.

Add 1 medium-size ripe tomato cut into ½-inch pieces to the basic recipe.

Shrimp makes a delicious addition to this dish. Shell and devein ½ pound medium-size shrimp. Warm 1 tablespoon olive oil and 1 clove garlic, quartered, in a sauté pan set over medium-high heat. When the oil is hot but not smoking, add the shrimp and cook, stirring frequently, until they turn pink, about 4 minutes. Remove the shrimp from the pan, reserving the garlic. Chop the shrimp into pieces slightly larger than the beans. Toss the shrimp with the beans, adding the reserved oil and garlic.

vegetable tart

torta salata

This wonderful tart emerged from one of Gianni's experiments just out of cooking school, when he would get together with friends to cook and experiment with unusual combinations of ingredients. "We'd end up with much more food than we could possibly eat, but it was a great learning experience," he recalls. "And after trying several dough recipes, we agreed that this one was the finest." We love the versatility of this tart. It may be filled with an infinite variety of cooked vegetable combinations, and you can serve it as a first course before roasted chicken or fish, or as the main dish of a light meal accompanied by a green salad.

Gianni recommends baking this tart in a springform pan. You can also roll the dough to fit a 9 x 15-inch baking sheet with a 1-inch rim; cut the baked tart into small cubes and serve it as an appetizer, hot or at room temperature.

FOR THE PASTRY:

2½ cups all-purpose flour

2 teaspoons kosher salt

Freshly ground black pepper

15 tablespoons cold butter,
   cut into small pieces

1 large egg yolk

½ cup water, or more as needed

¼ cup dry white wine

FOR THE FILLING:

2 tablespoons olive oil

2 cups thinly sliced onions (about 2 medium-
   size onions)

3 tablespoons chopped fresh Italian, flat
   leafed parsley

2 pounds Swiss chard, leaves and stems
   coarsely chopped

2½ cups fresh or frozen artichoke hearts cut
   into 1-inch pieces

Kosher salt and freshly ground black pepper

¼ cup freshly grated Parmesan cheese

¼ cup freshly grated pecorino Romano cheese

1 large egg, beaten

¼ cup light cream or milk

1 large egg yolk

2 tablespoons water

recipe continued on next page

1. To prepare the pastry: Combine the flour with the salt and pepper to taste in a large bowl or on a marble surface. Use your fingers or a pastry blender to cut the butter into the flour until it resembles coarse meal. Mound the flour mixture up and make a well in the center of it. Whisk together the egg yolk, water, and white wine. Pour this mixture into the well. Slowly incorporate the liquid ingredients by working the flour into them a little at a time. When the dough comes together, compact it into a large dish, wrap it in plastic wrap, and refrigerate it for at least 30 minutes or up to one day. If the dough does not come together add more water 1 tablespoon at a time.

2. To prepare the filling: Warm the olive oil in a large skillet set over medium-high heat. Add the onions and cook, stirring occasionally, until soft but not brown, about 5 minutes. Stir in the parsley. Reduce the heat to medium and add the Swiss chard and artichoke hearts; season with salt and pepper. Stir to combine, and cook until the vegetables have softened and most of the liquid has evaporated, about 20 minutes. Remove from the heat and cool completely. (This filling may be prepared up to one day in advance. Cover and refrigerate. Return to room temperature before proceeding with the recipe.)

3. Stir the cheeses, the beaten egg, and the cream into the vegetable mixture. Set aside.

4. Preheat the oven to 375° F. Lightly grease a 10-inch springform pan with butter and set aside.

5. Cut a quarter of the dough away from the disk and reserve it in the refrigerator. On a lightly floured surface, roll the remaining three quarters of the dough into a ⅛-inch-thick circle that will cover the bottom of the springform pan and come three quarters of the way up the sides. Line the pan with the dough.

6. Fill the shell with the vegetable mixture, patting it down with the back of a spoon so it is compact. Roll the remaining one quarter of dough into a circle slightly larger than the pan. Place it on top of the filling. Use your fingers to crimp together the sides and top of the dough. Pierce the top of the tart with a fork to make tiny air vents.

7. In a small mixing bowl, whisk the egg yolk and water. Brush this egg wash on the top and edges of the pastry. Bake until golden brown, about 1 hour. Allow to rest for 10 minutes before serving.

— MAKES 8 MAIN-COURSE SERVINGS, —

10 FIRST-COURSE SERVINGS

WINE PAIRING: Sparkling, full white, and light red

VARIATIONS: Ricotta salata cheese may be used in place of pecorino Romano.

Canned artichoke bottoms may be used in place of fresh or frozen artichoke hearts.

In place of Swiss chard and artichokes:

- cut 1 medium-size head of cauliflower into small florets and add to the cooked onions, along with 4 chopped anchovy fillets and 2 large potatoes, peeled, quartered, and thinly sliced. Cook until the cauliflower has softened, about 20 minutes, then proceed with the basic recipe.
- add 3 cups quartered mushrooms (such as cremini or portobello), 2 large potatoes, peeled, quartered, and thinly sliced, and ⅓ cup julienned pancetta to the cooked onions. Cook until the potatoes have softened, about 10 minutes, then proceed with the basic recipe.

To prepare an all-onion version of this tart, increase the onions to a total of 7 cups and cook until softened. Increase the pecorino Romano cheese to 1 cup, and stir it into the onions along with the Parmesan, beaten egg, and cream. Then proceed with the basic recipe.

roasted bell peppers

peperoni arrostiti

When we were selecting recipes to include in the book my mother came upon this simple preparation for roasted peppers. It brought to mind reminiscences of late summer days when she bottled tomatoes with her family. "We would all gather to pick the tomatoes, and then soak the ripe ones in a tub of water. Each tomato would then be cored and cut and put in a strainer to drain," Joan explained. "When the strainer was full, we'd dump the tomatoes into a pillowcase that was hanging from a tree limb, salt them, and then squeeze the pillowcase with our hands to extract the excess water. With one pass through a machine to reduce the pulp to a thick, seedless, skinless liquid, we were ready to bottle our own rich tomato puree—each topped with a fresh basil leaf. The bottles were then boiled in a huge drum over an outdoor fireplace to seal and preserve the fresh summer tomatoes all winter long."

While waiting for the sauce to boil, Joan's mother would roast fresh peppers over the coals and serve them to the family on toasted slices of homemade bread. I think they make a great complement to almost any sandwich. Also, if you have leftover pasta and not enough sauce, sauté garlic in some olive oil, add these peppers to heat them through, and toss this simple sauce over the pasta for a quick lunch dish.

10 red bell peppers	Kosher salt
½ cup olive oil	1 tablespoon chopped fresh Italian, flat leafed
2 cloves garlic, quartered	parsley

1. Preheat the oven broiler. Place a brown paper bag inside a plastic shopping bag and set aside.

2. Lay the peppers on their sides on an oven rack. Place a cookie sheet below the peppers to catch any juices. Broil the peppers, turning occasionally, until the skins are

recipe continued on next page

charred on all sides, including the tops and bottoms. Remove the peppers from the oven and immediately place them in the paper bag. Close the paper bag and the plastic bag around it, and allow the peppers to cool slightly, about 5 minutes.

3. Remove one of the peppers from the paper bag. Peel away and discard the charred skin, stem, and seeds. Tear the pepper lengthwise into ½-inch-wide strips, and place the strips in a bowl. Continue with this procedure until all of the peppers have been peeled. Set the bowl aside for 10 minutes.

4. Drain off all but ¼ cup of any liquid that may have accumulated in the bowl. Add the olive oil, garlic, salt to taste, and parsley to the bowl and toss to coat the peppers.

— SERVES 10 —

WINE PAIRING: Sparkling, medium white, light red, and rosé

NOTE: If you do not plan to serve these roasted peppers immediately, toss with the olive oil and place them in a jar. The peppers may then be stored in the refrigerator for up to 1 week. Bring to room temperature and add the remaining ingredients before serving.

Roasted peppers may also be frozen. Divide the peppers into two batches. Place in airtight containers or plastic freezer bags along with 2 tablespoons of the olive oil (or enough to cover) in each one. Freeze for up to 3 months. Thaw the peppers and then combine with the remaining ¼ cup olive oil and the other ingredients before serving.

spareribs

costicine di maiale

Often, in advance of a holiday celebration, my mother would get together with my father's sister Dora and his sister-in-law Teddy to cook. This recipe originated during one of those group cooking sessions. Even though this recipe isn't classically Italian, these savory spareribs have become a staple in our family, especially at summertime parties.

½ cup soy sauce

½ cup dry white wine

½ cup water

⅓ cup sugar

1 teaspoon kosher salt

2 cloves garlic, crushed

18 individual spareribs (about 3 pounds)

1. In a 2-cup measuring cup, whisk the soy sauce, wine, water, sugar, salt, and garlic. Place the spareribs in a single layer in a baking dish or in a tightly sealed plastic bag. Pour the sauce over the ribs, turning to coat them with the marinade. Cover and allow to marinate for at least 1 hour and up to 4 hours in the refrigerator.

2. Prepare a charcoal or gas grill. Cook the ribs, turning frequently, until well browned, 20 to 25 minutes. Serve immediately or at room temperature.

— SERVES 6 —

WINE PAIRING: Sparkling

VARIATION: This marinade may also be used on chicken wings or pork tenderloin for grilling. Instead of grilling, the spareribs or chicken wings may be cooked in the oven under the broiler, turning frequently.

stuffed mushrooms

funghi ripieni

When my father was a kid, in late August and early September his family would go to visit their relatives in Vermont and the entire extended family would venture out to the pine forests to gather wild mushrooms. As my father, Stan, recalls, "My task was to stay in a given place to receive and clean the treasures they found in the woods. We then placed them on large screens in the sun to air-dry." They would prepare them as suggested in this recipe, and they also are great in Milanese Risotto (page 194).

These mushrooms make the perfect hors d'oeuvres to serve with drinks before dinner or as part of a buffet. The filling may be prepared and the mushrooms stuffed several hours in advance. Drizzle with the oil just before baking. Always make more of these than you think you may need, as they can be addictive. Though most children dislike mushrooms, they can't seem to get enough of these. Watch them argue over the last one.

10 ounces medium-size white mushrooms

¼ cup plus 1 tablespoon olive oil

¾ cup plain dried bread crumbs, or more as needed

½ cup finely grated pecorino Romano cheese

1 teaspoon finely chopped garlic (about 2 small cloves)

2 tablespoons finely chopped fresh Italian, flat leafed parsley

Kosher salt and freshly ground black pepper

1 tablespoon extra virgin olive oil

1 tablespoon butter

1. Preheat the oven to 375° F.

2. Remove the stems from the mushroom caps and set the caps aside. Finely chop half the mushroom stems (discard the other half). Warm 1 tablespoon of the olive oil and the butter in a small sauté pan set over medium heat. Add the mushroom stems and cook, stirring, until they have softened and are lightly browned, about 5 minutes.

3. In a medium-size bowl, mix the cooked mushroom stems, bread crumbs, cheese, garlic, and parsley, and season with salt and pepper. Slowly stir in the remaining ¼ cup olive oil to form a moist dough. (If the dough is too oily, add more bread crumbs.)

4. Divide equally among the mushroom caps. Place the filled caps on a baking sheet. Drizzle the extra virgin olive oil over the mushrooms, and bake until the mushrooms are browned but still firm, about 8 minutes. Remove from the oven and serve warm. (If the tops of the mushrooms have not browned, place them under the broiler for 1 minute.)

— SERVES 6 —

WINE PAIRING: Sparkling, minerally white, and medium red

VARIATIONS: The chopped mushroom stems may be cooked in a microwave. Place them in a small dish and toss with the olive oil and melted butter. Cook on high power until firm but cooked through, about half a minute. Proceed with the recipe.

This same recipe may be prepared using large stuffing mushrooms. Chop one half of the mushroom stems and double the remaining filling ingredients. These mushrooms will take much longer to brown, about 12 minutes.

potato croquettes
crocchette di patate

The year my family was living in Italy, I came down with a stomach flu and was instructed to eat only crackers, bananas, water, and ginger ale. After what seemed a fortnight of eating this bland diet—okay, probably only two or three days—I began to yearn for many of my mother's and grandmother's dishes. I remember lying on the couch and rattling off some of my favorites. My mother looked at me sadly and told me, "All in good time." But what I wanted most of all were my grandmother's potato croquettes. I could see, smell, and taste them so clearly. I would try to rid my mind of them and concentrate on something else, but it was no use. The potato croquettes haunted me. I swore I could see them dancing, spinning mockingly around my head, their delicate aroma taunting my nostrils. I pleaded with my mother, telling her I was desperate for potato croquettes. "Soon," she said, "soon." If memory serves me, she did indeed make the croquettes within the week, but it's strange how one remembers the longing more than the eating.

4 medium-size all-purpose potatoes, peeled
    and quartered
2 large eggs, beaten
½ cup plain dried bread crumbs
2 tablespoons all-purpose flour

3 tablespoons finely grated pecorino Romano
    cheese
1 tablespoon chopped fresh Italian, flat leafed
    parsley
Kosher salt
¼ cup olive oil, plus more as needed

1. Place the potatoes in a large saucepan and fill with enough water to cover. Bring to a boil and cook until the potatoes are tender when pierced with a fork, 15 to 20 minutes. Drain the potatoes and mash them in a bowl with a potato masher. Add the eggs, bread crumbs, flour, cheese, parsley, and salt to taste. Mix them with your hands to make a firm, dry mixture, adding more bread crumbs or flour as necessary.

2. Heat the olive oil in a small frying pan (about 8 inches in diameter) set over medium heat. Roll tablespoons of the dough between the palms of your hands to form 3- to 4-inch-long logs. When the oil is hot but not smoking, add a few croquettes to the pan and fry until lightly browned on all sides, about 6 minutes. Transfer the cooked croquettes to a plate lined with paper towels to drain before serving. Continue to cook the croquettes in small batches. Add more oil to the pan if necessary, being sure to allow it to heat up before adding the croquettes. The croquettes are best served immediately, but they can be made ahead of time and reheated in the oven if necessary.

— SERVES 6 —

WINE PAIRING: Sparkling, medium white, and light red

VARIATION: The potatoes may be cooked whole. Peel and quarter them when cool to the touch and then proceed with the recipe.

fried zucchini fritters

frittelle di zucchine

Nonna (Grandma) Tropiano's fritters are best served warm immediately after frying; however, they may be made ahead of time and reheated in an oven at 350° F.

3 cups grated zucchini (about 2 medium-size zucchini)

2 teaspoons kosher salt

1 large egg

¼ cup finely grated pecorino Romano cheese

3 to 5 tablespoons all-purpose flour

¼ cup olive oil

1. Place the grated zucchini in a colander. Toss with salt. Place the colander over a bowl to catch any water, and let stand for 30 minutes.

2. Press all of the water out of the zucchini by squeezing small portions of it in your hand. Transfer the drained zucchini to a bowl. Add the egg, cheese, and 3 tablespoons of the flour to the bowl. Stir with a fork, adding more flour as necessary to create a mixture that holds together.

3. Warm the olive oil in a small sauté pan (about 8 inches in diameter) set over medium-high heat. When the oil is hot but not smoking, scoop out rounded tablespoons of the zucchini batter and add to the pan. Flatten the fritters slightly with a spatula. (It is best to cook only two or three fritters at a time to maintain the oil at an even heat.) Fry the fritters until they are golden brown on each side, about 3 minutes per side. Transfer to a paper-towel-lined plate to drain before serving.

— SERVES 6 —

WINE PAIRING: Sparkling, light white, and light red

VARIATION: Chopped zucchini blossoms may be prepared following this same recipe. Be sure to remove the blossoms' pistils first.

prosciutto with figs
prosciutto con fichi

I remember as a child observing the autumnal ritual of protecting the fig trees my mother's father had planted in his yard. They produced abundant quantities of luscious purple figs for decades. In early autumn, the trees were tightly wrapped in oilcloth, bent over, staked, and buried under dirt and leaves to protect them from the cold winter weather. Each spring the fig trees were righted and unwrapped in time to bloom and bear fruit for another season.

This simple recipe is a variation on the traditional prosciutto with melon. It may be served on individual plates to guests seated at the table or presented on a platter as part of a buffet. I find it to be an elegant and profoundly sexual appetizer—but since this is a family cookbook I'll leave it at that!

6 ripe figs   *8 very thin slices prosciutto*

Quarter each fig. Slice each piece of prosciutto lengthwise into thirds. Drape a slice of prosciutto over each fig quarter so that the prosciutto covers most of the fig.

— SERVES 6 —

WINE PAIRING: Sparkling and light white

VARIATIONS: Sections of peeled cantaloupe or honeydew melon, or sliced pears, persimmons, or peaches may be substituted for the fresh figs.

recipe pictured on page xxxviii

mussels, potatoes, and zucchini

cozze, patate, e zucchine

The best mussels to use when preparing this recipe are from Prince Edward Island or New Zealand when they are in season. Leave the mussels in their shells, making for a less formal, hands-on presentation, or remove the mussels from their shells before serving, return them to the pot to warm through, and then ladle them out with the vegetables and broth. Either way, this is a tasty warm appetizer or light luncheon dish. It may also be tossed with cooked short-cut pasta such as penne or ziti.

4 tablespoons extra virgin olive oil

2 tablespoons thinly sliced shallots

½ pound all-purpose potatoes, peeled and cut into ⅛-inch-thick slices

½ pound zucchini, cut into ⅛-inch-thick slices

1 clove garlic, thinly sliced

¼ cup dry white wine

3 tablespoons water

Kosher salt and freshly ground black pepper

48 mussels (about 4 pounds), scrubbed and debearded

½ cup cubed ripe tomatoes (about 2 plum tomatoes)

2 teaspoons fresh Italian, flat leafed parsley, chopped

6 slices country-style bread, toasted or grilled

1 clove garlic, cut in half

1. In a flameproof casserole set over medium-high heat, warm 2 tablespoons of the olive oil with the shallots, potatoes, zucchini, sliced garlic, wine, water, and salt and pepper to taste. Cook, stirring a few times, until the potatoes have softened, about 6 minutes. Place the mussels on top of the vegetables and sprinkle the tomatoes on top of the mussels. Cover and cook until the mussel shells have opened, about 5 minutes. Remove from the heat and discard any unopened mussels.

2. Remove the vegetables with a slotted spoon and distribute them evenly among six plates or shallow soup bowls. Top with equal portions of mussels. Add the remaining 2 tablespoons olive oil and the parsley to the liquid remaining in the casserole. Set the casserole over high heat and whisk the broth to combine the ingredients, adding more water if necessary. Cook just to warm through, about 1 minute, and pour on top of the mussels. Serve immediately, accompanied by toasted bread rubbed with the garlic halves.

— SERVES 6 —

WINE PAIRING: Sparkling and light white

clams baked on the half shell

vongole gratinate al forno

Top neck clams work best for this recipe, so be sure to ask your fishmonger for them by name. The topping may be prepared several hours in advance. Spoon it onto the clams just before broiling. When opening, place each clam over a big bowl so that you can collect the juice, which can be strained and reserved in the refrigerator or freezer to use to prepare Linguine with Clam Sauce (page 159).

12 top neck clams, scrubbed

1 cup plain dried bread crumbs

¼ cup chopped fresh Italian, flat leafed parsley

1 tablespoon finely chopped garlic

¼ cup olive oil

1. Pry the clams open and gently separate the top and bottom shells, loosening and allowing the clam to divide, with some remaining on the top shell and some remaining on the bottom shell. Save all of the juice from the clams and set aside to refrigerate or freeze for future use. You should have at least 16 clamshell halves to fill and bake. Arrange the clam-filled shells on a baking sheet.

2. Preheat the oven to 350° F.

3. In a small bowl, toss the bread crumbs, parsley, and garlic. Use a fork to stir the olive oil into this mixture. It should be moist but not oily.

4. Fill each clam with a portion of the topping mixture, spreading it evenly over the clam and to the edge of the shell. The filling should be about ⅛ inch thick. Bake until the topping begins to brown slightly, about 5 minutes. Remove from the oven and adjust the oven temperature to broil. Place the clams under the broiler and cook until golden brown, about 2 minutes. Serve immediately.

— SERVES 4 TO 6 —

WINE PAIRING: Sparkling, light white, and medium red

pan-seared calamari in its own broth

calamari affogati in brodetto

This is a quick dish to prepare in the summertime. Calamari can be tricky to cook because they become tough and rubbery if they are under- or overcooked. To ensure perfection, slice the calamari into rings, sauté for no more than two minutes, and then reheat in a flavorful broth. Calamari prepared this way may be served as a first course with grilled or fresh polenta or accompanied by toasted bread rubbed with fresh garlic. It may also be served over pasta.

3 tablespoons extra virgin olive oil

2 cloves garlic, thinly sliced

½ teaspoon red pepper flakes or 2 teaspoons seeded and chopped jalapeño peppers

1 tablespoon minced shallots

2 tablespoons chopped fresh Italian, flat leafed parsley

1 pound cleaned calamari, cut into bite-size rings

Kosher salt and freshly ground black pepper

¼ cup dry white wine

1½ cups diced ripe plum tomatoes (about 3 large tomatoes)

2 teaspoons chopped fresh basil leaves

2 tablespoons butter or extra virgin olive oil (optional)

1. Warm the olive oil in a large skillet set over high heat. When the oil is hot but not smoking, add the garlic and red pepper flakes. Cook until the garlic just begins to color, about 30 seconds (do not let it brown). Stir in the shallots and 1 tablespoon of the parsley. Cook until the shallots begin to color, about 10 seconds. Add the calamari and cook over high heat, stirring frequently, until it begins to soften, about 1 minute. Season with salt and generous grindings of black pepper. Add the wine and cook until the calamari absorbs the flavor of the wine, about 1 minute.

2. Remove the calamari from the pan with a slotted spoon and set aside. Stir the tomatoes into the skillet and continue boiling until slightly thickened, 2 to 3 minutes. Stir in the remaining 1 tablespoon parsley and the basil. Return the calamari to the skillet and adjust the seasoning with salt and pepper. For a slightly richer sauce, stir the butter into the calamari just before serving, or drizzle with the extra virgin olive oil just before serving. Serve immediately.

— SERVES 4 —

WINE PAIRING: Sparkling and light white

VARIATIONS: 1 cup cooked or canned white beans (drained and rinsed), such as cannellini, may be added to the sauce along with the tomatoes.

A pinch of ground cumin or paprika may be added in place of the red pepper flakes.

watercress, seafood, and mushroom casserole

stufatino di crescione con pesce e funghi

The idea of wilting bitter greens—such as escarole, spinach, and broccoli rabe—has long been a part of Italian cooking. To reduce the bitter taste of wilted watercress, Gianni pairs it with shrimp, which has a naturally sweet flavor.

1 tablespoon extra virgin olive oil, plus more for drizzling if desired

1 tablespoon chopped fresh Italian, flat leafed parsley

¼ cup chopped shallots

½ pound medium-size shrimp, shelled, deveined, and cut in half lengthwise

1½ cups thinly sliced white mushroom caps

Kosher salt and freshly ground black pepper

⅓ cup dry white wine

½ cup chicken broth

4 ounces watercress (about 2 bunches), tough stems removed

1 ripe plum tomato, diced

1 tablespoon butter

1. Warm the olive oil in a skillet set over high heat. Add the parsley and shallots and cook, stirring constantly, to wilt the shallots, about 2 minutes. Add the shrimp and cook, stirring frequently until the shrimp just begin to turn pink, about 2 minutes. Stir in the mushrooms, and season with salt and pepper. Cook until the shrimp are cooked through, 3 to 5 minutes. Add the wine, broth, and watercress. Cook, tossing the watercress until wilted, about half a minute. Remove from the heat.

2. Use tongs to remove the watercress from the skillet and distribute it evenly among four shallow bowls. Top with the shrimp. Return the skillet to the heat, and stir the tomato and butter into the remaining liquid. Cook, stirring frequently, to melt the butter and slightly thicken the sauce, about 2 minutes. Distribute the sauce evenly among the serving bowls. Serve immediately, drizzled with additional extra virgin olive oil if you like.

— SERVES 4 —

WINE PAIRING: Sparkling, light white, and light red

VARIATION: Whole bay scallops or quartered sea scallops may be used in place of shrimp.

venetian seafood salad

insalata veneziana ai frutti di mare

The seafood for this recipe may be prepared one day in advance. Toss it with the remaining ingredients one or two hours before serving. If your fishmonger cannot get fresh octopus, simply increase the amounts of calamari and shrimp.

FOR THE SEAFOOD AND POACHING LIQUID:

1 celery stalk

1 medium-size carrot

1 small onion, cut in half

1 bay leaf

3 tablespoons freshly squeezed lemon juice (from about 1 lemon)

1 teaspoon kosher salt

2 quarts water

1 pound cleaned calamari, cut into 1-inch-thick rings

½ pound sea or bay scallops, tough parts removed

1 pound medium-size or large shrimp

1 pound octopus

FOR THE SALAD:

1 cup julienned tender celery

1 cup julienned carrots

½ cup seeded and julienned red bell pepper

½ cup seeded and julienned yellow bell pepper

1 scallion (white part only), julienned

2 tablespoons chopped fresh Italian, flat leafed parsley

2 tablespoons chopped fresh basil leaves

2 cloves garlic, finely chopped

6 tablespoons freshly squeezed lemon juice (from about 2 lemons) or lime juice (from about 3 limes)

1 tablespoon white wine vinegar

½ cup extra virgin olive oil

½ teaspoon kosher salt

Freshly ground black pepper

6 to 8 cups baby lettuce

1. To poach the seafood, you will need a large saucepan fitted with a colander insert. In the bottom of the pan, combine the celery, carrot, onion, bay leaf, lemon juice, salt, and water. Bring to a boil.

recipe continued on next page

2. Place the calamari in the colander and cook in the boiling water for 2 minutes. Remove from the water, transfer to a large bowl, and set aside. Place the scallops in the colander and cook in the boiling water for 3 to 4 minutes. Remove from the water and transfer to the bowl with the calamari (large sea scallops may be cut in half horizontally after cooking; bay scallops may be left whole). Place the shrimp in the colander and cook in the boiling water until pink, about 3 minutes. Remove from the water. Peel, devein, and cut in half horizontally, adding them to the bowl with the calamari and scallops.

3. Remove the colander from the pan and place the octopus directly in the saucepan, adding more water if necessary to completely cover. Bring to a boil. Reduce the heat and gently simmer until you can easily push your finger through one of the thickest portions of the tentacles, 40 to 50 minutes. Transfer the octopus to a bowl and place under cold running water until cooled, about 5 minutes. Use your fingers and a small paring knife to remove the outer skin. Discard the hard mouth and the head sac. Cut the tentacles on the bias into 1-inch pieces and add to the bowl with the other seafood.

4. To prepare the salad, toss the julienned celery, carrots, bell peppers, scallion, parsley, basil, and garlic in a serving bowl. Add the seafood and toss. Add the lemon juice, vinegar, and olive oil, and toss well. Season with the salt and generous grindings of pepper. Arrange 1 cup of lettuce on each serving plate. Top with equal portions of the seafood-and-vegetable mixture, and serve immediately.

— S E R V E S 6 T O 8 —

WINE PAIRING: Sparkling and light white

VARIATIONS: Six to eight steamed mussels may be added to the basic recipe and tossed with the other seafood.

To extend the recipe and add a new texture dimension, ½ cup cubed, peeled, cooked Idaho potatoes can be added to the basic recipe. And although it isn't traditional, a hint of cilantro goes very well with this dish—2 teaspoons chopped should do it.

mushroom and white asparagus salad
insalata di funghi e asparagi bianchi

Gianni grew up near Bassano del Grappa, a town in northeastern Italy that is renowned for its white asparagus. "It's the best in the world," claims Gianni. "They are abundant from the end of April through the end of May. During that season every restaurant, trattoria, and osteria serves white asparagus." As Gianni explains it, the procedure for eating this local dish is almost like a religious ceremony. "Each person is served a plate on which are placed several very soft, warm asparagus, hard-boiled eggs, and some good olive oil. The eggs are crushed with the back of a fork and mixed with the oil and some salt and pepper to make a dressing. The asparagus (which is always eaten by hand) is dipped into the egg dressing and then consumed in one long bite. If you have never eaten asparagus this way," says Gianni "you must!"

This version of the recipe includes mushrooms and a delicate salad. It may be prepared with white or green asparagus. Pencil-thin asparagus do not need to be peeled.

16 white asparagus	Kosher salt and freshly ground black pepper
3 medium-size cremini or	1 teaspoon Dijon mustard
porcini mushrooms	2 tablespoons olive oil
¾ pound purslane, mâche, or a mixture of	2 tablespoons hot water
lettuce greens	¼ cup coarsely chopped toasted hazelnuts
1 tablespoon balsamic vinegar	(see note)

1. Bring a large pot of salted water to a boil.

2. Cut 1 inch of tough stalk off the bottom of each asparagus spear. Use a vegetable peeler to remove a thin layer of tough outer stalk from the lower third of the asparagus. Blanch the asparagus in the water until slightly tender, about 1 minute. Drain and run under very cold water to cool. Cut the asparagus on a sharp bias into 4-inch lengths and set aside.

3. Remove and discard the mushroom stems. If the variety you are using has soft brown gills on the underside of the mushroom cap, trim them away and discard. Cut the mushroom caps into very thin slices. Set aside.

4. Place the salad greens in a large bowl along with half the sliced mushrooms.

5. In a bowl, whisk together the vinegar and salt and pepper to taste. Add the mustard and whisk until smooth. Whisk in the olive oil and the water, 1 tablespoon at a time, beating to produce a smooth, emulsified dressing.

6. Pour the dressing over the salad and toss to coat evenly. Distribute the salad among four serving plates. Arrange the remaining mushrooms on top of each portion. Top with the asparagus. Sprinkle with the hazelnuts and serve.

— SERVES 4 —

WINE PAIRING: Sparkling, light white, and light red

VARIATIONS: As an addition to the basic recipe, 1 large portobello mushroom, with the stem removed, may be very thinly sliced, dusted in flour, and fried in 2 cups of hot but not smoking peanut or canola oil. Drain on paper towels before serving as a garnish on top of the salad.

In place of the hazelnuts, long, thin slices of aged ricotta salata or aged goat cheese may be arranged on top of the salad. I recommend using a vegetable peeler to create these slices (or you can simply grate the cheese).

NOTE: To toast the hazelnuts, preheat the oven to 300° F. Spread the nuts evenly in a small baking sheet or cake pan. Toast in the oven, stirring once or twice, until the nuts turn light gold and release their aroma, about 5 minutes. Allow to cool before chopping and sprinkling on the salad.

roasted mushroom salad with lettuce, balsamic vinaigrette, and parmesan shavings

insalata di funghi arrostiti

The key to this recipe is to prepare it using an assortment of mushrooms. Fall is a wonderful time of year to find freshly picked wild mushrooms. This recipe may be prepared several hours ahead and set aside until you are ready to toss the salad. I recommend selecting a butterhead lettuce for the salad and using a vegetable peeler to create the Parmesan shavings.

¾ pound any single variety of mushroom or a combination (shiitake, oyster, cremini, portobello, porcini, chanterelle, cinnamon cap), cut into wedges

5 tablespoons plus 2 teaspoons extra virgin olive oil

1 shallot, thinly sliced

1 tablespoon chopped fresh Italian, flat leafed parsley

Kosher salt and freshly ground black pepper

2 tablespoons balsamic vinegar

¾ pound Bibb or Boston lettuce

16 large shavings Parmesan cheese (about 2 ounces)

1. Preheat the oven to 450° F.

2. Toss the mushrooms in a baking dish along with 3 tablespoons of the olive oil, the shallot, and the parsley, and season with salt and pepper. Roast in the oven until the mushrooms are browned but still firm and the shallots have wilted, 6 to 8 minutes. Set aside.

3. In a large bowl, whisk the remaining 2 tablespoons plus 2 teaspoons olive oil, salt and pepper to taste, and the vinegar. Add the lettuce and toss thoroughly. Distribute the lettuce evenly among four salad plates. Top with the roasted mushrooms and Parmesan shavings. Serve immediately.

— SERVES 4 —

WINE PAIRING: Sparkling, light white, and light red

baby artichokes and arugula with parmesan cheese

carciofini e rucola con parmigiano

This is Gianni's twist on a traditional Roman recipe. Use tender artichokes, about 2½ inches tall, shaved very thin, ⅛ inch or less. Then add the arugula and Parmesan cheese to accent the flavor of the artichokes. Use a vegetable peeler to create large, thin shavings of Parmesan to garnish the salad.

1 lemon

10 baby artichokes (about 1 pound)

1 tablespoon finely grated Parmesan cheese

3 tablespoons freshly squeezed lemon juice
   (from about 1 lemon)

5 tablespoons extra virgin olive oil

Kosher salt and freshly ground black pepper

2 tablespoons balsamic vinegar

¾ pound arugula, stemmed

16 large shavings Parmesan cheese (about 2
   ounces)

1. Fill a large bowl with cold water. Cut the lemon in half and squeeze the juice into the water. Place the lemon halves in the water and set aside.

2. Cut away and discard the artichoke stems. Peel off and discard several layers of the tough outer leaves until you reach a layer where the artichoke leaves are half pale green and half pale yellow. Trim off the top pale green portion of the artichokes and discard. Slice the artichokes in half lengthwise, and remove any of the fine choke from the center. Place in the lemon water, rubbing each half with a bit of the lemon, and set aside.

3. In a large bowl, whisk the grated cheese, lemon juice, and 2 tablespoons of the olive oil. Season with salt and pepper.

4. Remove the artichokes from the water and pat dry. Slice the artichokes lengthwise into very thin strips—⅛ inch or less—and add the slices to the bowl with the dressing. Toss to coat evenly with the dressing and set aside for at least 15 minutes or for up to 2 hours.

5. In a large bowl, whisk the vinegar with salt and pepper to taste. Whisk in the remaining 3 tablespoons olive oil. Add the arugula and toss to evenly coat with this dressing. Distribute evenly among four salad plates. Top the arugula with equal portions of artichokes. Garnish each portion with 4 long strips of Parmesan cheese just before serving.

— S E R V E S 4 —

WINE PAIRING: Sparkling and light white

VARIATION: Celery root or jicama may be used in place of the artichokes. Peel the celery root or jicama, then cut into julienne strips using a food processor or knife. Toss with the dressing and proceed with the basic recipe. One quarter teaspoon red pepper flakes or ¼ fresh jalapeño pepper, seeded and finely chopped, may be added to the celery root or jicama just before tossing with the dressing.

arugula with prosciutto, pears, and parmesan

insalata di rucola, prosciutto, pera, e parmigiano

This recipe is based on the Italian tradition of serving seasonal fruits—such as pears, apples, grapes, or figs—with Parmesan cheese at the end of a meal. The sweet pears perfectly complement the tangy arugula and salty prosciutto. This refreshing, easy-to-assemble salad may be served either before or after a main course.

¾ pound arugula, stemmed

½ cup Sherry Shallot Vinaigrette (page 49)

8 thin slices prosciutto

2 firm ripe pears, peeled, cored, and thinly sliced

16 large shavings Parmesan cheese (about 2 ounces)

Toss the arugula with the vinaigrette in a large bowl. Distribute evenly among four plates. Garnish each plate with two slices of the prosciutto and equal portions of pear. Use a vegetable peeler to shave portions of the Parmesan on top.

— SERVES 4 —

WINE PAIRING: Sparkling, light white, and light red

VARIATIONS: Arugula tossed with shallot sherry vinaigrette is also delicious with sliced figs and crumbled goat cheese.

Toss the arugula with a balsamic vinaigrette and top with strawberries or orange sections and thin slices of fennel bulb and red onion.

Top arugula tossed with balsamic vinaigrette with thin slices of Granny Smith apples, coarsely chopped walnuts, and crumbled Gorgonzola or blue cheese. If you like, the walnuts may be toasted: Preheat the oven to 350° F. Place the chopped walnuts on a small baking sheet, and cook until they release their aroma and have browned slightly, about 5 minutes. Allow to cool before adding to the salad.

basic vinaigrette
vinaigrette all'italiana

I prepare this basic dressing almost every day to serve over a simple green salad. Our family maintains the Italian tradition of eating salad at the end of the meal. I think salad eaten at this point makes you feel less full, especially when tossed with a light dressing such as this one. I prepare the dressing in the bowl I plan to toss the salad in to coat the greens evenly. Just before serving I give the dressing a fresh whisk and then toss it with the greens. This recipe makes enough dressing for about ½ pound of salad greens.

½ small clove garlic

2 teaspoons kosher salt

Freshly ground black pepper

½ teaspoon dry mustard

2 tablespoons red wine vinegar

¼ cup extra virgin olive oil

Place the garlic and salt in the bottom of a salad bowl. Crush the garlic with the flat side of a knife blade and mash it into the salt to release its flavor. Whisk in pepper to taste, the mustard, and the vinegar. Then gradually whisk in the olive oil. Set aside for a few minutes before adding the salad greens. Toss evenly to coat with the dressing. Serve immediately.

— MAKES ½ CUP —

VARIATIONS: The dry ingredients may be combined in the salad bowl several hours before serving. Whisk in the vinegar just before adding the greens. Balsamic vinegar may be substituted for the red wine vinegar.

sherry shallot vinaigrette
vinaigrette allo scalogno

This dressing is appropriate for any simple green salad, and may also be used on the Arugula with Prosciutto, Pears, and Parmesan salad (page 47). It may be stored for up to two weeks in the refrigerator. However, the shallots should be removed after one day; this may be done by straining the dressing through a fine-mesh sieve. Allow the dressing to return to room temperature before whisking briskly and serving over tossed greens.

1 small shallot, finely diced

1 tablespoon Dijon mustard

¼ cup sherry vinegar

½ teaspoon kosher salt

Freshly ground black pepper

¼ cup canola oil

3 tablespoons extra virgin olive oil

1 tablespoon hot water

In a small bowl or wide-mouthed jar, whisk the shallot, mustard, vinegar, salt, and pepper. Slowly add the canola oil, olive oil, and the hot water, whisking to make a smooth, emulsified dressing. Set aside until needed.

— MAKES 1 CUP —

soups

zuppe

Ever since childhood I've loved soup, and I still find myself making it—even on the hottest of summer days. My grandmother Nonna Tropiano made a fresh batch once or twice a week year-round when my mom was growing up. Chicken soup was her favorite. She used every part of the chicken—even scraping and scrubbing the feet before adding them to the pot. While not as resourceful as she in the kitchen, when I was struggling as an actor in New York after college, I found that making a large pot of chicken soup or buying a bowl of split pea soup from a deli provided a nutritious, filling, and inexpensive meal. It was a comfort to know that a little soup could go a long way. Whether you're on a tight budget or a tight schedule, our family soup recipes are varied, delicious, cheap, and easy to make.

chicken soup with tiny chicken meatballs

brodo di gallina con polpettine di pollo

My grandfather never quite learned to speak English properly, primarily because he was surrounded by Italians and didn't have to rely on it to get by. My sisters and I loved his thick Italian accent. In Nonno Tropiano's mouth, "vegetable soup" became "dirigible soup"—which, of course, sent all of us, my grandfather included, into fits of laughter. This is my grandmother's basic chicken soup recipe, made special by the addition of her signature tiny, delicious chicken meatballs.

FOR THE SOUP:

One 3-pound free-range chicken, quartered

4 quarts water

2 large celery stalks, cut into thirds

2 medium-size carrots, cut into thirds

4 sprigs fresh Italian, flat leafed parsley

1 large onion

Kosher salt

2 very ripe or canned plum tomatoes, quartered

FOR THE MEATBALLS:

½ boneless, skinless chicken breast (or 1 pound ground chicken breast)

1 large egg, lightly beaten

¼ cup chopped fresh Italian, flat leafed parsley

¼ cup plain dried bread crumbs

2 tablespoons freshly grated pecorino Romano cheese

Freshly ground black pepper

Freshly grated Parmesan or pecorino Romano cheese (optional)

1. Place the quartered chicken in a large pot and cover with the water. Set the pot over medium-low heat and slowly bring the water to a simmer, skimming off any foam that accumulates on top. Add the celery, carrots, parsley, onion, and salt to taste. Simmer, uncovered, to soften the vegetables, about 10 minutes. Add the tomatoes and continue to simmer, with the lid slightly askew, about 30 minutes.

2. Remove the chicken, carrots, and onion to a platter and set aside. Strain the broth through a fine-mesh sieve, discarding the celery, parsley, and tomatoes. Transfer 1 cup of the broth to a small pot. Return the rest of the broth to the large pot. Shred the cooked chicken, discarding bones and skin, and add to the large batch of broth. Dice the cooked carrots and onions. Add them to the remaining broth along with the shredded chicken. Cover the pot and keep the broth warm while you cook the meatballs.

3. In a food processor, finely chop the chicken breast. Transfer to a small bowl and add the egg, parsley, bread crumbs, cheese, and salt and pepper to taste. Stir with a fork to combine into a soft mixture.

4. Use a ½-teaspoon measuring spoon to scoop out a small portion of the mixture and roll between the palms of your hands to form small, ½-inch balls. Continue rolling until all of the mixture has been made into meatballs, setting finished ones on a wax paper–lined plate or cutting board as you proceed. This recipe will make 20 or more ½-inch small meatballs. Bring the small pot containing the 1 cup of broth to a gentle boil and cook the meatballs, 8 to 10 at a time, in the broth, until they are cooked through, about 5 minutes. If the broth begins to evaporate, water may be added as needed. As they finish cooking, transfer them with a slotted spoon to the large pot of broth.

5. Serve with grated Parmesan or Romano cheese if desired.

— SERVES 8 —

WINE PAIRING: Light white, medium white, and light red

VARIATIONS: The beauty of soup is that it can be varied to accommodate ingredients you have (or don't have) on hand. Here are a few suggestions:

- The cooked chicken may be served separately, rather than shredding it and adding it to the soup. Serve the soup, containing the vegetables and the chicken meatballs, as a first course.
- 2 cups cooked pasta, such as orzo, or 2 cups cooked rice may be added to the strained broth and warmed through just before serving.

recipe continued on next page

- 2 medium-size all-purpose potatoes, peeled and quartered, may be added to the soup with the tomatoes. Return to the pot with the carrots and onion, and serve with the soup.

This soup may be prepared using any fowl. Allow an additional 30 minutes of cooking time to tenderize the meat.

NOTE: This rich broth may be strained and frozen for up to 3 months and used in recipes that call for chicken broth.

potato and cabbage soup

zuppa di patate e cavoli

This is a meal typical of ones that my mother's family would eat on Fridays, when they abstained from eating meat as part of the Catholic tradition. I serve this as a lunch dish or as a vegetable course that comes before the entrée, accompanied by bread, olives, and cheese.

1 small head Savoy or green cabbage, trimmed, cored, and quartered

1 clove garlic, cut in half

2 tablespoons chopped fresh or canned plum tomatoes

2 tablespoons olive oil

Kosher salt and freshly ground black pepper

2 small potatoes, quartered

Place the cabbage in a medium-size saucepan. Add the garlic, tomatoes, olive oil, and salt and pepper to taste. Pour in enough water so three quarters of the cabbage is immersed in water. Cover and bring to a boil. Reduce the heat to medium-low and simmer for 5 minutes. Add the potatoes, pushing them down into the water. Cover and continue to simmer until the cabbage and potatoes are just tender, about 25 minutes. Distribute the vegetables and broth among four shallow soup bowls and serve.

— SERVES 4 —

WINE PAIRING: Medium white

VARIATION: For a hearty variation on this soup, dumpling dough (*canederli;* see Italian Bread Dumpling Soup, page 60) may be shaped into teaspoon-size balls and added to the broth during the last 5 minutes of cooking.

summer vegetable soup

minestra estiva

This soup makes for a refreshing lunchtime meal on a hot summer day. Accompanied by bread, cheese, and olives, it may be served hot or cold and will keep in the refrigerator for three or four days. I like to drizzle a tiny bit of extra virgin olive oil over each portion just before serving to enhance the flavor.

2 tablespoons extra virgin olive oil

¾ cup chopped onion, cut into ¼-inch cubes (about 1 medium-size onion)

½ cup chopped carrot, cut into ¼-inch cubes (about 1 medium-size carrot)

1½ cups chopped celery, cut into ¼-inch cubes (about 2 stalks)

¾ cup chopped potato, cut into ¼-inch cubes (about 1 medium-size potato)

2 tablespoons chopped fresh Italian, flat leafed parsley

1 tablespoon chopped fresh basil leaves

¾ cup ripe tomato, cut into ¼-inch cubes (about 1 medium-size tomato)

6 cups vegetable broth (see note) or water

3 cups zucchini, cut into ¼-inch cubes (about 2 medium-size zucchini)

¼ cup fresh peas

1 cup asparagus, woody bottoms discarded and remaining tender spears cut into ¼-inch cubes (about 6 spears)

Kosher salt and freshly ground black pepper

Place a large flameproof casserole over medium-high heat. Add the olive oil and the onion, carrot, and celery. Cook, stirring occasionally, until the vegetables soften, about 7 minutes. Stir in the potato, parsley, and basil and cook, stirring occasionally, to season the vegetables with the herbs, about 2 minutes. Add the tomato and 3 cups of the stock or water. Bring to a boil, reduce the heat to medium-low, and simmer to warm through, about 5 minutes. Add the zucchini, peas, and asparagus along with the remaining 3 cups stock or water. Season with salt and pepper. Cover with the lid slightly askew and return to a boil. Reduce the heat to medium-low and simmer to heat through and soften the vegetables, about 10 minutes. Remove from heat. Allow to cool and serve at room temperature, or keep in the refrigerator for up to four days.

— S E R V E S   6   T O   8 —

WINE PAIRING: Medium white, light red, and medium red

NOTE: While you are chopping the vegetables for this soup, you can make homemade vegetable stock with little extra effort. Place 10 cups water in a stockpot. Add the peelings from the carrot and potato. Add the tops and bottoms of the zucchini, along with the tough asparagus bottoms. Then add:

    1 carrot, broken in half
    1 small potato, quartered
    ½ small onion
    5 sprigs fresh Italian, flat leafed parsley
    4 small celery stalks with their leaves
    5 black peppercorns
    ½ teaspoon kosher salt

Bring to a boil, then reduce the heat to medium-low and simmer, with the lid slightly askew. By the time it is called for in the recipe, the stock will be done. Strain, measure, and add it to the soup.

cremini mushroom and bean soup

zuppetta di funghi e fagioli

When you are obsessed with food, fresh ingredients are a must and you will go to absurd lengths to get them. As Gianni recounts, "When I am in Italy in the late summer, I drive an hour from my home to a village, Lamon, known for wonderful fresh and dried beans. Along the streets and roadsides old men sit beneath market umbrellas selling beans and potatoes on stands they construct from upturned vegetable crates. Between selecting beans at two or three different stands and talking with the old men, a simple task becomes an all-day excursion."

For this recipe, which Gianni created, he recommends cooking the beans separately from the vegetables so the beans do not become overcooked and muddy the crisp flavors of the other vegetables. If possible, use shelled fresh beans, both for their flavor and because they take less time to cook. However, dried beans can be used in this recipe and may be purchased anywhere at any time of year. Gianni favors cranberry beans (called *borlotti* in Italy), but pinto or white beans will do as well. This soup may be prepared several hours in advance. Combine and heat through just before serving.

1½ cups dried cranberry beans, or pinto beans or white beans such as cannellini

12 cups chicken broth or water

1 clove garlic, lightly crushed

1 tablespoon finely chopped fresh sage leaves

½ cup thinly sliced celery (about 1 stalk)

½ cup thinly sliced onions

2 tablespoons olive oil

1 tablespoon finely chopped fresh rosemary leaves

1 tablespoon finely chopped fresh Italian, flat leafed parsley

1 pound cremini mushrooms, cut into ¼-inch-thick slices

¾ cup canned whole plum tomatoes

2 cups potato, cut into ½-inch cubes

Kosher salt and freshly ground black pepper

1. Rinse the beans, removing any stones or grit, and place them in a bowl or saucepan. Fill the pan with water to a level 2 inches above the beans, and allow them to soak for 6 to 8 hours. Drain and proceed with the recipe. (A quick method for soaking beans is to place them in a pot of cold water, cover the pot, bring the water to a boil, and allow the beans to boil for 2 minutes. Remove from the heat and let the beans stand, covered, for 1 hour before draining and proceeding with the recipe.)

2. Combine the beans, 8 cups of the broth, the garlic, and the sage in a large pot. Bring to a boil, reduce the heat to medium-low, cover, and simmer until the beans are soft, about 50 minutes. Up to 1 cup of the remaining broth may be added to the beans, ½ cup at a time, to maintain a constant level during the cooking.

3. Meanwhile, in a wide sauté pan set over medium heat, cook the celery and onions in the olive oil until soft, about 7 minutes. Add the rosemary, parsley, and mushrooms, and cook, stirring to soften the mushrooms, about 10 minutes. Stir in the tomatoes, crushing them with your hands or the back of a slotted spoon as you add them to the pan. Add the potato cubes and cover the vegetables with the remaining 3 to 4 cups chicken broth. Bring to a boil, reduce the heat to medium-low, and simmer until the potatoes are soft when pierced with a fork, about 10 minutes.

4. Stir the mushroom mixture into the beans, season with salt and pepper, warm through, and serve immediately.

— SERVES 4 —

WINE PAIRING: Medium white and light red

italian bread dumpling soup

zuppa di canederli

This is a very traditional soup from the Veneto region of northern Italy, which is close to the Austrian border, and the influence on northern Italian cuisine is evident. This soup is very practical, relying principally on dry bread, and is often served as a pasta course. This dumpling dough (*canederli* in Italian) also may be rolled into a 3-inch-thick log, wrapped in a clean dish towel, and simmered for about 1 hour. When cooked through, it is then sliced and served with a meat-based pasta sauce, such as ragù.

2½ cups diced dry Italian white bread
    (about 4 ounces)

6 cups chicken broth

1 cup all-purpose flour

½ cup thinly sliced, then finely chopped
    pancetta (about 2 ounces)

⅓ cup thinly sliced, then finely chopped hard
    salami (about 1 ounce)

1 large egg, lightly beaten

1 cup milk

1 tablespoon chopped fresh chives

2 tablespoons chopped fresh Italian, flat
    leafed parsley

Pinch of ground nutmeg

½ teaspoon kosher salt

1. Air-dry the bread cubes overnight, or place them on a baking sheet and bake in an oven preheated to 300° F, stirring occasionally, until dry but not brown, about 20 minutes. Set aside.

2. Place the chicken broth in a medium-size saucepan set over medium-high heat. Cover with the lid askew and bring to a boil, then reduce the heat to a simmer.

3. Meanwhile, in a medium-size bowl, combine the bread with the flour, pancetta, salami, egg, milk, chives, parsley, nutmeg, and salt. Mix well, using your hands if necessary to evenly incorporate the ingredients. The dough should be moist and malleable. Scoop out rounded tablespoons of the dough and roll into balls.

4. Add the dough to the simmering chicken broth. Cook until all the balls are floating on the surface of the broth and are cooked though, about 8 minutes. Do not stir.

5. Remove the dumplings from the broth with a slotted spoon and distribute them equally among four soup bowls. Ladle the broth into the bowls and serve immediately.

— SERVES 4 —

WINE PAIRING: Medium white

VARIATIONS: Other fresh herbs, such as thyme or sage, may be substituted or added to the dough.

Speck, prosciutto, mortadella, and other similar meats may be added.

Dumpling dough may be shaped into teaspoon-size balls and added to Joan's Potato and Cabbage Soup recipe (page 55).

peasant soup
ribollita

Ribollita means "reboiled" and describes a hearty traditional soup that is usually cooked over two or three days. In this recipe, Gianni has devised a short cooking method that still achieves the rich flavor attained by many hours of simmering.

The recipe calls for black cabbage, which is shaped like romaine lettuce, when it is in season. However, it may not be as widely available in America as it is in Italy, so we recommend Savoy cabbage, which has a short growing season but can be found in supermarkets here. If you cannot find either of these, use very thinly sliced tender green cabbage. (Do not use red cabbage, which has a strong flavor that tends to overpower the other vegetables in this soup.)

In Italy ribollita has a thick consistency, closely resembling a vegetable stew. If you prefer a soupier dish, add more broth as desired. Top each serving with a wedge of sweet red onion.

½ pound dry bread, crusts removed, cut into ½-inch cubes

1 cup coarsely chopped celery (about 2 stalks)

1 cup diced carrots (about 2 medium-size carrots)

1 cup diced red onions (about 1 medium-size onion)

3 cloves garlic, chopped

2 tablespoons olive oil

1½ pounds Swiss chard, leaves and stems coarsely chopped

¾ pound Savoy or black cabbage, trimmed, cored, and coarsely chopped

1 tablespoon coarsely chopped fresh Italian, flat leafed parsley

2 teaspoons coarsely chopped fresh sage leaves

½ teaspoon chopped fresh thyme leaves

One 3-ounce rind Parmesan cheese (optional)

1½ cups canned whole plum tomatoes

6 cups chicken broth or water

1½ cups cooked cannellini beans or great Northern beans (½ cup dried; see note)

Extra virgin olive oil to drizzle

1. Air-dry the bread cubes overnight, or place them on a baking sheet and bake in an oven preheated to 300° F, stirring occasionally, until dry but not brown, about 20 minutes. Set aside.

2. Place the celery, carrots, onions, garlic, and olive oil in a large, heavy-bottomed soup pot set over medium heat. Cook the vegetables until softened but not browned, about 15 minutes. Stir in the Swiss chard and cabbage, and cook to wilt slightly, about 1 minute. Add the parsley, sage, thyme, cheese rind, if using, and tomatoes. Simmer gently until the Swiss chard leaves have completely wilted, about 10 minutes. Add the chicken broth and the beans. Cover the pot, with the lid slightly askew. Slowly bring the soup to a boil and then simmer gently until the cabbage and chard are tender, about 20 minutes. The soup may be prepared up to this point and allowed to cool to room temperature for a few hours before reheating and serving.

3. Just before serving, add the bread cubes. Simmer for 5 minutes. Remove the cheese rind, if using. Spoon the soup into bowls, and drizzle some extra virgin olive oil on top of each bowl. Serve immediately.

— SERVES 8 —

WINE PAIRING: Medium white and medium red

NOTE: Canned beans that have been drained and rinsed may be substituted for cooked beans in this recipe.

grace's chicken soup with mozzarella

zuppa di pollo con mozzarella alla grazia

This recipe is named for my Aunt Grace, my mother's sister, who created this variation based on my grandmother's original chicken soup recipe. This tasty soup is a meal in itself when served with a slice of crusty bread. For this recipe, you can use homemade broth (see Chicken Soup with Tiny Chicken Meatballs, page 52) or you can substitute a store-bought broth. These days there are several excellent varieties available—I always select the organic brands sold at my local supermarket. The chicken meatballs called for in this recipe are optional—the soup is very tasty prepared either way.

2 small heads escarole, chopped

7 cups chicken broth

1 whole chicken breast, bone in, skin removed

20 small chicken meatballs (page 52)

1 cup grated mozzarella cheese

4 tablespoons finely grated pecorino Romano cheese

1 large egg, lightly beaten

1. Bring a large pot of salted water to a gentle boil. Blanch the escarole until tender, about 5 minutes. Drain and set aside.

2. Bring 3 cups of the chicken broth to a gentle boil in a large saucepan. Add the chicken breast, cover, and poach until cooked through, about 12 minutes. Skim off and discard any foam that rises to the surface. Remove the chicken with a slotted spoon and set aside to cool.

3. Add the meatballs to the chicken broth and poach until cooked through, about 1 minute. Remove with a slotted spoon and set aside.

4. Strain the chicken broth through a fine-mesh strainer into a large saucepan or mixing bowl, add the remaining 4 cups broth, and set aside.

5. Shred the chicken meat into bite-size pieces and set aside, discarding the bone.

6. Preheat the oven to 350° F.

7. Pour ½ cup of the chicken broth into a small casserole or soufflé dish. Layer one quarter of the escarole over the broth. Add one quarter of the meatballs, one quarter of the shredded chicken, 1 cup of the broth, one quarter of the mozzarella, and 1 tablespoon of the pecorino Romano cheese. Top with another quarter of the escarole and continue to layer the ingredients, ending with mozzarella and pecorino Romano cheese. Pour the beaten egg over the top. Bake until the cheese has melted and the broth is heated through, about 20 minutes. Serve immediately.

— SERVES 6 —

WINE PAIRING: Light white, medium white, and light red

VARIATION: This is also wonderful prepared without the meatballs.

recipe pictured on page 50

venetian-style fish soup
zuppa di pesce alla veneziana

"The uglier the fish, the better the soup." That's the Italian rule of thumb. The fish that live closer to the rocks are the tastiest and also the ugliest. And the type of fish used determines how this recipe will proceed, so there isn't really a set recipe to follow. The basic idea is to cook the firmest fish first, adding the more delicate fish and seafood later on to produce a soup with great flavor and texture.

It also helps to purchase the smallest, sweetest clams available. Littlenecks are a good choice. Some specialty fish markets may be able to supply Manila clams, which are ideal. This simple soup goes well with grilled or toasted bread that has been rubbed with garlic. Venetian-Style Fish Soup may be prepared several hours in advance. Store it at room temperature and slowly reheat it before serving.

¼ cup extra virgin olive oil, plus more to drizzle over each serving

5 cloves garlic, lightly crushed

2 tablespoons chopped fresh Italian, flat leafed parsley

1 small jalapeño pepper, seeded and diced, or ½ teaspoon red pepper flakes

2 lobster tails (1 pound each), each cut into 3 pieces with shell

12 littleneck clams, scrubbed

½ cup dry white wine

2½ cups peeled and chopped fresh or canned tomatoes

18 ounces white-fleshed fish fillets (see note), such as scrod, cut into 1-inch cubes

12 mussels, scrubbed and debearded

6 jumbo shrimp, shelled and deveined

6 large sea scallops

½ teaspoon chopped fresh oregano leaves

½ teaspoon chopped fresh marjoram leaves

1 tablespoon chopped fresh basil leaves

Kosher salt and freshly ground black pepper

1. Heat the olive oil and garlic in a large flameproof casserole set over medium-high heat. When the oil is warm, add the parsley and jalapeño. When the garlic begins to brown lightly, add the lobster and clams. Stir and begin to warm the clams, about 2 minutes. Stir in the wine and cook, allowing the lobster to absorb the flavor, about 2 minutes. Add the tomatoes. When they begin to simmer, add the fish. Cover and simmer until the fish is no longer translucent, about 5 minutes.

2. Add the mussels, shrimp, and scallops along with the oregano, marjoram, and basil. Gently push this new layer of seafood down into the broth. Cook until the mussel shells have opened and the shrimp are pink, about 5 more minutes. Season with salt and pepper to taste, discard any clams and mussels that haven't opened, and serve immediately.

— SERVES 6 —

WINE PAIRING: Light white and medium white

NOTE: Halibut, bass, or red snapper may be used. Monkfish is also a good substitute, but it will require more cooking time. Add it to the soup along with the lobster.

fish stew in the style of the marche region
brodetto di pesce alla marchigiana

Our wonderful photographer, Francesco Tonelli, contributed this recipe, which was handed down to him from his mother. It is essentially a "poor man's" tomato sauce made with onions, garlic, and tomato paste—an excellent base for a variety of lunch dishes. It also makes for a quick, flavorful sauce in the winter, when there are no fresh tomatoes available, and can be made a day ahead of time and then reheated. I like to use an assortment of fish and seafood in this stew, but it may also be prepared using just one type of fish. Select any you like—although I would not recommend oily fish, such as salmon, tuna, or bluefish. Serve it as a main course over boiled rice or pasta or over slices of toasted bread that have been drizzled with olive oil.

¼ cup extra virgin olive oil

1 cup finely chopped onions

2 bay leaves

2 cloves garlic, thinly sliced

¼ cup tomato paste

Freshly ground black pepper

3 cups water

Kosher salt

1 pound rockfish, halibut, or striped bass

steak, bone in, skin removed, cut into 6 to 8 portions

1¼ pounds scrod, snapper, or cod fillets, cut into 3-inch chunks

½ pound cleaned calamari, cut into 2-inch chunks

6 to 8 jumbo shrimp, shelled and deveined

3 tablespoons torn fresh basil leaves

1. Warm the olive oil in a large, wide saucepan over medium-low heat. Stir in the onions, bay leaves, and garlic and cook until the onions soften and are golden yellow, about 8 minutes. Stir in the tomato paste and generous grindings of pepper. Cook, stirring constantly, to sweeten the paste with the onions, about 2 minutes. Stir in the water and season the sauce with salt. Bring to a slow simmer over low heat. Cook to thicken and reduce the sauce, about 20 minutes.

2. Add the rockfish (or other fish), cover the pan, and cook over low heat to soften slightly, about 5 minutes. Add the scrod (or other fish) and the calamari. Do not stir the fish, as it may break. Instead, shake the pan back and forth to incorporate the new fish and coat it with some of the sauce. Cover and cook to soften slightly, about 7 minutes. Add the shrimp, cover, and cook until they just begin to turn pink, about 3 minutes. Remove from the heat and set aside, allowing the fish to finish cooking off the heat, about 5 minutes more. Season with salt and garnish with the basil leaves. Serve immediately.

— SERVES 6 TO 8 —

WINE PAIRING: Light white and medium white

VARIATION: This dish may be served as a hearty soup appetizer. Reduce the amount of fish by half. Slice the shrimp in half lengthwise. Proceed with the recipe as written, serving the finished, slightly soupier stew in shallow bowls.

eggs

uova

My parents were never big on eggs for breakfast. Both of their families typically prepared egg-based dishes for lunch or light suppers, particularly on Friday evenings when abstaining from meat. But the frittata was always one of my favorite dishes.

To prepare for *Big Night,* I worked with Gianni in the kitchen at Le Madri, and the first thing I asked to be taught was how to cook a frittata. After a few attempts ended up on the kitchen floor, I started to get the hang of it. Somehow, however, I seldom seem to accomplish this culinary feat with the ease that I did when the camera was rolling. The scene was filmed in a five-and-a-half-minute-long master shot, with no coverage (therefore there could be no cutaways), so I knew I must perform this task perfectly. I had found that a very high heat was the key to success with a frittata. We did seven takes, two of which were aborted halfway through—but not because of the cooking, which luckily was successful every time. It is because of this scene that people believe I can really cook. If they only knew!

poached eggs on country bread with pecorino toscano

crostone di pane "all'occhio di bue"

All'Occhio di Bue means "the eyes of the bull," which is a colorful way of describing what poached eggs look like. In this recipe, simple poached eggs are taken to a higher level with the addition of fresh herbs and pecorino Toscano cheese. Pecorino Toscano is a soft, mild sheep's milk cheese. Unfortunately, it is very difficult to find in the United States, so instead you may substitute Asiago, Fontina, Emmenthaler, or even an extra-sharp cheddar. For this recipe, use a vegetable peeler to shave paper-thin slices of cheese.

4 slices country-style bread

1 clove garlic, cut in half

1 tablespoon chopped fresh herbs (rosemary, sage, parsley, oregano, marjoram, tarragon, or chives)

1 quart water

3 tablespoons white or cider vinegar

Kosher salt

4 large eggs

½ teaspoon white truffle oil (available in specialty food stores)

½ teaspoon extra virgin olive oil

Freshly ground black pepper

16 large shaving pecorino Toscano cheese (about 3 ounces)

1. Toast the bread. Rub with the garlic and sprinkle the herbs over the toast. Set aside.

2. Place the water, vinegar, and some salt in a 2-quart saucepan and bring to a boil. Reduce the heat to a simmer. Break 1 egg into a small bowl and gently slide it into the water. Do the same one at a time with the other 3 eggs. Cook until the whites of the eggs are solid but the yolks are still runny, 3 to 5 minutes. Remove with a slotted spoon and place one egg on top of each slice of bread.

3. In a small dish, whisk the truffle oil and olive oil. Drizzle over the eggs. Season with the salt and pepper, and top with the cheese shavings. Serve immediately.

— SERVES 4 —

WINE PAIRING: Sparkling and light white

VARIATION: More extra virgin olive oil may be used in place of the truffle oil.

recipe pictured on page 70

eggs with peppers
frittata con peperoni

Frittata was a staple for lunch when I was growing up—each slice was filled with different vegetables. Though I loved it, I must confess that at times I traded it for a sandwich of peanut butter and Marshmallow Fluff. Frittata is perfect when served with focaccia and a green salad.

¼ cup olive oil

2 red or green cubanelle or bell peppers, seeded and cut into ½-inch-wide strips

4 large eggs

Kosher salt and freshly ground black pepper

Warm the olive oil in a medium-size nonstick or regular frying pan set over medium heat. Add the peppers, cover, and cook until softened, about 20 minutes. In a small bowl, beat the eggs and salt and pepper to taste. Add the eggs to the softened peppers in the pan. Allow the eggs to set, about 2 minutes, then turn over and continue cooking on the other side until firm, about 2 minutes more.

— SERVES 4 —

WINE PAIRING: Sparkling, light white, and medium white

VARIATIONS: Here is how my mother prepared asparagus frittata—her childhood favorite:

Cut about ½ pound asparagus on the bias into 1-inch pieces. Blanch in boiling water for about 1 minute. Drain, pat dry, and cook in the oil to soften, about 5 minutes. Proceed with the basic recipe, adding 2 tablespoons finely grated pecorino Romano cheese to the egg mixture.

One small potato, peeled, or 1 small zucchini, cut into ⅛-inch-thick slices (about ½ cup each) may be used instead of the peppers.

One small onion, coarsely chopped (about ½ cup), may be sautéed with the peppers or other vegetables.

One tablespoon finely grated pecorino Romano cheese may be added to the eggs before frying.

If you are really hungry, *all* of the above ingredients may be added to the frittata.

eggs with tomato

uova al pomodoro

As a kid I looked forward to this Friday night meal. Not only was it unusually beautiful, but its sweet flavor, thanks to the onions, would linger long after the last bite. This recipe uses a simple method of poaching the eggs in tomato sauce. It makes a terrific lunch dish, served with slices of bread for dipping in the sauce and accompanied by a tossed salad.

¼ cup olive oil

1 small onion, thinly sliced

1 cup canned whole plum tomatoes

4 large eggs

Kosher salt and freshly ground black pepper

Warm the olive oil in a medium-size nonstick frying pan over medium heat. Add the onion and cook until soft, about 3 minutes. Add the tomatoes, crushing them with your hand or the back of a slotted spoon. Cook until the tomatoes have sweetened, about 20 minutes, stirring occasionally. Gently break the eggs into the pan and cover. Cook until the whites are opaque and the yolks are moderately firm, about 5 minutes. Serve immediately, seasoned with salt and pepper to taste.

— SERVES 2 —

WINE PAIRING: Sparkling and light white

VARIATIONS: One cup Gianni's Basic Tomato Sauce (page 118) or Sailor's-Style Sauce (page 120) may be substituted for the olive oil, onion, and canned tomatoes. Warm the sauce over medium heat for 5 to 7 minutes before adding the eggs.

To make a heart-healthy and tasty version of this dish, follow the basic recipe but use 6 egg whites in place of the whole eggs.

egg tart with spinach and potatoes

tortino di uova, patate e spinaci al forno

This recipe is a variation on one that Gianni's father used to make for the patrons of his family-run bar. "He would cut the *tortino* into small squares and place it on top of the counter to be eaten as a snack with a glass of wine," Gianni recalls. "At home it was served to us children as a snack after school along with a slice of bread." This is scrumptious eaten warm from the oven, at room temperature, or even cold.

1 large Yukon Gold potato, peeled

8 large eggs

½ pound fresh spinach, stems removed, leaves washed well, coarsely chopped, and blanched in boiling water for 1 minute

Kosher salt and freshly ground black pepper

2 teaspoons chopped fresh Italian, flat leafed parsley

1 tablespoon butter

1 tablespoon canola oil

1. Preheat the oven to 375° F.

2. Place the potato in a pot filled with cold salted water. Bring to a boil and cook the potato until just tender when pierced with a fork, 20 to 25 minutes. Cut the potato in half lengthwise and then into thin half-moon-shaped slices.

3. In a medium-size bowl, whisk the eggs until frothy. Squeeze all the water out of the spinach and add to the eggs along with the potato slices, salt and pepper to taste, and the parsley. Stir briskly to incorporate all the ingredients.

4. Heat a 10- to 12-inch nonstick ovenproof frying pan or well-seasoned cast-iron skillet over medium-high heat. Add the butter and oil. When the butter has melted and is foaming, pour the egg mixture into the pan, stirring well. Continue to cook and stir until the eggs become slightly scrambled, about 2 minutes. Transfer the pan to the oven and bake until the eggs are firm but still moist, about 6 minutes. Remove from the oven and flip the egg tart onto a serving plate. Slice and serve immediately.

— SERVES 4 —

WINE PAIRING: Sparkling, light white, and medium white

eggs with salad and soppressata

uova, insalata, e soppressa

In this dish the soppressata and eggs are cooked together and tossed with a lightly dressed salad. It makes a simple meal that may be served for lunch or for a casual Sunday supper. Pancetta, other hard salamis, or bacon may be substituted for soppressata.

4 tablespoons olive oil

1 tablespoon balsamic or red wine vinegar

Kosher salt and freshly ground black pepper

¾ pound mixed bitter salad greens, washed, patted dry, and coarsely chopped (see note)

¼ pound soppressata, sliced, or lean pancetta or bacon, cut into strips

1 tablespoon chopped fresh herbs (see note)

2 tablespoons coarsely chopped scallions (white part only)

8 large eggs, lightly beaten

1. In a salad bowl, whisk 3 tablespoons of the olive oil with the vinegar and salt and pepper to taste. Add the salad greens and toss to coat evenly with the dressing.

2. In a large nonstick sauté pan or a well-seasoned cast-iron skillet set over medium heat, cook the soppressata in the remaining 1 tablespoon olive oil. When it is crisp, add the herbs, scallions, and eggs. Cook, stirring the eggs to scramble. When the eggs are firm but not dry, spoon them over the salad. Toss quickly but gently. Serve immediately.

— SERVES 4 —

WINE PAIRING: Sparkling, medium white, and light red

NOTE: Any of the following fresh herbs may be used individually or in combination when preparing this dish: chives, basil, parsley, oregano, or marjoram. Some of the bitter salad greens I recommend using include frisée, radicchio, dandelion greens, endive, and romaine.

pastina with eggs

pastina con uova

In Italy, *pastina* is any of the little pastas given to babies and small children, such as orzo or small star shapes. My father, Stan, remembers his mother making this dish for him for a quick warm lunch or if he wasn't feeling too well. My mother, Joan, who walked home for lunch from school each day, remembers her grandmother preparing plain warm pastina drizzled with olive oil as a lunchtime meal. So you can try this dish the Tucci way, with eggs, or the Tropiano way, without eggs.

½ cup pastina pasta

Kosher salt

2 large eggs (optional)

1 teaspoon butter or olive oil

1. Fill a small saucepan with salted water and bring to a boil over medium-high heat. Add the pastina and cook according to the package instructions.

2. Reserve 1 cup of the cooking water before draining the pastina. Return the cup of hot water and the drained pastina to the saucepan over medium-high heat. Break the eggs, if using, directly into the saucepan. Whisk and simmer to cook the eggs, about 1 minute. Divide between two plates, and top with equal portions of the butter. Serve immediately.

— SERVES 2 —

WINE PAIRING: Sparkling, light white, and medium white

bread and pizza

pane e pizza

They say "man cannot live on bread alone." I wonder if this is true, because sometimes I think I might be able to pull it off, I love it so much. Its pure simplicity is its attraction. Bread is a before, an in-between, and an after. It is the first food that most of us turn to when hunger begins to gnaw. The baguettes of France, the flatbreads of the Middle East, the soda breads of Ireland, and the countless Italian breads: focaccia, schiacciata, pizza, the bland saltless bread of Florence (made this way so as not to interfere with the flavor of the sauce when used for dipping)—the varieties are endless. But what is constant is that we all find comfort in this most basic and spiritual of foods.

Homemade bread and pizza were staples in my mother's home when she was growing up. My grandmother worked during the week, so on the weekends she would bake several loaves at once to be eaten throughout the week, topped with jellies made from fruit my grandfather grew or generously spread with homemade ricotta made from fresh goat's milk.

As Joan recalls: "When she was done baking, my mother would put aside one or two loaves of bread for slicing. She would return these slices to the oven to be baked a second time. We called this bread *biscotto*. It was excellent eaten like a cracker with soup or topped with chopped fresh tomatoes and olive oil. To me it tasted better than a cookie."

bread sticks

grissini

Using a pasta machine to make these bread sticks guarantees they will be of uniform width and will make them easy to roll out. Of course they may also be made by rolling sections of the dough on a floured surface and then cutting them into long, thin strips. Bread sticks that are twisted into shapes or that are more than ¼ inch wide will take slightly longer to bake.

1 package dry yeast

1 tablespoon sugar

1⅓ cups warm water

3 cups all-purpose flour

½ cup semolina flour, plus extra for dusting

1 tablespoon kosher salt

1 tablespoon chopped fresh rosemary leaves

¼ cup extra virgin olive oil

2 teaspoons grappa or vodka

1. Stir the yeast and sugar in a 2-cup measuring cup. Stir in the warm water and set aside for 5 minutes.

2. In a large bowl or on a clean work surface, mix the all-purpose flour, semolina flour, salt, and rosemary. Mound the mixture, and make a well in the center. Add the yeast mixture, olive oil, and grappa to the well. Using a fork at first and then your hands, gradually blend the flour mixture into the wet ingredients. Turn the dough out onto a lightly floured work surface and knead until it is smooth and not sticky. Place in a clean bowl. Cover with plastic wrap and a clean dish towel. Set aside in a warm place to rise until doubled in size, about 1 hour.

3. Preheat the oven to 350° F. Dust several baking sheets with semolina flour and set them aside.

4. Turn the dough out onto a lightly floured surface. Cut the dough into six equal pieces. Flatten one piece to the width of the pasta machine opening. Lightly flour the dough and pass it through the widest opening of the machine to produce a flat 12-inch-long piece of dough. Lightly flour the dough again and pass it through the wide noodle setting to create individual strands of dough. Arrange them ½-inch apart on a prepared baking sheet. Repeat this procedure with the remaining pieces of dough. Bake until golden brown on the bottom, about 5 minutes. Turn and continue baking until evenly brown, about 5 minutes more. Allow to cool on wire racks before serving or storing in an airtight container.

— SERVES 8 —

WINE PAIRING: Sparkling

VARIATIONS: If you'd like to serve an assortment of flavored bread sticks, divide the risen dough into quarters, setting one quarter aside to be baked as in the basic recipe. To one of the remaining quarters add ¼ cup finely grated Parmesan or cheddar cheese. To another quarter add 1 teaspoon chopped fresh herbs such as sage, thyme, oregano, or marjoram. To the last quarter add 1 teaspoon olive paste. Knead each quarter well to incorporate these ingredients. Allow to rest for 10 minutes before passing through the pasta machine.

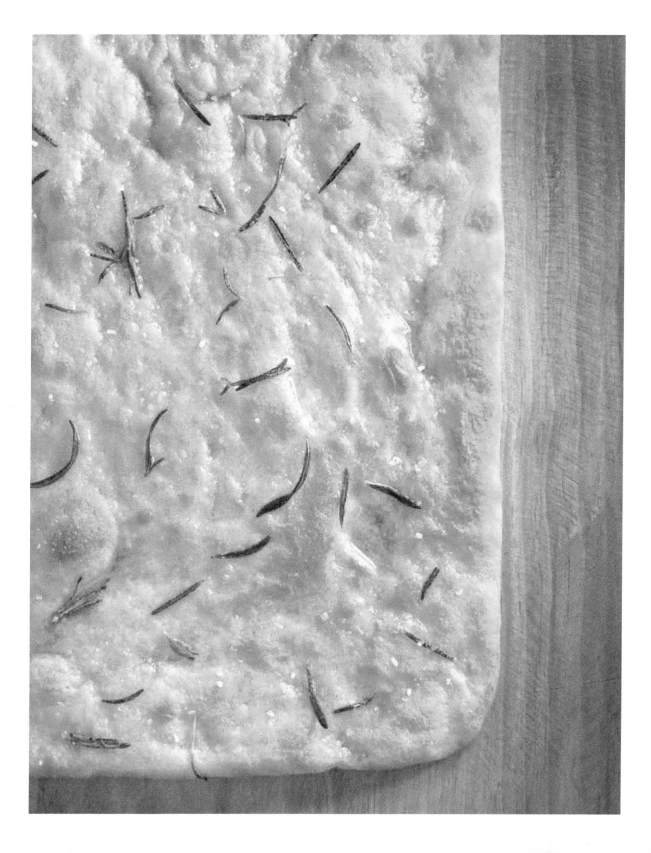

rosemary focaccia

focaccia al rosmarino

During one year in Italy it seems to me that I lived on focaccia. I would buy a piece after school every day. Though mass-produced and sold from a cart, this hearty oiled and salted bread was the perfect treat. This basic recipe can be changed by adding different herbs or toppings, sometimes becoming a meal in itself (see variations, below).

1 package dry yeast

2¼ teaspoons sugar

½ cup warm water

2 cups all-purpose flour

2 cups bread flour

4 teaspoons kosher salt

1 cup milk

5 tablespoons olive oil, plus more for oiling the bowl

Leaves from one 5-inch sprig fresh rosemary

1. In a measuring cup, stir the yeast, sugar, and warm water. Set aside for 5 minutes.

2. In the bowl of an electric mixer fitted with a dough hook, mix the all-purpose and bread flours with 2 teaspoons of the salt. Stir in the yeast mixture. Gradually stir in the milk and 3 tablespoons of the olive oil. Mix at low speed until the dough has come together and is smooth, about 5 minutes.

(To mix by hand: Combine the all-purpose flour, bread flour, and 2 teaspoons of the salt in a large bowl. Make a well in the center of these dry ingredients and add the yeast mixture. Mix with a fork while adding the milk and 3 tablespoons of the olive oil to form a soft, dry dough. Turn the dough out onto a lightly floured surface and continue mixing it with your hands. Knead until the dough has come together and is smooth, about 8 minutes.)

3. Lightly grease a bowl with olive oil. Place the dough in the bowl, cover tightly with plastic wrap, and drape a dish towel over the bowl. Set aside in a warm place and allow to double in size, about 2 hours.

recipe continued on next page

4. Lightly grease a large baking sheet (about 9 x 15-inch). Gently punch down the dough. Place it on the baking sheet and roll it out to fit evenly on the sheet. Cover with a dish towel and allow the dough to rise for 20 minutes.

5. Preheat the oven to 375° F.

6. Use your fingertips to make random indentations in the dough. Drizzle the top with the remaining 2 tablespoons olive oil. Sprinkle with the remaining 2 teaspoons salt and the rosemary leaves. Bake until golden brown, about 30 minutes. Allow to cool slightly before slicing and serving warm.

— SERVES 10 —

VARIATIONS: Before baking, top the focaccia with any combination of the following ingredients: ¼-inch-thick slices ripe plum tomatoes; 24 pitted kalamata olives; ¼ cup very thinly sliced red onions; ⅓ cup crumbled goat cheese; ¼-inch-thick slices peeled eggplant; ¼-inch-thick slices zucchini; ¼-inch-thick slices bell peppers; ⅓ cup pesto.

For a sweet variation on this recipe, gently press 1 cup dried fruit such as raisins, cherries, or blueberries, or 1 cup chocolate chips, into the rolled and risen focaccia. Brush with 3 tablespoons melted butter and bake.

tropiano family focaccia

focaccia tropiano

The wonderful aroma of fresh breads and pizzas wafting from my grandmother's kitchen was a staple of my mother's childhood. This recipe makes two medium-size focaccias, which may be served with lunch, as an appetizer, or with dinner. For variety, fresh herbs such as rosemary, sage, marjoram, or basil may be added to the dough when the focaccia is first kneaded, or combined with the olive oil that is drizzled on top just before baking.

My mother mixes this dough by hand. However it may also be prepared in a stand mixer fitted with a dough hook.

*1 package dry yeast
    or 1 cake fresh yeast
2 cups warm water
4 cups all-purpose flour*

*1 tablespoon kosher salt, plus more for
    sprinkling
4 tablespoons cornmeal
4 tablespoons olive oil*

1. In a measuring cup, combine the yeast with ½ cup of the warm water. Stir until the yeast dissolves.

2. In a large bowl, combine the flour and salt. Make a well in the center and add the yeast mixture. Begin by mixing with a fork and then use your hands while adding enough of the remaining 1½ cups water to form a soft, dry dough.

3. Turn the dough out onto a lightly floured surface and continue mixing it with your hands. Add flour as necessary to keep the dough from being too sticky. Knead until the dough is no longer sticky. Form the dough into a ball and place in a large bowl. Cover loosely with a clean dish towel or with plastic wrap that has been brushed with olive oil on the side that faces down into the bowl. Set aside in a warm place and allow to rise until it has doubled in size, about 2 hours.

recipe continued on next page

4. Preheat the oven to 400° F.

5. Divide the risen dough in half. Roll one half of the dough on a lightly floured surface to a size that will roughly fit a baking sheet, about 9 x 13 inches. Sprinkle the baking sheet with 2 tablespoons of the cornmeal. Place the dough on the baking sheet and cover with plastic wrap or a clean dish towel. Allow to rise for 30 minutes. Proceed in the same fashion with the other half of the dough.

6. Use your fingertips to make random indentations in the risen dough. Drizzle approximately 2 tablespoons of the olive oil over each piece of dough, and sprinkle with additional kosher salt. Bake on the bottom rack of the oven until golden brown, about 15 minutes.

7. Serve sliced, warm or at room temperature.

— S E R V E S 1 2 —

N O T E : Dough that has risen once may be wrapped in plastic and stored in the refrigerator for up to 3 days, or frozen for up to 1 month. Allow the dough to come to room temperature before rolling it out to fit on a baking sheet. Then set it aside to rise for half an hour before proceeding with the recipe.

walnut bread

pane di noci

The dry milk in this recipe produces a light, airy loaf and the walnuts release a rich aroma while the bread is baking. It is excellent served with assorted cheeses and a tossed salad, or dipped in a flavorful olive oil. Save some to toast in the morning, and top with marmalade or your favorite jam.

2½ cups warm water

1 package dry yeast

6 cups whole wheat flour, or more as needed

1 teaspoon kosher salt

⅓ cup whole milk powder

3 tablespoons honey

¼ cup olive oil

½ cup walnut oil

1½ cups coarsely chopped walnuts

1. In a small bowl, stir ¼ cup of the warm water and the yeast. Set aside for 5 minutes.

2. In a large bowl, toss 3 cups of the flour, the salt, and the milk powder. Stir in the yeast mixture along with the remaining 2¼ cups warm water, the honey, olive oil, and walnut oil. Mix with a fork or the dough hook of a stand mixer until well combined. Add the walnuts and 1 cup of the remaining flour to the mixture, kneading to combine. Continue adding the remaining 2 cups flour, ¼ cup at a time, until the dough is moist and slightly sticky. Set aside to rest for 5 minutes.

3. Turn the dough out onto a lightly floured surface. Knead until the dough is soft and elastic, about 8 minutes. If the dough is very sticky, add more flour, ¼ cup at a time, while kneading.

4. Place the dough in a clean bowl and cover with plastic wrap and a clean dish towel. Set aside in a warm place and allow to rise for 1 hour.

recipe continued on next page

5. Preheat the oven to 375° F. Line two baking sheets with parchment paper and set aside.

6. Divide the risen dough in half and shape each half into a round loaf. Place on baking sheets and cover with a dish towel. Set aside and allow to double in size, about 40 minutes.

7. Bake the loaves until they are deep golden brown and firm, 40 to 45 minutes.

— MAKES 2 LOAVES —

VARIATIONS: This bread is also delicious when you replace the walnuts with an equal amount of coarsely chopped fennel leaves and 2 tablespoons fennel seeds or replace them with coarsely chopped sun-dried tomatoes or chopped pitted mixed olives. With either of these variations, regular olive oil may be used in place of the walnut oil. All versions of this bread freeze well.

maria pia's easter bread

anello di pasqua di maria pia

My grandmother Nonna Tucci baked this cakelike bread, decorated with eggs, every Easter. Now my cousin Maria Pia has taken over the tradition. She knows just how soft and sticky the dough should feel to create a light, not-too-sweet bread, and she serves it along with other desserts and coffee. Leftovers are great for breakfast, too.

The raw eggs in their shells can be dyed prior to being inserted in the dough or left plain. They bake along with the bread and can be removed from their shells and eaten just like hard-boiled eggs.

When I was growing up, my other grandmother, Nonna Tropiano, or my aunt Angie would give us each one of these breads as an Easter gift. We would carry them around, munching on the sweet dough for hours.

9 large eggs, at room temperature

½ cup granulated sugar

1 teaspoon pure vanilla extract

4 cups all-purpose flour

½ teaspoon kosher salt

4 teaspoons baking powder

12 tablespoons (1½ sticks) butter, softened

1½ cups confectioners' sugar

2 tablespoons milk or water

½ teaspoon pure lemon extract

1. Preheat the oven to 350° F.

2. In a medium-size bowl, beat 6 of the eggs, the granulated sugar, and the vanilla until pale yellow and frothy. Set aside.

3. In a large bowl, stir together 3 cups of the flour, the salt, and the baking powder. Add the butter and blend with an electric mixer to form a crumbly mixture. Gradually beat in the egg mixture. Add up to ½ cup of the remaining flour to form a soft dough that is dry on the outside but still sticky on the inside.

recipe continued on next page

4. Gently roll the dough into a log about 15 inches long and 2 inches in diameter. Cut off a 1-inch-long piece of the dough and set aside. Place the log on a baking sheet. Bring the ends of the log together to form a circle, pinching the dough together to seal the ends. Press 1 of the remaining eggs into the dough at this joint. Place the other 2 eggs an even distance apart on either side of the joint, gently pressing them into the dough.

5. Roll the reserved dough into six ropes about ½ inch wide and 4 inches long. Place two ropes over each egg to form an X, or cross, pinching gently to seal the ends of the ropes to the bread dough. Bake until the bread is light golden brown and a skewer inserted in the center comes out clean, about 30 minutes. Remove from the oven and allow to cool completely.

6. In a small bowl mix the confectioners' sugar, milk, and lemon extract, until smooth. Drizzle the icing back and forth over the bread to create a decorative topping. Allow the icing to set for 30 minutes before slicing and serving.

— SERVES 10 —

VARIATIONS: Nonna Tucci made several different types of confections from this same dough: *Cicirata,* also known as *struffoli,* are deep-fried teaspoon-size balls of this dough that are dipped in honey and mounded together to create an Italian version of croquembouche.

This dough should not be sticky in the center; an additional ½ cup flour may need to be kneaded into the dough before rolling small sections into ½-inch-thick ropes. Cut the ropes into ½-inch sections. Fill a small frying pan with vegetable oil to a depth of 1 inch. Warm over medium-low heat until the oil is hot but not smoking. Fry batches of the cookies in the oil until golden.

While the oil is warming before frying the cookies, place 1 cup honey, 1 cup sugar, and 1 cup water in a medium-size saucepan and slowly bring to a boil. Boil to dissolve the sugar and thicken the mixture slightly, about 20 minutes. Use a fork or tongs to dip the fried cookies into the honey syrup. Shape the cookies into a mound on a serving plate. Decorate with colorful sugar sprinkles and serve in the middle of the table.

Anellini are small ring-shaped cookies. Preheat the oven to 350° F. Roll small sections of this dough into ½-inch-thick ropes. Cut the ropes into 2-inch lengths. Wrap each length around the ends of your two middle fingers and pinch together to form a small ring. Place the cookies on a baking sheet and bake until lightly browned, about 12 minutes. Allow to cool completely before drizzling with the same icing mixture used in the bread. Garnish with colorful sugar sprinkles if you like.

kate's banana bread

This recipe is from my late wife, Kate, who passed away in 2009. Not only was she an extraordinary person, she was also a great cook and a wonderful baker. Making this recipe is just one of the ways we keep her close to us.

Kate's banana bread was devoured weekly by our kids and by the endless stream of their friends who came through our doors over the years. Serve warm with a dollop of butter.

1¼ cups all-purpose flour

1 teaspoon baking soda

½ cup (1 stick) butter, softened

½ cup sugar

2 large eggs

1 teaspoon pure vanilla extract

3 ripe bananas

¼ cup Grape-Nuts cereal

1. Preheat the oven to 350° F. Grease a 4 x 8-inch loaf pan and line with parchment paper.

2. In a medium-size bowl, sift the flour and baking soda. In another medium-size bowl, use a wooden spoon or whisk to mix together the butter and sugar. Add the eggs, one at a time, beating after each addition. Add the vanilla and the bananas, mashing them into the batter. Stir in the Grape-Nuts.

3. Spoon the batter into the prepared loaf pan. Bake until golden brown on top and a cake tester comes out clean, about 45 minutes.

Kate in the kitchen

fried dough

zeppole

My mother claims, "In all modesty, my mother's *zeppole* were the best I've ever tasted. They were lighter than all others and not laden with oil." My grandmother prepared these fritters for holidays and special occasions, such as Christmas Eve. Her family ate them plain, while the Tucci family dusted them with granulated sugar. Zeppole are good either way, and taste best if you eat them right after they've been fried. You can also fry them earlier in the day and reheat in the oven.

4 medium-size all-purpose potatoes (about 1⅓ pounds)

1 package dry yeast

1 cup warm water

4 cups all-purpose flour

Kosher salt

Corn oil for frying

1. Place the potatoes in a pot, cover with cold water, and bring to a boil. Cook the potatoes until tender when pierced with a knife, about 15 minutes. Drain, peel, and quarter. Season with salt before mashing until smooth with a potato masher or electric mixer. Transfer to a large bowl.

2. In a measuring cup, dissolve the yeast in the warm water. Set aside for 5 minutes.

3. Mix 1 cup of the flour into the mashed potatoes. Stir in the yeast mixture. Mix in 2 cups more of the flour. Turn the dough out onto a floured work surface. Gradually knead in as much of the remaining cup of flour as necessary to form a soft, dry dough. Slice the dough in half to test the center. If it is still sticky, knead in some more flour.

4. Place the dough in a clean bowl. Cover with plastic wrap and then with a clean dish towel. Set aside in a warm place to rise until doubled in size, about 2 hours.

recipe continued on next page

5. Line a baking sheet with two layers of paper towels and set aside. Fill a medium-size frying pan with corn oil to a depth of 1 inch. Warm the oil over medium-high heat until hot but not smoking.

6. Gently deflate the risen dough. It will be sticky—lightly dust your fingers with flour. Scoop out a 2-tablespoon-size portion of the dough. Shape it with your fingers to create a doughnut shape. Place it in the oil. If the oil is hot enough, the dough will rise to the surface and bubble. Fry until golden on both sides, turning once, 3 to 5 minutes on each side. Remove from the oil with a slotted spoon and place on the paper-towel-lined baking sheet to drain before serving.

7. Continue frying the dough in batches of two zeppole at a time. Add more oil to the pan as necessary. Allow the oil to return to frying heat before adding more dough. Serve in small batches after allowing to cool slightly.

— SERVES 10 —

VARIATION: Mixing 1 or 2 chopped anchovies with each zeppole creates a nice savory version of this recipe.

Gianni was at our house when we were testing this fried dough recipe for the book. He made a few additional serving suggestions: You may prepare a delectable sandwich by cutting the fried dough in half and filling it with a slice of prosciutto, salami, mortadella, or Asiago cheese.

pizza

pizza

In her neighborhood, my grandmother Tropiano's pizza was considered the best—quite an accomplishment in a largely Italian community. She began making dough on an almost daily basis at the age of nine or ten and was still doing it at eighty-five. My mother follows my grandmother's example, kneading the dough by hand, but it may also be prepared in a stand mixer fitted with a dough hook.

This is my family's basic recipe for pizza. Of course, an infinite number of toppings may be used. Even the marinara sauce is optional. Roll your pizza as thick or thin as you like. My grandmother rolled hers thin enough to be cut with scissors.

1 package dry yeast or 1 cake fresh yeast

2 cups warm water

4 cups all-purpose flour

1 tablespoon kosher salt

4 tablespoons cornmeal

4 tablespoons olive oil

2 cups Sailor's-Style Sauce (page 120)

4 cloves garlic (optional)

½ teaspoon dried oregano

1 pound mozzarella cheese, grated

½ cup finely grated pecorino Romano cheese

1. In a measuring cup, combine the yeast with ½ cup of the warm water. Stir until the yeast dissolves.

2. In a large bowl, combine the flour and salt. Make a well in the center and add the yeast mixture. Begin by mixing with a fork and then by hand while adding enough of the remaining 1½ cups water to form a soft, dry dough.

3. Turn the dough out onto a lightly floured surface and continue mixing it with your hands. Knead to form a smooth dough, adding more flour as necessary to keep the dough from being too sticky. Form into a ball and place in a clean bowl. Cover the bowl loosely with a clean dish towel. Set it aside in a warm place and allow to rise until it has doubled in size, about 2 hours.

recipe continued on page 102

4. Preheat the oven to 500° F.

5. Divide the risen dough in half. Roll one half of the dough on a lightly floured surface into a rectangle that will fit on a 9 x 13-inch or 12-inch round baking street. Sprinkle the baking sheet with 2 tablespoons of cornmeal. Transfer the rolled dough to the baking sheet. Drizzle with 2 tablespoons of the olive oil. Spread 1 cup of the marinara sauce evenly over the dough to within 1 inch of the edge. Squeeze 2 of the garlic cloves, if using, through a press and sprinkle over the marinara. Sprinkle ¼ teaspoon of the oregano over the marinara. Sprinkle half the mozzarella and half the Romano cheese over the marinara. Bake until the edges and bottom of the dough are lightly browned, about 15 minutes.

6. While the first pizza is baking, roll out the other half of the dough and top it with the remaining ingredients. Bake the second pizza. Allow each pizza to cool for 5 minutes before slicing so all the cheese doesn't slide to the middle.

— SERVES 8 —

VARIATIONS: A pound of Fontina, grated, may be substituted for the mozzarella. If you have scraps of leftover dough, shape them by hand into thin 4-inch rounds. Warm 2 tablespoons olive oil in a small frying pan set over medium-low heat. When the oil is hot but not smoking, add the dough and fry until golden brown and puffy on one side. Turn and continue browning. Sprinkle with granulated sugar and serve as a snack. Stan's family ate fried dough with eggs, as though it was toast.

Stanley preparing pizza to cook in his backyard brick oven

stuffed pizza

pizza ripiena

My grandmother Nonna Tropiano made these stuffed pizzas for large family gatherings to be eaten as an appetizer. She would buy an eight- to ten-pound ham, boil it for fifteen to twenty minutes, trim away any fat, then dice enough meat into cubes to use as a filling for three or four pizza ripiene. Soppressata or diced ham steaks may be substituted.

This pie may be refrigerated for one day. Bring it to room temperature or reheat before serving.

1 package dry yeast or 1 cake fresh yeast
2 cups warm water
4 cups all-purpose flour
1 tablespoon kosher salt
2 tablespoons cornmeal
4 cups ½-inch cubes smoked ham

2 cups ricotta cheese (about 1 pound)
¼ cup finely grated pecorino Romano cheese
2½ cups ½-inch cubes mozzarella cheese
  (about ¾ pound)
2 large eggs, lightly beaten
Freshly ground black pepper

1. In a measuring cup, combine the yeast with ½ cup of the warm water. Stir until the yeast dissolves.

2. In a large bowl, combine the flour and salt. Make a well in the center and add the yeast mixture. Begin by mixing with a fork and then by hand while adding enough of the remaining 1½ cups water to form a soft, dry dough. The dough may be prepared in a stand mixer fitted with a dough hook. Dough prepared this way may require less water.

3. Turn the dough out onto a lightly floured surface and continue mixing it with your hands. Knead to form a smooth dough, adding more flour as necessary to keep the dough from being too sticky. Form into a ball and place in a clean bowl. Cover the bowl loosely with a clean dish towel. Set it aside in a warm place and allow the dough to rise until it has doubled in size, about 2 hours.

4. Preheat the oven to 350° F. Sprinkle a large (about 9 x15-inch) baking sheet with the cornmeal and set aside.

5. In a large bowl, mix together the ham, ricotta, Romano, and mozzarella. Mix in the eggs. Season with pepper and set aside.

6. Divide the risen dough in half. Roll one half of the dough on a lightly floured surface into a rectangle that is slightly larger than the baking sheet. Transfer the rolled dough to the baking sheet. Spread the filling evenly over the dough to within 1 inch of the edge.

7. Roll the second half of the dough on a lightly floured work surface into a rectangle that will fit on top of the pie. Place it on top of the filled dough in the baking sheet. Gently press the two layers together. Trim away any thick portions of dough to create an even edge. Use the tines of a fork to completely seal the edges.

8. Bake until the dough is golden brown on the top and bottom, about 1 hour. Allow to cool slightly and set before serving, about 30 minutes.

— SERVES 10 —

WINE PAIRING: Sparkling, light white, and light red

recipe pictured on page 82

pasta

pasta

As for most Italians, pasta is a staple in our family's daily life. We eat it all the time, primarily as a first course. It is one of the simplest yet most complex and varied foodstuffs ever. Each time you make it, you are presented with a blank canvas that can be given so many shapes, sizes, and textures, and that is enhanced by each sauce accompanying it.

In Italy, every region has its own array of pasta shapes that are served with a variety of stuffings and sauces. Some pasta names vary from region to region—*strozzapreti,* for example, or "priest stranglers," are called *strangolapreti* in some towns. In the north, they are strands of pasta the width of fettuccine twisted into a coil; in the south, they are big ricotta dumplings. Other shapes of pasta, such as *garganelli* or *maccheroni,* have the same name all over Italy but the size of the noodles varies from region to region.

The traditional pasta recipes that follow are some of the finest I've eaten. Most are simple to prepare, calling for ingredients that I usually keep in the pantry, such as canned tomatoes, canned tuna, beans, capers, and olives. The portions are modest, with a pound of pasta serving as many as six people. Try them and let them be an inspiration to create your own versions.

mediterranean pasta salad with arugula and tomatoes

penne con rucola e pomodori

I love any dish prepared with arugula—hot or cold. This pasta may be prepared a day in advance. Cover and store it in the refrigerator until one hour before tossing and serving.

1 pound penne

6 tablespoons extra virgin olive oil

4 cups packed stemmed arugula, coarsely cut
    or torn

½ cup chopped fresh basil leaves

3 cups peeled and seeded ripe tomatoes cut
    into ½-inch dice (about 4 large tomatoes)

3 teaspoons kosher salt

Freshly ground black pepper

1 tablespoon freshly squeezed lemon juice

Freshly grated Parmesan or ricotta salata
    cheese

Bring a large pot of salted water to a rapid boil. Add the pasta and cook until al dente, following the package instructions. Drain and transfer to a wide serving bowl. Toss with 1 tablespoon of the olive oil. Add the arugula, basil, tomatoes, the remaining 5 tablespoons olive oil, the salt, pepper to taste, and the lemon juice. Toss well. Serve at room temperature, garnish with Parmesan.

—SERVES 6 TO 8—

WINE PAIRING: Sparkling, light white, and light red

VARIATIONS: Fusilli, farfalle, or conchiglie pasta may be substituted for the penne. Red or yellow cherry tomatoes, or a combination of both, cut in half, may be substituted for the whole tomatoes. (Note: You will need about 1½ pints.) Another great addition to this dish is ½ pound diced fresh mozzarella. Toss it in the salad along with 1 teaspoon grated lemon zest and 1 tablespoon balsamic vinegar for a zesty, hearty dish.

summer pasta salad

insalata di pasta estiva della salute

Serve this as a first course before grilled chicken or fish or as a main course for lunch. All of the vegetables except the tomatoes may be prepared one day in advance. Store in the refrigerator before tossing with the remaining ingredients.

Here's a trick I learned from Gianni: Do not rinse cooked pasta under cold water. This washes away the pasta's natural starch and flavor and sauces will not adhere as well. Instead, drain the cooked pasta and toss it with a small amount of olive oil. Then spread it on baking sheets and allow it to cool completely.

1 pound short-cut pasta, such as fusilli or penne

4 tablespoons olive oil

½ medium-size eggplant, peeled in intermittent strips and cut into ½-inch cubes (about 3 cups)

2 medium-size carrots, peeled

2 medium-size zucchini

½ cup fresh or frozen peas

1 roasted red bell pepper, diced (page 21)

1 roasted yellow bell pepper, diced (page 21)

2 cups finely diced tender celery hearts

2 cups chopped ripe plum tomatoes (about 4 tomatoes)

3 tablespoons chopped fresh basil leaves

2 tablespoons chopped fresh Italian, flat leafed parsley

1 tablespoon chopped fresh oregano leaves

½ cup extra virgin olive oil

Kosher salt and freshly ground black pepper

6 ounces fresh mozzarella cheese, cut into ¼-inch cubes

1. Bring a pot of salted water to a boil. Cook the pasta, following the package instructions, until al dente. Drain well. Toss the pasta with 1 tablespoon of the olive oil and spread it out in a single layer on baking sheets to cool. Set aside.

2. Warm the remaining 3 tablespoons olive oil in a large skillet set over high heat. When the oil is hot but not smoking, add the eggplant and cook, tossing frequently, until

recipe continued on next page

golden brown and somewhat softened, about 6 minutes. Transfer to a paper-towel-lined plate and set aside.

3. Fill a 3-quart saucepan with water, salt it, and bring to a boil. Add the carrots and boil to soften slightly, about 5 minutes. Add the zucchini and cook until the vegetables are tender but still firm, about 5 minutes. Add the peas and cook until just tender, about 1 minute. Drain the water from the pan and cover the vegetables with cold water, allowing the water to run for 2 to 3 minutes to cool the vegetables and arrest the cooking.

4. Cut the cooled carrots and zucchini in half lengthwise and then into ⅛-inch-thick slices. Place in a large serving bowl. Add the drained peas, the eggplant, and the roasted peppers, celery, and tomatoes. Add the basil, parsley, oregano, extra virgin olive oil, and cooked pasta. Toss well to combine. Season with salt and pepper. Gently mix in the mozzarella and serve.

— SERVES 8 TO 10 —

WINE PAIRING: Light white, medium white, and light red

VARIATIONS: Blanched asparagus, cut on the bias into 1-inch pieces, makes a nice addition to this salad.

pasta salad niçoise

insalata di pasta alla nizzarda

Salad Niçoise is an excellent appetizer and a terrific lunch dish. The entire salad may be prepared one day ahead of time: Toss all of the ingredients except the dressing. Refrigerate overnight and allow the salad to return to room temperature before tossing with the dressing.

¾ pound shell-shaped pasta

4 tablespoons extra virgin olive oil

2 tablespoons balsamic vinegar

1 tablespoon freshly squeezed lemon juice

2 cloves garlic, finely chopped

½ teaspoon kosher salt

½ teaspoon freshly ground black pepper

2 tablespoons drained capers

¼ cup pitted kalamata or niçoise olives

½ cup diced Roasted Bell Peppers (page 21)

One 7-ounce can solid white tuna packed in olive oil

¼ cup chopped fresh basil leaves

2 tablespoons chopped fresh Italian, flat leafed parsley

1. Cook the pasta in a pot of rapidly boiling salted water until al dente, according to the package instructions. Drain and toss with 2 tablespoons of the olive oil. Spread on baking sheets and set aside to cool.

2. In a deep serving bowl, whisk the remaining 2 tablespoons olive oil, the vinegar, lemon juice, garlic, salt, and pepper. Add the capers, olives, and roasted peppers. Do not drain the tuna, but pour the oil into the bowl while using a fork to flake the tuna as you add it to the other ingredients. Add the basil and parsley. Add the pasta and toss well. Serve immediately.

— SERVES 6 TO 8 —

WINE PAIRING: Sparkling, light white, and light red

homemade pasta
pasta fresca fatta in casa

Tender homemade pasta is a real treat. My grandmother never used a machine to mix the dough or to roll it out. She kneaded the dough by hand and then rolled small pieces into strips and spread them out to dry on a clean sheet she had placed across a bed. This family recipe has been adapted so it can be made in a food processor.

My parents like to make pasta together. My mother mixes it in the food processor and my father rolls it through the pasta machine. They arrived at this efficient method when they were both working and still wanted to make fresh pasta for dinner.

1½ cups all-purpose flour

½ teaspoon kosher salt

2 large eggs plus 1 egg yolk

1 teaspoon olive oil

1 tablespoon water (optional; add if dough does not blend)

1. Place 1 cup of the flour and the salt in food processor and pulse to combine. Add the eggs, egg yolk, and olive oil, and mix until the dough comes together to form a ball. Turn the dough out onto a lightly floured surface. Gradually knead the remaining ½ cup flour into the dough by hand. The dough should be smooth, not sticky. Break the dough ball in half to test the center of the dough. If the center is sticky, continue to knead more flour into the dough. Knead for an additional 5 to 7 minutes.

2. Wrap the dough in plastic and set it aside to rest for 20 minutes. (Or wrap it in plastic and refrigerate for several hours. Return to room temperature before proceeding with the recipe.)

3. Line a large table or work surface (or bed) with a clean sheet or towels. Lightly flour the surface.

4. Break off one third of the dough. (Rewrap unused sections.) Sprinkle it lightly with flour and pass it through a pasta machine, following the manufacturer's instructions. (Stan's procedure with a hand-crank machine is to begin with the machine set at the widest opening by one notch, dusting with flour each time so it does not stick to the machine. He continues to narrow the opening one notch at a time until the dough is the desired thickness. For lasagna and cannelloni it is best to stop one short of the narrowest setting on the machine.)

5. Cut the pasta into 12-inch lengths as wide as you wish. For lasagna, the pasta may now be spread out on the table to dry. For long strands of pasta, pass the dough through the cutting portion of the machine and then lay the strands out to dry. (Scraps may be passed through the machine to make shorter strands that may be dried and cooked that day.) Or spread the strands on baking sheets and freeze. Once the strands are stiff, they may be packed in airtight containers and frozen for up to 1 month.

6. Roll out the remaining two thirds of the dough, one third at a time, following the same procedure.

— MAKES ABOUT 1 POUND —

(ENOUGH FOR 2 RECIPES OF GREEN LASAGNA)

white sauce

besciamella

This recipe makes a medium-consistency *besciamella* (béchamel) sauce, which may be used in many recipes in place of cream. It can be prepared a few hours ahead of time and kept at room temperature. Place a piece of plastic wrap or waxed paper directly on the surface of the sauce to prevent a skin from forming.

6 tablespoons (¾ stick) butter

6 tablespoons all-purpose flour

3 cups whole or skim milk, warmed

Kosher salt and freshly ground black pepper

¼ teaspoon ground nutmeg

Melt the butter in a medium-size saucepan set over medium-low heat. When the butter is foaming, whisk in the flour. Whisk in the milk. Cook, whisking frequently, until the sauce thickens, about 20 minutes. Remove from the heat and stir in salt and pepper to taste and the nutmeg.

— SERVES 4 (MAKES ABOUT 3 CUPS) —

WINE PAIRING: Full white

NOTE: This recipe may be easily cut in half or in thirds when smaller amounts are called for in various recipes throughout this book. Smaller quantities will require less cooking time.

uncooked fresh tomato sauce

passata di pomodoro

The best time to prepare this dish is summertime, when sweet, flavorful tomatoes are in abundance. This sauce is wonderful over pasta, but is also delicious served on bruschetta.

1½ pounds ripe tomatoes
kosher salt

1 pound pasta (spaghetti, linguine, or fettuccine)
2 tablespoons extra virgin olive oil

1. Bring a large pot of salted water to a boil. Use a sharp knife to score the bottoms of the tomatoes with an X. Gently place the tomatoes in the boiling water. When the skin begins to unfurl at the X, remove the tomatoes from the water with a slotted spoon and plunge into a bowl of cold water. Allow the tomatoes to cool slightly; then peel away the skins.

2. Cut the tomatoes into several small pieces. Remove and discard the seeds. Place the tomatoes in a food mill fitted with a coarse blade. Grind the tomatoes through the mill (or finely chop by hand) into a bowl. Place the tomatoes in a fine mesh sieve placed over a bowl. Allow the tomatoes to drain for several hours at room temperature or overnight in the refrigerator.

3. Bring a large pot of salted water to a boil. Add the pasta and cook, following the package instructions. Drain well and toss with the olive oil. Distribute evenly among four plates. Discard the water accumulated in the bowl below the tomatoes, and spoon equal portions of the concentrated tomatoes on top of the pasta. Serve immediately.

— SERVES 4 —

WINE PAIRING: Light red and medium red

gianni's basic tomato sauce

salsa pomodoro di gianni

One might think that all tomato sauces are basically alike, but slight variations can make a big difference in texture and flavor. This recipe makes a slightly chunky tomato sauce. If you like a smoother consistency, cool the sauce and pass it through a food mill, process it with an electric mixer, or pulse it in a blender. I prefer to use fresh peeled and chopped plum tomatoes or ripe summer heirloom tomatoes from the farmer's market rather than canned tomatoes. When tomatoes are in season, prepare a double batch and freeze the sauce in several small airtight containers for up to six months.

1 tablespoon butter

2 tablespoons olive oil

¾ cup diced onions

3 pounds ripe plum tomatoes, coarsely chopped

10 large fresh basil leaves, cut into long thin strips

Kosher salt and freshly ground black pepper

Place the butter and olive oil in a medium-size saucepan set over medium-high heat. When the butter begins to foam, add the onions and cook, stirring frequently, until they have softened but not browned, about 6 minutes. Stir in the tomatoes, crushing them with your hand or the back of a slotted spoon as you add them to the pan. Add half the basil and bring to a boil. Reduce the heat to medium-low and simmer until most of the water has evaporated, about 25 minutes. Season with salt and pepper. Just before serving, stir in the remaining basil. Briskly whisk the sauce to create a chunky puree.

— SERVES 8 —

WINE PAIRING: Light red and medium red

VARIATIONS: Possible additions include 4 cloves garlic, chopped; 1 teaspoon chopped fresh oregano leaves; a pinch of red pepper flakes or ¼ teaspoon seeded and diced fresh jalapeño pepper—all of which may be added to the sauce after the onions.

joan's basic tomato sauce

salsa pomodoro di joan

There are many similarities between this recipe and the one for marinara sauce (Sailor's-Style Sauce, page 120). The most important difference between them is the size pot they are cooked in. The uncovered 12-inch sauté or frying pan called for in the marinara sauce allows the tomatoes' juices to reduce or cook off, resulting in a thick, densely flavored sauce. This recipe calls for the sauce to be cooked in an 8-inch covered saucepan so the tomatoes retain their juices, resulting in a less thick and slightly milder sauce.

Because this sauce freezes well, consider making extra to have on hand. It may also be cooled and then pureed in the blender for a finer consistency.

¼ cup olive oil

2 cloves garlic, chopped

1 tablespoon chopped onions

1 tablespoon seeded and chopped green bell
   pepper (optional)

3½ cups canned whole plum tomatoes
   (about one 28-ounce can)

1 fresh basil leaf

Kosher salt and freshly ground black pepper

Warm the olive oil in a medium-size saucepan (about 8 inches in diameter) set over a medium-low heat. Add the garlic, onions, and bell pepper, if using. Cook until softened but not browned, about 2 minutes. Stir in the tomatoes, crushing them with your hands or with the back of a slotted spoon as you add them to the pan. Add the basil and season with salt and pepper. Bring to a boil, cover, and reduce the heat to a gentle simmer. Cook the tomatoes until they sweeten, about 35 minutes. Uncover and continue to simmer for 5 minutes to thicken the sauce slightly.

— SERVES 6 —

WINE PAIRING: Light red and medium red

sailor's-style sauce

salsa marinara

This sauce takes its name from the fresh, simple marinara sauces that fishermen's wives would prepare to accompany the catch of the day. We call it Sailor's-Style to distinguish it from Joan's Basic Tomato Sauce (page 119). The ingredients for both sauces are essentially the same—the difference lies in the cooking technique. This Sailor's-Style marinara sauce is cooked in a large uncovered pan so the tomatoes break down, creating an intensely flavored, thick sauce. Joan's Basic Tomato Sauce is cooked in a small covered saucepan, resulting in a lighter, soupier sauce. For either sauce, whenever I shop for canned tomatoes, I look for ones from the San Marzano area of Italy. They are the finest. This sauce may be prepared several days ahead and refrigerated or frozen. Reheat slowly before serving. Serve over pasta or with other dishes as noted throughout the book.

¼ cup olive oil

3 cloves garlic

1 tablespoon chopped onions

4 cups canned whole plum tomatoes (about one 35-ounce can)

2 teaspoons chopped fresh oregano leaves or ½ teaspoon dried (optional)

3 fresh basil leaves

Kosher salt and freshly ground black pepper

Warm the olive oil in a large sauté or frying pan (about 12 inches in diameter) set over a medium-high heat. Add the garlic and onions and cook until the onions are soft but not browned, about 2 minutes. Stir in the tomatoes, crushing them with your hands or with the back of a slotted spoon as you add them to the pan. Stir in the oregano (if using) and basil, and season with salt and pepper. Simmer until the tomatoes have thickened and sweetened, about 25 minutes (the longer you cook this sauce, the thicker it will become). Remove from the heat and allow to rest so the sauce thickens slightly and the flavors come together, about 5 minutes.

— SERVES 6 —

WINE PAIRING: Light red and medium red

tropiano ragù sauce

ragù tropiano

My mother, a Tropiano, makes a recipe for *ragù* that is lighter than the Tucci version. It is served the same way—spooning just the tomato sauce over pasta as a first course, followed by the stewed meat as a second course. She also uses it in lasagna by shredding the tender cooked meat into smaller pieces and ladling it between layers of homemade pasta and ricotta cheese for a traditional lasagna casserole.

¼ cup olive oil

½ pound stewing beef, trimmed of fat, rinsed, patted dry, and cut into pieces

½ pound pork chops or spareribs, trimmed of fat, rinsed, and patted dry

2 cloves garlic, finely chopped

1 tablespoon finely chopped onions

½ cup dry red wine

3½ cup canned whole plum tomatoes (about one 28-ounce can), pureed in a blender or food mill

1 fresh basil leaf

Kosher salt and freshly ground black pepper

1. Warm the olive oil in a medium-size flameproof casserole set over a medium-low heat. Add the stewing beef and brown evenly on all sides, about 10 minutes. Remove the beef to a bowl and set aside.

2. Add the pork to the pot and brown evenly on both sides, about 10 minutes. Remove from the pan and add to the bowl with the beef.

3. Stir the garlic and onions into the pot and cook until softened but not browned, about 2 minutes. Add the wine and stir to loosen any bits of meat that may have stuck to the bottom of the pan. Stir in the tomatoes and basil. Return the meat to the pot, along with any juices that have accumulated in the bottom of the bowl. Season with salt and pepper. Bring to a boil, then cover, reduce the heat to medium-low, and simmer until the tomatoes have sweetened and the meat is very tender, about 1½ hours.

— SERVES 8 —

tucci ragù sauce

ragù tucci

This is the traditional recipe for the Tuccis' *ragù* sauce, though my grandmother made a lighter version of this same sauce. It calls for spareribs and stewing beef, but different cuts of meat may be added depending on what is on hand—pork chops, sausage, pig's feet. It is delicious with Meatballs (*polpette*) (page 252), which may be added to the sauce during the last half hour of cooking.

This sauce, which is used in Timpano alla *Big Night* (see note on facing page), may be prepared two days ahead of serving. Refrigerate it overnight and reheat before tossing with the pasta. It may also be frozen with the meat and meatballs.

¼ cup olive oil

1 pound stewing beef, trimmed of fat, rinsed, patted dry, and cut into pieces

1 pound country-style spareribs, trimmed of fat, cut in half, rinsed, and patted dry

1 cup coarsely chopped onions

3 cloves garlic, coarsely chopped

½ cup dry red wine

One 6-ounce can tomato paste

1½ cups warm water

8 cups canned whole plum tomatoes (about two 35-ounce cans), passed through a food mill, or pureed in a blender or food processor

3 fresh basil leaves

1 tablespoon chopped fresh oregano leaves or 1 teaspoon dried

1. Warm the olive oil in a stew pot set over medium-high heat. Sear the stewing beef until brown on all sides, about 10 minutes. Remove from the pot and set aside in a bowl.

2. Add the spareribs to the pot and sear until they are brown on all sides, about 10 minutes. Remove the ribs and set aside in the bowl with the stewing beef. (If your pot is big enough to hold all of the meat in a single layer, it may be cooked at the same time.)

3. Stir the onions and garlic into the pot. Reduce the heat to low and cook until the onions begin to soften, about 5 minutes. Stir in the wine, scraping the bottom of the pot clean. Add the tomato paste. Pour ½ cup of the water into the can to loosen any residual paste and then pour the water into the pot. Cook to warm the paste through, about 2 minutes. Add the tomatoes along with the remaining 1 cup water. Stir in the basil and oregano. Cover with the lid slightly askew and simmer to sweeten the tomatoes, about 30 minutes.

4. Return the meat to the pot, along with any extra juices that have accumulated in the bowl. Cover with the lid slightly askew and simmer, stirring frequently, until the meat is very tender and the tomatoes are cooked, about 2 hours. Warm water may be added to the sauce, in ½-cup portions, if the sauce becomes too thick. (If you have made meat-balls, sauté separately to warm through and then they may be added during the last half hour of cooking. The meatballs will soften and absorb some of the sauce.)

— SERVES 8 —

WINE PAIRING: Light red and medium red

VARIATION: Sweet Italian sausage may be added to this sauce. Sauté it after the spareribs and then proceed with the recipe as written.

NOTE: When preparing Tucci Ragù Sauce for Timpano alla *Big Night* (Drum of Ziti, page 181), only the sauce is used and the meat is served as a separate course. The sauce for timpano should be thin, so measure out 7½ cups of prepared sauce and stir in ½ cup water before proceeding with the timpano recipe.

maria rosa's sauce

salsa alla maria rosa

The year my family was living in Florence my sister Gina became friends with a young girl named Mirca. My parents in turn became friends with Mirca's parents—Vittorio, who was a policeman, and his wife, Maria Rosa. To this day they remain friends, phoning throughout the year and visiting whenever they have the opportunity. Maria Rosa taught my mother how to make this sauce. We serve *Salsa alla Maria Rosa* with penne, farfalle, ziti, or any other long tubular pasta such as rotini or fusilli. It can also be used to prepare Green Lasagna (page 164). This sauce freezes very well.

2 tablespoons butter

¼ cup olive oil

1 cup diced carrots (about 2 medium-size carrots)

½ cup diced celery (about 2 small tender stalks)

1 cup diced onions (about ½ large onion)

2 cloves garlic, chopped

2 tablespoons chopped fresh Italian, flat leafed parsley

4 cups canned whole plum tomatoes (about one 35-ounce can)

Kosher salt and freshly ground black pepper

In a large saucepan set over a medium heat, melt the butter in the olive oil. When the butter is foaming, add the carrots, celery, onions, and garlic and cook, stirring often, until they have softened, 8 to 10 minutes. Stir in the parsley. Stir in the tomatoes, crushing them with your hands or with the back of a slotted spoon as you add them to the pan. Bring the sauce to a boil. Season with salt and pepper. Reduce the heat to medium-low and simmer, partially covered, until the tomatoes are sweetened and cooked, about 45 minutes.

— SERVES 6 —

WINE PAIRING: Light red and medium red

VARIATIONS: To create a less coarse version of this sauce, puree the tomatoes in a food mill or food processor before proceeding with the recipe. Also, 1 pound ground beef may be added to the sauce before the tomatoes. Cook until the beef is lightly browned and then proceed with the recipe.

basil pesto
pesto al basilico

This is a classic summer pasta dish, which may be served before grilled fish or meats. In Liguria, a northwestern region of Italy, I have had it served over pasta that has been cooked with string beans and thinly sliced half-moons of peeled potatoes. The beans add a crisp texture to the pasta, while the potatoes add creaminess to the sauce. (Add the vegetables to the pasta during the last 5 minutes of cooking.) Sometimes broccoli florets are cooked in the same way. If you like to freeze pesto sauce, I recommend preparing this recipe without the cheese. Freshly grated cheese may then be stirred into the thawed sauce before tossing with pasta.

4 cups well-packed fresh basil leaves

1¼ cups well-packed fresh Italian, flat leafed
  parsley

½ cup pine nuts

6 cloves garlic, peeled

¼ cup very finely grated pecorino Romano
  cheese

1 cup finely grated Parmesan cheese

2 teaspoons kosher salt

1¼ cups extra virgin olive oil

1 pound pasta (spaghetti, linguine, or
  fettuccine)

1. Place the basil, parsley, pine nuts, and garlic in a food processor or blender. Process until the basil and parsley are coarsely chopped. Add the Romano, Parmesan, and salt, and process. With the machine running, add the olive oil in a steady stream. Do not overprocess. Set aside.

2. Bring a large pot of salted water to a rapid boil. Add the pasta and cook until al dente, following the package instructions. Drain well and toss with a small amount of the pesto. Distribute evenly among plates and top with additional pesto before serving.

— SERVES 6 —

VARIATIONS: **If** you like a richer sauce, you may add butter to this basic recipe. Just replace ¼ cup of the extra virgin olive oil with softened butter. If the pesto is slightly brown instead of bright green, add a few leaves of fresh spinach and process. This should help restore the color. Also, you may use Parmesan cheese instead of the pecorino Romano called for in this recipe. And coarsely chopped hazelnuts, toasted in an oven at 350° F for 5 minutes, may be used in place of the pine nuts.

tomato pesto for pasta or fish

pesto di pomodoro per pasta o pesce

I prepare this recipe only in the summer, when the tomatoes are ripe and flavorful. It is a delectable lunch dish or pasta course served before grilled fish or meat. This pesto may also be served as a type of salsa with freshly grilled fish: Spoon a portion onto a serving plate and top with the fish and some coarsely chopped fresh tomatoes. This pesto may be prepared up to three days in advance; cover and store it in the refrigerator. Return the sauce to room temperature before serving.

¾ cup packed fresh basil leaves

⅓ cup packed fresh Italian, flat leafed parsley

4 cloves garlic

Kosher salt

½ cup extra virgin olive oil

1 cup peeled, seeded, and finely diced ripe tomatoes (about 3 medium-size tomatoes)

Freshly ground black pepper

1 pound pasta (penne, fusilli, spaghetti, or other pasta of your choice)

1. Place the basil, parsley, garlic, and salt in a food processor or blender. Turn on the machine and coarsely chop. With the machine running, add the olive oil in a steady stream. Turn off the machine and scrape down the sides. With the machine running again, gradually add the tomatoes. Process just until the tomatoes have been blended into the other ingredients. Season with pepper and set aside.

2. Bring a large pot of salted water to a boil. Add the pasta and cook until al dente, following the package instructions. Drain well and toss with a small amount of the pesto. Distribute evenly among six dinner plates, topping with additional pesto before serving.

— SERVES 6 —

WINE PAIRING: Medium white, light red, and medium red

VARIATION: Thinly slice ½ pound fresh mozzarella cheese and serve it on top of the sauced pasta.

tomato sauce with mushrooms

marinara con funghi

This is the first sauce I learned to make. It is simple and inexpensive. During the lean years when I was just starting out in New York, I found it a great comfort nutritionally and economically. This recipe makes enough sauce for 1 pound of linguine or spaghetti. It may be made one day ahead; refrigerate it and reheat before serving. This sauce also pairs well with Polenta (page 175): Cook the polenta and then stir in one third of the sauce. Distribute among four dinner plates and top with remaining sauce.

3 tablespoons olive oil

1 clove garlic, sliced

10 ounces white mushrooms, cut into ¼-inch-
   thick slices

4 cups canned whole plum tomatoes (about
   one 35-ounce can)

3 fresh basil leaves

1 teaspoon chopped fresh oregano leaves or
   ½ teaspoon dried (optional)

Kosher salt and freshly ground black pepper

Freshly grated Parmesan or pecorino
   Romano cheese for garnish (optional)

1. Warm the olive oil in a large sauté pan set over medium-high heat. Add the garlic and cook until softened and lightly colored, about 2 minutes. Stir in the mushrooms and cook until lightly colored and softened, about 5 minutes. Remove the mushrooms to a plate and set aside.

2. Add the tomatoes to the sauté pan, crushing them with your hands or the back of a slotted spoon as you stir them into the pan. Add the basil and oregano (if using), and season with salt and pepper. Bring to a boil, then reduce the heat and simmer until the sauce thickens slightly, about 15 minutes. Return the mushrooms to the pan and continue to simmer until the sauce is sweet, about another 15 minutes. Serve over pasta garnished with Parmesan or pecorino Romano cheese if desired.

— SERVES 4 —

WINE PAIRING: Light red and medium red

spaghetti with fresh tomatoes

spaghetti alla crudaiola

This is a wonderful pasta to serve in the summer when fresh ripe tomatoes are widely available. The amount of salt you need to add to the tomatoes is determined by how juicy they are.

8 large ripe tomatoes

¾ cup plus 2 tablespoons extra virgin olive oil

1 teaspoon balsamic vinegar

6 fresh basil leaves, torn in half

1 clove garlic, quartered

Kosher salt

1 pound spaghetti or linguine

1. Cut the tomatoes in half and then into ½-inch-wide wedges. Cut these wedges in half to create chunks. Place them in a large bowl and toss with ¾ cup of the olive oil, the vinegar, basil, and garlic. Set aside for 15 minutes. Then season with salt and let stand until the salt has drawn out the tomatoes' juices, about 10 minutes.

2. Bring a large pot of salted water to a rapid boil. Cook the pasta until al dente, following the package instructions. Drain and toss with the remaining 2 tablespoons olive oil. Distribute among four serving plates. Top with equal portions of the tomato mixture and serve immediately.

— SERVES 4 —

WINE PAIRING: **Light red**

VARIATIONS: Just before topping off the pasta, ¼ cup Basil Pesto (page 126) may be added to the tomato mixture.

spaghetti with garlic

spaghetti aglio e olio

Believe it or not, the Tucci family would actually cook pasta at picnics! My father remembers setting out early in the morning, having loaded my grandfather's truck with food, beer, wine, bocce balls, and musical instruments. "Once we had secured our favorite spot we would build a fire," recalls Stan. "A large cauldron would be filled with water and placed on the fire. Once it came to a boil we would cook the pasta—enough for up to thirty people." But you don't need to go camping to make this flavorful sauce.

1 pound spaghetti or linguine

½ cup olive oil

3 cloves garlic, cut into ⅛-inch-thick slices

¼ teaspoon paprika

Kosher salt

1. Bring a large pot of salted water to a boil and cook the pasta, following the package instructions, until al dente.

2. Meanwhile, warm the olive oil in a small sauté pan set over medium-high heat. Add the garlic and cook until it colors slightly but does not brown, about 3 minutes. Remove from the heat and set aside.

3. Drain the pasta and place in a serving bowl. Add the oil and garlic and toss. Sprinkle with the paprika and serve immediately, adding salt to taste.

— SERVES 4 —

WINE PAIRING: Medium white and light red

angry penne

penne arrabbiata

The ingredients for this classic *arrabbiata*, or "angry," pasta are inexpensive, but the flavor is rich. I like to prepare this sauce with jalapeño pepper because I like the heat, but it is also good with red pepper flakes. I recommend serving this as a first course followed by a hearty meat dish or stewed fish.

¾ pound penne

5 tablespoons extra virgin olive oil

3 cloves garlic, minced

¼ teaspoon red pepper flakes or ½ jalapeño
   pepper, seeded and chopped

1½ cups Gianni's Basic Tomato Sauce (page
   118) or use your favorite

2 tablespoons chopped fresh Italian, flat
   leafed parsley

Kosher salt and freshly ground black pepper

Finely grated Parmesan cheese for garnish
   (optional)

1. Bring a large pot of salted water to a rapid boil. Add the pasta and cook, following the package instructions, until al dente.

2. While the pasta is cooking, warm the olive oil in a medium-size saucepan set over medium-high heat. Add the garlic and red pepper flakes. When the oil is hot but before the garlic has browned add the tomato sauce and 1 tablespoon of the parsley. Bring to a boil and cook to heat through and evaporate any water, about 2 minutes.

3. Drain the pasta well and add to the sauce. Add the remaining 1 tablespoon parsley and toss well. Season with salt and pepper. Serve with Parmesan cheese, if desired.

— SERVES 4 —

WINE PAIRING: Light red and medium red

desperate sauce
salsa disperata

This sauce is easy and quick to prepare. A little bit of spicy sauce goes a long way, and believe me, if you use enough jalapeño you'll understand why it's called "desperate." I recommend serving this over a long pasta such as spaghetti, bucatini, fettuccine, or linguine. It is also nice spooned over sautéed veal, chicken breast, or pork chops.

¼ cup olive oil

1 tablespoon finely chopped shallots or
    onions

2 cloves garlic, chopped

1 tablespoon chopped fresh Italian, flat leafed
    parsley

1 tablespoon chopped fresh basil leaves

½ jalapeño pepper, seeded and chopped, or
    ¼ teaspoon red pepper flakes

1 teaspoon finely chopped anchovies (3 to 4
    fillets)

2 cups canned whole plum tomatoes, crushed

1 teaspoon chopped fresh oregano leaves or
    ¼ teaspoon dried

1 teaspoon capers, drained and rinsed

Kosher salt and freshly ground black pepper

1½ pounds spaghetti

1. Warm the olive oil with the shallots in a sauté pan set over medium-low heat. When the oil begins to gently bubble, cover the pan and cook to soften the shallots, about 1 minute. Stir in the garlic, parsley, basil, jalapeño, and anchovies. When the mixture begins to bubble, add the tomatoes and oregano and cover. Reduce the heat to medium-low and cook to blend the flavors and sweeten the tomatoes, about 15 minutes. Stir in the capers, cover, and cook to flavor the sauce, another 5 minutes. Season with salt and pepper.

2. While the sauce is simmering, cook the pasta. Bring a large pot of salted water to a boil. Add the pasta and cook, following the package instructions, until al dente. Drain and transfer to a deep serving bowl. Add the sauce and toss well to coat the pasta. Serve immediately.

— SERVES 6 —

WINE PAIRING: Light white and light red

VARIATION: Any of the following ingredients may be added to the sauce along with the capers, or for a hearty sauce, try adding all three: 18 pitted olives, cut in half; 1 roasted red bell pepper, coarsely chopped; 7 ounces good-quality Italian tuna packed in olive oil (drained).

ziti with broccoli

ziti con broccoli

This recipe is a good example of how the Tucci and Tropiano cooking styles have come to be melded. The Tucci family prepared this dish with ziti and no garlic. The Tropiano family prepared it using spaghetti broken into 2½-inch lengths, so now my mother sometimes serves it with broken spaghetti. Either way, it's very tasty.

1 large head broccoli (about 1 pound)
1 pound ziti
¼ cup olive oil
1 clove garlic (optional), chopped

Freshly ground black pepper
Extra virgin olive oil to drizzle on each
 portion

1. Trim off 2 to 3 inches of the tough broccoli stems and discard. Cut the broccoli florets away from the remaining tender stems. Cut the florets into large bite-size pieces. Peel the tender stems as you would carrots, then cut into short sections and then into thin, bite-size lengths. Set all of the prepared broccoli aside.

2. Bring a large pot of salted water to a boil. Add the stems and then the broccoli florets. Cook until tender but firm, about 4 minutes. Remove with a slotted spoon to a bowl and set aside.

3. Add the pasta to the same water and cook, following the package instructions, until al dente. Reserve 1 cup of the cooking water before draining the pasta.

4. Return the drained pasta to the pot and toss with the olive oil. Add the garlic (if using), broccoli, and ½ cup reserved cooking water. Toss, adding more olive oil and water if the mixture is too dry. Serve immediately, garnished with freshly ground black pepper and drizzled with extra virgin olive oil.

— SERVES 4 —

WINE PAIRING: Light white, light red, and rosé

linguine with capers and olives

linguine con capperi e olive

This sauce is similar to puttanesca sauce, which traditionally includes anchovies. Since my father is not fond of anchovies, my mother, Joan, created this recipe, which may be prepared earlier in the day and reheated while the pasta is cooking. It is delicious served as a first course before grilled chicken.

½ cup olive oil

2 tablespoons chopped onions

1 large clove garlic, quartered

10 kalamata olives, pitted and halved

2 teaspoons capers, drained and rinsed

4 cups canned whole plum tomatoes (about
   one 35-ounce can)

Kosher salt and freshly ground black pepper

3 fresh basil leaves

1 pound linguine

Freshly grated Parmesan cheese for garnish
   (optional)

1. In a large frying pan, warm the olive oil over medium-low heat. Add the onions and garlic and cook until the onions soften slightly but do not brown, about 5 minutes. Stir in the olives and capers and cook to warm through, about 1 minute. Add the tomatoes, crushing them with your hands or the back of a slotted spoon as you stir them into the pan. Season with salt and pepper, then stir in the basil leaves. Bring the sauce to a low boil, and then simmer slowly until the sauce has thickened and the tomatoes have sweetened, about 30 minutes.

2. Bring a large pot of salted water to a rapid boil. Add the linguine and cook until al dente, following the package instructions. Drain well and toss in a bowl with a ladleful of the sauce. Distribute evenly among four dinner plates. Top with the remaining sauce and serve immediately. Garnish with grated Parmesan cheese if you like.

— SERVES 4 —

WINE PAIRING: Light white or rosé

ditalini with peas

ditalini e piselli

As children, my sister Gina and I enjoyed this dish, but our younger sister, Christine, never could decide how she felt about it. One week she would eat all the peas and leave the pasta, another week she would eat all the pasta and leave the peas. Sorting the peas from the *ditalini,* which is a short tubular pasta (aka "little thimbles"), was a time-consuming task, but somehow Christine managed.

½ pound ditalini

1½ cups Joan's Basic Tomato Sauce (page 119)

2 cups frozen or drained canned peas (if frozen, run under warm water briefly to defrost)

Kosher salt and freshly ground black pepper

Freshly grated Parmesan cheese for garnish (optional)

1. Bring a large pot of salted water to a boil. Cook the pasta until al dente, following the package instructions. Reserve ½ cup of the cooking water before draining the pasta.

2. Meanwhile, in a large saucepan set over medium-high heat, bring the tomato sauce to a simmer. Add the peas and simmer until tender, about 5 minutes. Add the drained pasta to the sauce. Stir in enough of the reserved pasta water to create a slightly soupy sauce. Season with salt and pepper, and serve immediately. Garnish with Parmesan cheese if desired.

— SERVES 4 —

WINE PAIRING: Light white or light red

ditale with beans

ditale con fagioli

My father recalls that this is one of the first dinners he had with my mother at her parents' house. "When I got home I told my parents that the Tropianos made this dish quite differently than we did, but that it was very tasty," says Stan. "My father asked how it was prepared. When I told him it was served in a light tomato liquid, he responded immediately, 'That's just how my mother prepared it in Italy.'"

This is a quick pasta-with-beans recipe, especially since the sauce may be prepared up to one day in advance. Add the beans and celery and warm the sauce while the pasta is cooking. I like to use ditale, but any tubular pasta may be substituted. This dish has a souplike consistency and should be served immediately so the pasta doesn't soak up all the sauce.

¼ cup olive oil

1 clove garlic, chopped

4 cups canned whole plum tomatoes (about one 35-ounce can)

Kosher salt

1 fresh basil leaf

1 tender 5-inch-long celery stalk with leaves, cut into 1-inch pieces (optional)

One 19-ounce can cannelloni beans, drained and rinsed

1 pound ditale

Freshly ground black pepper

Freshly grated Parmesan cheese for garnish (optional)

1. Warm the olive oil in a large saucepan set over medium-high heat. Add the garlic and cook until soft but not browned, about 2 minutes. Stir in the tomatoes, crushing them with your hands or the back of a slotted spoon as you add them to the pan. Season with salt, stir in the basil, and bring to a boil. Reduce the heat to a simmer, cover, and cook until the tomatoes sweeten, about 20 minutes. Stir the celery (if using) and beans into

the sauce. Return to a simmer, cover, and cook until the beans are heated through and have blended with the tomato sauce, about 10 minutes.

2. Meanwhile, bring a large pot of salted water to a boil. Cook the pasta until al dente, following the package instructions. Reserve 1 cup of the cooking water before draining the cooked pasta.

3. Add the drained pasta to the bean sauce, and stir in enough of the reserved cooking water as necessary to make a soupy consistency. Simmer until the ingredients are combined, about 2 minutes. Serve immediately, garnishing with pepper and, if you like, Parmesan cheese.

— SERVES 4 TO 6 —

WINE PAIRING: Light white or light red

VARIATION: I often use dried beans to make this dish and I like to prepare the beans using the following quick-soak method. Place the dried beans in a saucepan and fill the pan with cold water to a level 2 inches above the beans. (If you like, a few tender celery leaves may be added to the beans.) Cover the pot and bring the water to a boil. Allow the beans to boil for 2 minutes. Remove from the heat and let the beans stand, covered, for 1 hour. Reserve 1 cup of the cooking liquid before draining the beans and proceeding with step 3 of the recipe.

pasta casserole
farfalle al forno

My mother created this recipe and it is one of my children's favorite dishes. "I was inspired to create this recipe because I wanted a dish that would serve a group and still allow me time to visit with company," explains Joan. It may be prepared one day in advance—just cover and refrigerate overnight. Allow the casserole to return to room temperature before baking.

4 tablespoons (½ stick) butter

¼ cup all-purpose flour

2 cups whole or skim milk

Kosher salt and freshly ground black pepper
    to taste

⅛ teaspoon nutmeg

1 pound Swiss chard, tough stems removed
    and discarded and leaves coarsely chopped

1 pound farfalle

2 tablespoons olive oil

2 cups Maria Rosa's Sauce (page 124)

½ cup grated Fontina cheese

½ cup grated Jarlsberg cheese

½ cup grated mozzarella cheese

½ cup finely grated Parmesan cheese

1. Preheat the oven to 350° F.

2. Melt the butter in a medium-size saucepan set over medium-low heat. Whisk in the flour, then slowly whisk in the milk. Cook the sauce, whisking frequently, until it thickens, about 10 minutes. Season with salt and pepper, and stir in the nutmeg. Cover with plastic wrap and set this *besciamella* sauce aside.

3. Bring a large pot of salted water to a boil. Add the Swiss chard and cook until tender but firm, 8 to 10 minutes. Remove with a slotted spoon to a fine-mesh sieve. Drain, pressing out any excess water.

4. Return the water to a boil. Add the pasta and cook until al dente, following the package instructions. Drain well and place the pasta in a large bowl and toss with the olive oil. Toss the pasta with the Swiss chard, 1 cup of Maria Rosa's Sauce, the white sauce, and the grated Fontina, Jarlsberg, and mozzarella cheeses.

5. Spread the remaining 1 cup Maria Rosa's Sauce over the bottom of a large casserole or baking dish. Spread the pasta mixture on top of the sauce and sprinkle with the Parmesan cheese. Bake until the sauce is bubbly and the casserole is warmed through, about 30 minutes.

— SERVES 6 —

WINE PAIRING: Medium white or light red

VARIATION: Penne or *mezzani* pasta may be substituted for the farfalle.

farfalle with artichokes, potatoes, and prosciutto

farfalle con carciofi, patate, e prosciutto

Potatoes are a traditional ingredient in northern Italian cooking, just as the tomato is crucial to unique flavors of southern Italian cooking. In this recipe inspired by Gianni's mother, who would prepare it in the late fall at the beginning of the artichoke season, the potatoes create a creamy sauce that does not compete with the subtle flavor of the artichokes.

4 large artichokes, or one 9-ounce package
    frozen artichoke hearts, thawed, or one
    15-ounce can artichoke bottoms, drained
1 tablespoon freshly squeezed lemon juice
    (for fresh artichokes)
¼ cup extra virgin olive oil
1 cup thinly sliced onions (about 1 medium-
    size onion)
1 cup julienned prosciutto, pancetta, or bacon
    (about 3 ounces)

2 tablespoons chopped fresh parsley
2 medium-size potatoes, peeled, halved, and
    sliced ¼ inch thick and quartered (about
    2 cups)
Kosher salt and freshly ground black pepper
2 cups chicken broth or water
1 pound farfalle
¼ cup freshly grated Parmesan cheese
1 tablespoon extra virgin olive oil

1. If using fresh artichokes, peel off and discard the hard outer leaves. Cut off the top of each artichoke at the point where the leaves become almost white. Discard the top. Cut the remaining artichoke into ⅛-inch-thick wedges. Remove any fine hairs (choke) from each wedge. Place the trimmed artichoke pieces in a bowl of cold water along with the lemon juice. Set aside.

2. Warm the olive oil in a large skillet or large saucepan set over medium heat. Add the onions, cover, and cook until soft but not browned, 5 to 8 minutes. Stir in the prosciutto

and cook to soften, about 1 minute. Stir in the parsley and potatoes. Drain the fresh artichokes, pat dry, and stir them into the pan. Season with salt and pepper. Cover and cook to allow the flavors to combine, about 2 minutes. Add the broth and simmer slowly, with the lid on, until the potatoes and artichokes are tender, 5 to 10 minutes. (If you are using frozen or canned artichokes, add them now, allowing them to warm through while the sauce reduces.)

3. Meanwhile, bring a large pot of salted water to a boil. Add the pasta and cook, following the package instructions, until al dente. Drain, and stir the pasta into the vegetable mixture. Gently stir the pasta and sauce over low heat to coat and thicken slightly. Add the Parmesan cheese and adjust the seasoning with salt and pepper. Distribute among plates or pasta bowls, drizzle with the extra virgin olive oil, and serve.

—SERVES 4 AS A SECOND COURSE—

6 AS A FIRST COURSE

WINE PAIRING: Light white or light red

VARIATIONS: Other pastas that hold sauce well, such as rigatoni, fresh fettuccine, or fusilli, may be substituted for farfalle. And adjustments to the ingredients can be made according to taste and preference. For example:

- 1 tablespoon chopped fresh mint, thyme, or marjoram leaves may be sprinkled on top of the pasta along with the Parmesan cheese.
- The prosciutto may be eliminated to make a flavorful vegetarian pasta.
- Broccoli or cauliflower may be added to the sauce: Add 1 head trimmed cauliflower florets to the salted boiling water along with the pasta and cook until the pasta is al dente. Trimmed broccoli florets will require less cooking time than cauliflower and may be added to the pasta during the last 5 minutes of cooking.

fusilli with ricotta, prosciutto, and spinach

fusilli con ricotta, prosciutto, e spinaci

This creamy sauce is also a tasty filling for cannelloni (page 168). It may be prepared up to two days in advance. Refrigerate it and let it return to room temperature before tossing with the pasta or filling cannelloni. This sauce reheats well even after it has been tossed with the pasta: Place the leftover pasta in a saucepan set over medium heat, add ½ cup hot water, and cook to warm through, stirring frequently.

2 tablespoons olive oil

2 cups finely chopped onions

1 pound spinach, washed well and tough stems removed

1 cup ricotta cheese

1 cup finely chopped prosciutto (about 6 ounces)

1 cup finely grated Parmesan cheese

Freshly ground black pepper

½ cup plain dried bread crumbs

2 teaspoons extra virgin olive oil

1 pound fusilli

1. Warm the olive oil in a saucepan set over medium-high heat. Add the onions and cook, stirring occasionally, until softened but not browned, about 5 minutes. Add the spinach and cook until wilted, about 5 minutes. Remove from the heat and cool completely.

2. Squeeze out any liquid retained by the spinach by pressing it between your hands or by placing it in a fine-mesh sieve and pressing the spinach with the back of a spoon. Place the spinach in a food processor. Add the ricotta and prosciutto and process until smooth. Stir in the Parmesan and season with pepper. Set aside.

3. Preheat the oven to 350° F. In a bowl, toss the bread crumbs and extra virgin olive oil. Spread on a baking sheet. Toast the bread crumbs in the oven, stirring once or twice, until lightly browned, about 8 minutes. Set aside.

4. Bring a large pot of salted water to a boil. Cook the fusilli until al dente, following the package instructions. Reserve ½ cup of the cooking water before draining well. Return the drained pasta to the pot. Stir in the sauce and the reserved cooking water. Heat over low heat, stirring constantly, until the sauce is creamy and evenly coats the pasta, about 3 minutes. Serve immediately, topped with the toasted bread crumbs.

— SERVES 6 —

WINE PAIRING: Light red or medium red

VARIATIONS: In place of the spinach, 1 pound chopped broccoli florets, broccoli rabe, or asparagus may be used. Similarly, 1 pound cauliflower florets that have been boiled until tender, about 10 minutes, may be used in place of the spinach. Puree 4 anchovy fillets in the processor along with the cauliflower and the other ingredients in the original recipe.

linguine with veal rolls

linguine con topolini

My grandfather Stanislao originated the recipe for these savory veal rolls. After your guests have eaten this delightful meal, you can inform them that *topolini* is the Italian word for "mice"! These rolls are the best when prepared several hours in advance and then slowly warmed through while the pasta is cooking. The veal and sauce may be cooled and refrigerated overnight or frozen for up to one month.

Spoon the sauce onto the pasta and serve it as a first course, and then serve the veal rolls as a second course with a vegetable side dish. Or if you prefer, the pasta and veal rolls may be served together as one course.

1½ pounds veal scallops

3 cloves garlic, finely chopped

6 tablespoons finely chopped provolone cheese

6 tablespoons grated pecorino Romano cheese

6 tablespoons chopped fresh Italian, flat leafed parsley

Kosher salt and freshly ground black pepper

½ cup olive oil

1 cup dry white wine

2 cups chicken broth

½ cup coarsely chopped tender celery leaves

1½ pounds linguine

Freshly grated pecorino Romano cheese for garnish

1. Cut the veal into squares measuring about 3 inches across. Pound each piece, flattening it to form a slightly larger square, about 4 inches.

2. Sprinkle each veal square with equal portions of the garlic. Then sprinkle with about 1 teaspoon each of the provolone, pecorino Romano, and parsley, placing these ingredients near one edge of each piece of veal. Season with salt and pepper. Roll each square tightly to make a small sausage shape. Tie snugly with butcher's string.

3. Warm the olive oil in a large frying pan set over a medium-high heat. When the oil is hot but not smoking, add half the veal rolls and cook until well browned on all sides, about 8 minutes. Remove the veal to a plate and set aside. Cook the remaining veal rolls in the same manner, remove to the plate, and set aside.

4. Add the wine and stir, loosening any pieces of meat that may have been stuck to the bottom of the pan. Add the chicken broth and celery leaves to the pan and cook, stirring constantly, to soften slightly, about 2 minutes. Return the veal rolls to the pan along with any juice that has accumulated on the plate. Bring to a boil and then simmer gently until the meat is cooked through, about 20 minutes. Turn the veal rolls two or three times while they cook to keep them evenly moist.

5. Bring a large pot of salted water to a boil. Add the linguine and cook until al dente, following the package instructions. Drain the pasta and return it to the pot. Spoon a small amount of the veal sauce onto the pasta and toss.

6. Distribute the pasta equally among six plates. Top with more sauce and serve, garnishing with freshly grated pecorino Romano cheese.

7. Serve the veal as a second course, removing the strings and spooning any remaining sauce over the meat.

— SERVES 6 —

WINE PAIRING: Medium white and light red

VARIATION: This dish may also be prepared using boneless chicken breasts in place of the veal. Slice each breast in thirds horizontally, creating three thin slices. Cut and pound the chicken as necessary to achieve the recommended dimensions given for the veal. Proceed with the basic recipe.

spaghetti with tomato and tuna

spaghetti con pomodoro e tonno

The basic tomato sauce for this recipe—excluding the tuna—may be made in advance and kept in the refrigerator for one week or frozen for future use. The tuna should sit in the sauce for ten to fifteen minutes before being ladled over the pasta so the flavor develops. If it sits longer than that, however, the tuna absorbs too much of the tomato and the sauce gets too thick.

¼ cup plus 2 tablespoons olive oil

1 tablespoon coarsely chopped onions

4 cups canned whole plum tomatoes (about one 35-ounce can)

Kosher salt and freshly ground black pepper

2 fresh basil leaves

One 6-ounce can Italian tuna packed in olive oil

1 pound spaghetti or linguine

1. Warm ¼ cup of the olive oil in a small saucepan set over medium-high heat. Add the onions and cook, stirring, until softened, about 3 minutes. Add the tomatoes, crushing them well with the back of a slotted spoon or by squeezing them through your fingers while adding them to the pan. Season with salt and pepper, and stir in the basil. Cover and bring to a boil. Reduce the heat to medium-low and simmer to sweeten the tomatoes, about 20 minutes. Remove the cover and simmer to slightly thicken the sauce, an additional 5 minutes. Drain half of the olive oil from the canned tuna. Pour the remaining oil into the sauce as you use a fork to flake the tuna into the tomato sauce. Cover and simmer to heat through, 8 to 10 minutes. Remove from the heat and set aside.

2. Bring a large pot of salted water to a boil. Add the pasta and cook until al dente, following the package instructions. Drain, then toss the pasta with the remaining 2 tablespoons olive oil. Add about 3 ladles of sauce and continue tossing. Distribute evenly among four dinner plates. Ladle the remaining sauce on top, and serve immediately.

—SERVES 4—

WINE PAIRING: Medium white or light red

VARIATIONS: Fresh tuna may be used: Warm 1 tablespoon olive oil in a nonstick sauté pan set over medium-high heat. Add a 6-ounce tuna steak and cook until medium to medium rare, about 2 minutes per side. Flake the cooked tuna into the sauce during the last 15 minutes of cooking time. Proceed with the basic recipe.

fettuccine with asparagus and shrimp

fettuccine con asparagi e gamberetti

This is an elegant but simple spring pasta. The sauce cooks in the time it takes to boil the pasta. The shrimp may be replaced by bay scallops, crabmeat, lobster, or squid. Or substitute thinly sliced white mushrooms for the seafood to create a purely vegetarian meal.

An easy way to peel the fresh tomatoes called for in this recipe is to plunge them into the boiling water the pasta will be cooked in. It will not affect the flavor of the pasta and eliminates boiling a second pot of water just to remove the skins.

1 pound fettuccine

12 medium-size asparagus (about 1 pound)

5 tablespoons extra virgin olive oil, plus extra
    to drizzle on top of the pasta

2 tablespoons finely diced shallots

2 cloves garlic, thinly sliced

⅛ teaspoon red pepper flakes

1 tablespoon chopped fresh Italian, flat leafed
    parsley

1 tablespoon chopped fresh basil leaves

¾ pound medium-size shrimp, shelled,
    deveined, and sliced in half lengthwise

Kosher salt and freshly ground black pepper

½ cup dry white wine

1 cup peeled and coarsely chopped ripe
    tomatoes (1 large or 2 plum tomatoes)

1. Bring a large pot of salted water to a boil and add the fettuccine. Cook until al dente, following the package instructions.

2. Meanwhile, cut 1 inch off the bottoms of the asparagus. Use a vegetable peeler to trim away the tough outer layer of the asparagus, beginning about 1 inch below the tender tip. Cut the asparagus on an acute angle to create 2-inch-long slices. Set aside.

3. Warm 3 tablespoons of the olive oil in a large sauté pan set over medium-high heat. Add the shallots, garlic, red pepper flakes, parsley, and basil and cook, stirring frequently, to flavor the oil with the aromatics, about 1 minute. Stir in the asparagus and shrimp, and season with salt and pepper. Cook, stirring and tossing frequently, until the shrimp are pink, 2 to 3 minutes. Add the wine and cook until it evaporates, about 1 minute. Add the tomatoes and return the sauce to a gentle boil. Drain the pasta and add it to the sauce. Stir in the remaining 2 tablespoons olive oil. Gently toss to coat the pasta with the sauce.

4. Serve immediately, placing the shrimp decoratively on top of the pasta and drizzling with additional extra virgin olive oil.

— SERVES 4 —

WINE PAIRING: Medium white

VARIATIONS: Canned whole plum tomatoes may be substituted for fresh ripe tomatoes. And ½ pound shelled fresh or frozen peas, or young summer zucchini that has been finely julienned or diced into ¼-inch pieces, may be substituted for the asparagus. Two thin, round slices of seeded fresh jalapeño pepper may be substituted for the red pepper flakes. Remove the pepper slices from the pan just before tossing pasta with the sauce.

fettuccine with shrimp and tomato

fettuccine con gamberetti e pomodoro

This is a simple, quick, and outstandingly delicious meal. If you don't have marinara sauce in the freezer, it will take about thirty minutes to prepare before proceeding with the rest of the recipe. If you have the marinara sauce already made, just warm it on the stove before adding the shrimp.

1 pound fettuccine

¼ cup plus 1 tablespoon olive oil

2 cloves garlic, cut in half

1 pound large shrimp, shelled and deveined

½ cup dry white wine

4 cups warm Sailor's-Style Sauce (page 120)
or your favorite tomato sauce

2 fresh basil leaves

Kosher salt and freshly ground black pepper

1. Bring a large pot of salted water to a boil. Cook the pasta until al dente, following the package instructions.

2. Meanwhile, warm ¼ cup of the olive oil in a large sauté pan set over medium-high heat. Add the garlic and cook to flavor the oil but do not brown, about 2 minutes. Add the shrimp and cook, stirring constantly, until they turn pink, about 1 minute. Add the wine and simmer, allowing the shrimp to absorb the wine, about 1 minute. Stir in the marinara and basil, and season with salt and pepper. Reduce the heat to medium-low and gently simmer the sauce until the shrimp are cooked through but not chewy, about 5 minutes.

3. Drain the pasta and place in a serving bowl. Toss with the remaining 1 tablespoon olive oil. Distribute the pasta equally among four dinner plates. Top with equal portions of the sauce, and serve immediately.

— SERVES 4 —

WINE PAIRING: Light white and medium white

VARIATIONS: Here is a simple and very tasty variation on this dish that does not call for marinara sauce. Follow the basic recipe, adding ½ cup chopped fresh parsley and ¼ cup chopped fresh basil to the shrimp. Toss the pasta with the sauce, along with an additional ¼ cup olive oil. Cover and set aside for 5 minutes to allow the pasta to absorb the flavor of the sauce.

linguine with "angry lobster"

linguine all'aragosta arrabbiata

What makes these lobsters angry comes after they're cooked: the spicy red pepper flakes, garlic, and herbs. Gianni perfected this scrumptious recipe, which provides the home cook with the opportunity to present a restaurant-worthy dish—served in the main part of the lobsters' shell—that can be prepared with surprising ease.

The lobster may be cooked and the meat removed from the shells one day in advance. Cover and refrigerate the meat and shells overnight, bringing them to room temperature before finishing the dish. After cooking the lobsters and removing the meat, cut each lobster in half lengthwise with a heavy, sharp knife. Place each lobster half, with the cavity facing up, on a serving plate and then fill the cavity with the cooked pasta.

2 fresh lobsters (about 1½ pounds each)

1 pound linguine

⅔ cup extra virgin olive oil

⅓ cup minced shallots

¼ cup minced garlic

½ cup chopped fresh Italian, flat leafed parsley

⅓ cup chopped fresh basil leaves

1 teaspoon red pepper flakes

Kosher salt and freshly ground black pepper

½ cup dry white wine

1 cup chopped canned tomatoes (with some of the juice)

1. Bring a large pot of water to a boil. Add the lobsters, cover, and cook until the shells are bright red, about 15 minutes. Drain and set aside to cool.

2. Separate the claws from the body and extract the claw meat. Set aside. Cut the lobsters in half lengthwise. Remove the tail meat and roe. Chop the tail and claw meat into bite-size pieces and set aside. Finely chop the roe and set aside. Discard the green tomalley, and rinse the shells thoroughly under cold running water. Reserve the shells until ready to serve.

3. Bring a large pot of salted water to a boil. Add the linguine and cook until al dente, following the package instructions. Reserve ½ cup of the pasta cooking water before draining.

4. Warm ⅓ cup of the olive oil in a large saucepan set over medium-high heat. Add the shallots and cook to flavor the oil, stirring frequently, about 30 seconds. Stir in the garlic, ¼ cup of the parsley, half the basil, and the red pepper flakes. Cook to soften the garlic slightly, about 2 minutes. Add three quarters of the lobster meat and all of the roe. Cook, stirring frequently, to flavor the lobster with the aromatics, about 2 minutes. Season with salt and pepper. Add the wine and bring to a boil. Add the tomatoes and simmer, stirring frequently. Stir in the remaining lobster meat. Add the drained pasta, the remaining ¼ cup parsley, the remaining basil, and the remaining ⅓ cup olive oil. Toss to coat the pasta with the sauce. If the pasta seems dry, add the reserved pasta water. Spoon onto plates and serve immediately.

— SERVES 4 —

WINE PAIRING: Light white and full white

linguine with clam sauce

linguine con vongole

According to my father, this was one of Nonno Tucci's favorite sauces to make. "He preferred to open the clams himself," recalls Stan. "He would remove the clam meat, making certain to collect all the juice. In the summer when we had large outdoor parties, we often served a bushel of raw clams on ice. Any remaining clams were prepared following my father's methods and frozen. They defrost quickly, providing a meal in the time it takes to cook the pasta."

If your fish market will open the clams and reserve the juice, it will save a lot of preparation time. If not, wash the clamshells thoroughly. Open the clams over a large bowl to catch the juices. Remove clams, discarding the dark sac, and set aside. Strain the juice through a fine-mesh sieve to remove sand and shells. Add the clams to the strained juice. Begin to prepare the sauce when the pasta is halfway cooked.

1 pound linguine

½ cup plus 1 tablespoon olive oil

6 cloves garlic, finely chopped

¼ cup dry white wine

18 littleneck or chowder clams

Kosher salt and freshly ground black pepper

1 tablespoon chopped fresh Italian, flat leafed parsley

1. Bring a large pot of salted water to a boil and cook the pasta, following the package instructions, until al dente.

2. Meanwhile, warm ½ cup of the olive oil in a high-sided saucepan set over medium-high heat. Add the garlic and cook until softened, about 2 minutes. Add the wine and allow it to cook away slightly, about 1 minute. Add the clams and their juice, and season with salt and pepper. Cook until the broth froths to a level of 1 to 2 inches. Remove from the heat. Stir in the parsley.

recipe continued on next page

3. Drain the pasta and toss in a serving bowl with the remaining 1 tablespoon olive oil. Distribute evenly among six dinner plates. Top with equal portions of the sauce, and serve immediately.

— SERVES 6—

WINE PAIRING: Light white and full white

VARIATIONS: The same dish may be prepared without removing the clams from their shells, making for a less formal, hands-on meal. Warm the olive oil in a pot large enough to hold the clams in a single layer. Add the garlic and cook until softened but not browned, about 2 minutes. Add the wine and allow to simmer and sweeten, about 2 minutes. Add the clams and parsley, and cover the pot. Cook until the clams open, about 5 minutes. Season with salt and pepper. Remove from the heat and spoon over cooked pasta. Be sure to discard any unopened clams.

spaghetti with lentils

spaghetti e lenticchie

This recipe was a staple at Nonna Tropiano's home. She used tomatoes she had grown and bottled, along with items that she kept on hand in the pantry. The lentils for this recipe may be prepared one day in advance and then combined with the sauce.

1 cup dried brown lentils, rinsed and picked over to remove stones

½ pound spaghetti, broken into 1- to 1½-inch pieces

1½ cups Joan's Basic Tomato Sauce (page 119) or Sailor's-Style Sauce (page 120) or your own favorite tomato sauce

Freshly ground black pepper

1. Place the lentils in a medium-size saucepan. Fill the pan with cold water to a level 1 inch above the lentils. Slowly bring to a simmer, and cook until the lentils are just tender, about 20 minutes. Remove from the heat and set aside.

2. Bring a large pot of salted water to a boil. Cook the spaghetti until al dente, following the package instructions. Reserve ½ cup of the cooking water before draining the pasta.

3. Meanwhile, drain the lentils and combine them with the tomato sauce in a saucepan large enough to hold the pasta. Bring to a simmer, cover, and cook until the lentils have blended with the sauce, about 10 minutes. Add the drained pasta, along with the reserved pasta water to make a liquid consistency. Season with pepper. Simmer the pasta and sauce together to allow the flavors to combine, about 3 minutes. Serve immediately.

— SERVES 4 —

WINE PAIRING: Medium white or medium red

NOTE: Lentils should not have much water left after cooking; draining may not be necessary.

lasagna with chicken and mushrooms
lasagne di pollo e funghi misti

This lasagna recipe may be served as a pasta course before roasted pork or grilled fish. When served with bread and a tossed green salad, it makes a meal all by itself. It may be baked up to one day in advance. Cover it and refrigerate overnight, then allow to return to room temperature before reheating. It also freezes well.

FOR THE CHICKEN:

1 whole boneless, skinless chicken breast, split

Kosher salt and freshly ground black pepper

2 teaspoons butter

2 teaspoons olive oil

3 fresh sage leaves

FOR THE WHITE SAUCE:

4 tablespoons (½ stick) butter

½ cup all-purpose flour

4 cups whole milk, at room temperature

Pinch of ground nutmeg

FOR THE LASAGNA:

12 strips lasagna pasta, dried or fresh,
  cooked al dente and rinsed in cold water

1 recipe Tomato Sauce with Mushrooms
  (page 129)

⅓ cup freshly grated Parmesan cheese

¼ cup chopped fresh Italian, flat leafed
  parsley

TO PREPARE THE CHICKEN:

The chicken breast should be about ½ inch thick. If necessary, place it between two sheets of plastic wrap and pound to achieve the desired thickness. Season the chicken on both sides with salt and pepper. Heat the butter and oil in a medium sauté pan set over medium heat. When the butter is foaming, add the sage and then place the chicken in the pan. Cook over medium heat so the chicken slowly browns on one side, about 5 minutes. Turn and continue cooking until browned and cooked through, about 5 more minutes. Remove from the pan and allow to cool. Dice into ½-inch cubes (there should be about 1½ cups).

Melt the butter in a 2-quart saucepan set over medium-high heat. When the butter is foaming, whisk in the flour. Gradually whisk in the milk and nutmeg. Reduce the heat to medium and continue whisking until the sauce thickens, about 8 minutes. (If you plan to bake the lasagna a day before serving, or if you plan to freeze it, the sauce may be of slightly thinner consistency because it will thicken as it cools. To make a thinner sauce, cook for less time.) Remove from the heat and set aside.

TO PREPARE THE LASAGNA:

1. Preheat the oven to 350° F. Butter a 9 x 13-inch baking pan.

2. Evenly spread ½ cup of the white sauce over the bottom of the prepared pan. Place three lasagna noodles side by side on top of the sauce. Spread a layer of white sauce on top of the noodles. Spread one quarter of the mushroom sauce on top of the white sauce. Sprinkle half the chicken on top of the mushroom sauce. Sprinkle with some of the Parmesan and parsley.

3. Top with three lasagna noodles and spread a layer of white sauce on top of the noodles. Spread one quarter of the mushroom sauce on top of the white sauce. Sprinkle the remaining half of the chicken on top of the mushroom sauce. Sprinkle with Parmesan and parsley.

4. Top this layer with three lasagna noodles. Spread a layer of white sauce on top of the noodles. Spread one quarter of the mushroom sauce on top of the white sauce. Sprinkle with Parmesan and parsley.

5. Place the final layer of noodles on top. Spread with the remaining white sauce, then the remaining mushroom sauce, and sprinkle with the remaining Parmesan and parsley.

6. Bake until bubbly and lightly browned on top, about 30 minutes. Allow to cool for 10 minutes before slicing and serving.

— SERVES 8 —

WINE PAIRING: Light red and medium red

green lasagna

lasagne vérde

During our family stay in Italy, we found ourselves in Bologna—the only city, it seemed, where there was an orthodontist who could replace my sister's retainer. During this day trip we ate lunch at a restaurant that specialized in *lasagne vérde*. I can only say that to this day, it remains one of the finest meals I have ever eaten. Soon my mother had perfected the recipe, and this dish tops the request list when she prepares family birthday dinners.

This dish can be made using Homemade Pasta (page 114), but it is also very tasty made with commercial fresh pasta or dried pasta. Either way I recommend using a combination of both egg, or standard yellow, noodles and spinach, or green, noodles for a colorful and flavorful dish.

If you are using homemade noodles, leave them the width they are when they come out of the pasta machine and then trim them to fit the length of the pan. This way you will need only two of these wider noodles to complete each layer of lasagna. The directions in this recipe are based on using commercial pasta that is narrower, so each layer will require three noodles. The lasagna may be prepared, cooled completely, and refrigerated for two days before baking and serving. It may also be frozen and should be defrosted before baking.

1 recipe Maria Rosa's Sauce (page 124)

7 standard lasagna noodles, cooked al dente, chilled in cold water, and drained on dish towels

1 recipe White Sauce (page 116)

1 cup finely grated Parmesan cheese

8 green lasagna noodles, cooked al dente, chilled in cold water, and drained on dish towels

1. Preheat the oven to 350° F. Butter a 9 x 13-inch baking pan.

2. Ladle ½ cup of Maria Rosa's Sauce over the bottom of the prepared pan. Place three standard lasagna noodles side by side on top of the sauce. Spread a layer of one quarter of the remaining Maria Rosa's Sauce on top of the noodles. Spread one quarter of the White Sauce on top of the sauce. Sprinkle with ¼ cup of the Parmesan.

3. Top with three green lasagna noodles, and spread a layer of Maria Rosa's Sauce, a layer of White Sauce, and another ¼ cup of the Parmesan on top of these noodles.

4. Top this layer with three standard lasagna noodles, and spread a layer of Maria Rosa's Sauce, a layer of White Sauce, and ¼ cup Parmesan on top of these noodles.

5. For the final layer, place one standard lasagna noodle in the center and a green lasagna noodle on either side of it. Top with remaining Maria Rosa's Sauce, the remaining White Sauce, and the remaining ¼ cup Parmesan.

6. Bake until bubbly and lightly browned on top, about 30 minutes. Allow to cool slightly before cutting.

— SERVES 8 —

WINE PAIRING: Light red and medium red

potato gnocchi

gnocchi

This recipe is for two variations of gnocchi—the regular small ones that are rolled off a fork and the larger hand-rolled ones that are stuffed. The stuffed version freezes very well and may be cooked in boiling water directly from the freezer. Both types may be topped with any number of sauces and served either as a pasta dish or as a main course.

2 large all-purpose potatoes (about 1½ pounds), peeled

Kosher salt

1 large egg plus 1 large egg yolk, lightly beaten

2 teaspoons olive oil

¼ teaspoon ground nutmeg

¾ to 1 cup all-purpose flour, as needed

1 cup finely grated Parmesan cheese

Melted butter or heated sauce, for serving

1. Place the potatoes in a medium-size pot and cover with cold water. Season with salt and bring to a low boil. Cook until the potatoes are very tender when pierced with a fork but not breaking apart, about 35 minutes.

2. Drain the potatoes and press through a ricer or mash well with the back of a fork. Spread the potatoes out on a work surface and allow to cool. Gather the cooled potatoes into a shallow round, forming a well in the center. Place the beaten egg and yolk, olive oil, salt to taste, and nutmeg in the well. Distribute ¾ cup of the flour and the grated cheese around the outer edge of the round. Use your hands to gradually incorporate all of the ingredients into the potatoes to form a smooth dough. (Making gnocchi is similar to making bread, so the amount of flour you will need will vary. Up to ¼ cup of additional flour may be necessary to make a smooth dough.) Form the dough into a short, thick log.

3. Bring a large pot of salted water to a boil.

4. Lightly flour your work surface. Cut the thick log into quarters. Roll each quarter of the dough into a long ½-inch-diameter log. Cut into ½-inch pieces. The gnocchi may be cooked in these cylindrical shapes or individually rolled off a fork to form the traditional gnocchi shape—three or four shallow stripes on one side, a small indentation on the other.

5. Cook the gnocchi in small batches in the pot of boiling water. They will sink to the bottom of the pot at first. When they rise to the top, they are done. Use a skimmer or slotted spoon to remove them from the water, and set them aside on a warm serving dish until all of the gnocchi are cooked. Toss with butter or sauce and serve immediately.

6. For stuffed gnocchi, cut the thick log in half. Roll each half into a 2-inch-thick log. Cut a 1-inch-deep slit down the length of the log. Fill this slit with a semisoft cheese (such as Robiola, smoked mozzarella, Brie, Fontina, or Asiago). Firmly pinch the slit closed. Cut the filled log into 3-inch lengths. Firmly pinch the cut ends closed to seal in the cheese. The stuffed gnocchi may be cooked immediately in boiling water following the instructions for traditional gnocchi, or they may be frozen.

7. To freeze, place the small logs on a baking sheet and place in the freezer. When the logs are firm, they may be transferred to a container and kept frozen for up to 2 months. Cook in boiling water directly from the freezer. Serve as an appetizer topped with butter or your favorite sauce.

— SERVES 6 —

WINE PAIRING: Depends on the sauce

VARIATIONS: Gnocchi may also be served topped with these warmed sauces: Joan's Basic Tomato Sauce (page 119); 2 tablespoons chunky sweet Gorgonzola cheese melted in 1 cup heavy cream until thickened, 6 to 8 minutes.

For an elegant version of stuffed gnocchi, fill the split log with smoked salmon. Serve topped with sour cream and a dollop of caviar.

cannelloni with two fillings

cannelloni in due maniere

Tasty homemade cannelloni are versatile and, because they may be prepared one day in advance, great to make when you are entertaining. Cannelloni are a terrific dish for a buffet. This recipe will prepare twenty cheese-filled and twenty meat-filled cannelloni. Serve one of each kind as an appetizer, or two of each kind as a pasta course. If you are planning to freeze the cannelloni, prepare a slightly thinner white sauce, as it will thicken while it cools.

Another variation is to serve the cannelloni as a passed appetizer with cocktails. After rolling the cannelloni as described below, cut each long roll into 1-inch sections. Place them filling side down on a baking sheet. Sprinkle with Parmesan cheese and bake in a preheated oven at 350° F, until heated through and lightly browned, about ten minutes.

1 recipe Homemade Pasta (page 114)
2 recipes White Sauce (page 116)
1 cup finely grated Parmesan cheese
1 recipe Spinach Ricotta Filling (page 170)

½ cup Joan's Basic Tomato Sauce (page 119)
1 recipe Meat Filling (page 171)

1. Bring a large pot of salted water to a boil. Preheat the oven to 400° F.

2. Roll out the homemade pasta as instructed. Cut each long strip of pasta into pieces that are 4 inches by the width created by your pasta machine. There will be about 40 pieces. Cook the pasta in batches just until tender, about 3 minutes. Cool the cooked pasta under cold running water. Drain and lay out on a dish towel to dry.

3. Butter two large baking dishes. Evenly spread a thin layer of white sauce on the bottom of each dish and set aside.

4. Place a piece of cooked pasta on a dry cloth with the short end toward you. Dust the top end of the pasta with a small amount of Parmesan cheese. Place 2 tablespoons of the spinach ricotta filling ½ inch above the short end of the pasta and spread it to within ¼ inch of either edge. Roll the pasta up toward the Parmesan-dusted edge to form a neat roll. Place each completed roll, seam side down, in one of the prepared baking dishes.

5. When all of the cheese-filled cannelloni are rolled and in the baking dish, top with half of the remaining white sauce. Dot ½ teaspoon of the tomato sauce in the center of each cannelloni. (The cannelloni may be covered and frozen at this point. When reheating frozen cannelloni, bake at 350° F for 15 minutes, then broil to brown as described below.)

6. Fill the remaining pasta with the meat filling, following the same procedure. Arrange in the other prepared baking dish and cover with the remaining white sauce.

7. Sprinkle the remaining Parmesan cheese on top of both dishes of cannelloni before baking. Cook until the sauce begins to bubble, about 10 minutes. Turn on the oven broiler and cook until lightly browned, about 3 minutes. Serve immediately.

— SERVES 8 TO 10 —

WINE PAIRING: Full white (with white sauce) and medium red (with basic tomato sauce)

VARIATION: The shape of homemade pasta that has been cut and boiled in the method used for cannelloni is called *fazzoletti,* which means "handkerchief." Fazzoletti may also be used to prepare individual portions of an informal lasagna: Place a sheet of cooked pasta on a serving plate. Top with sauce, such as Pan-Seared Calamari in Its Own Broth (page 34) or Tucci or Tropiano Ragù Sauce (pages 122 and 121), and lay another piece of pasta on top. Top with more sauce and serve immediately.

FAZZOLETTI LASAGNA MAY ALSO BE FROZEN: Place individual portions of this informal lasagna a few inches apart on a baking sheet and place in the freezer to set, about 30 minutes. Transfer to an airtight container and store for up to 1 month.

recipe continued on next page

Place the frozen fazzoletti in a preheated oven at 300° F and bake to soften, about 10 minutes. Increase the temperature to 350° F and cook until browned, about 8 to 10 minutes. Serve immediately.

spinach ricotta filling

2 tablespoons olive oil

½ cup finely chopped onions

1 pound fresh spinach, washed well and
*   tough stems removed*

2 cups ricotta cheese

¾ cup finely grated Parmesan cheese

¼ cup plain dried bread crumbs

Kosher salt and freshly ground black pepper

1. Warm the olive oil in a medium-size skillet set over high heat. Add the onions and cook, stirring constantly to wilt them, about 2 minutes. Add the spinach and cook, stirring frequently, to wilt the spinach, about 4 minutes. Remove from the heat and cool completely.

2. Squeeze out any liquid retained by the spinach by pressing it between your hands or by placing it in a fine-mesh sieve and pressing on it with the back of a spoon. Place the spinach in a food processor and chop. Add the ricotta and process to combine. Stir in the Parmesan and bread crumbs, season with salt and pepper, and set aside.

— MAKES APPROXIMATELY 2 ½ CUPS —

WINE PAIRING: Light white and full white

VARIATIONS: Use 1 cup ricotta cheese and 1 cup grated smoked mozzarella, grated Fontina, or grated Asiago cheese in place of the 2 cups ricotta. If the ricotta is very wet, place it in a fine-mesh sieve placed over a bowl and allow to drain for approximately 30 minutes.

meat filling

If you have any leftover filling you can make tiny *polpette,* or fried meatballs. Stir ¼ cup plain dried bread crumbs into the meat to form a dough and then scoop out rounded tablespoons and shape them into small patties. Dip the patties in lightly beaten egg and roll them in more bread crumbs, fry them in olive oil, and serve.

2 tablespoons olive oil

1½ cups coarsely chopped celery

1½ cups coarsely chopped carrots

1½ cups coarsely chopped onions

½ cup coarsely chopped fresh Italian, flat leafed parsley

3 cloves garlic, crushed

¼ cup coarsely chopped fresh sage leaves

¼ cup coarsely chopped fresh rosemary leaves

1 pound stewing beef, veal, lamb, pork, or venison, trimmed of fat and cut into cubes

Kosher salt and freshly ground black pepper

½ cup dry red wine

1 cup water

½ cup dried porcini mushrooms

1 large egg, lightly beaten

½ cup freshly grated Parmesan cheese

1. Warm the olive oil in a medium saucepan set over medium-high heat. Stir in the celery, carrots, onions, and parsley. Cook, stirring occasionally, to soften the onions, about 5 minutes. Add the garlic, sage, and rosemary and continue cooking until the onions begin to brown, about 10 minutes. Stir in the beef. Cook, stirring occasionally, to brown the meat, 6 to 8 minutes. Season with salt and pepper, then add the wine, water, and mushrooms. Cover, and reduce the heat to a simmer. Cook until most of the water has evaporated and the meat is beginning to fall apart, about 1 hour.

2. Remove the cover and increase the heat to medium. Stir the meat and cook to make sure all the water has evaporated, about 10 minutes. Remove from the heat and allow to cool. Place in a food processor and process until very smooth. Blend in the egg and Parmesan cheese. Taste, and season with more salt and pepper if necessary. Set aside.

— MAKES APPROXIMATELY 3 CUPS —

recipe continued on next page

WINE PAIRING: Light red and medium red

VARIATIONS: When preparing this filling with lamb, 1½ cups coarsely chopped cabbage may be added to the celery, carrots, and onions at the beginning of the recipe. When preparing this filling with venison, ½ cup currants or raisins that have been soaked for 5 minutes in boiling water and drained may be stirred into the completed puree.

stuffed crepes

m a n i c o t t i

During my family's stay in Italy in 1974, we went to visit my mother's cousin Catherine in Calabria. "I remember working with her in the kitchen and watching as she made these light, delicious stuffed crepes," says Joan. "Before that I had used this stuffing to make cannelloni or stuffed shells."

This is a terrific first course or buffet dish. It may be prepared earlier in the day or may be frozen for several weeks before bringing to room temperature and baking.

FOR THE CREPES:

3 large eggs

1¾ cups water

1½ cups all-purpose flour

Kosher salt

Olive oil for the pan

FOR THE FILLING:

2 pounds whole-milk or part-skim ricotta cheese

1 cup grated mozzarella cheese (about 4 ounces)

1 large egg

2 teaspoons chopped fresh Italian, flat leafed parsley

½ cup White Sauce (page 116)

½ cup chopped cooked spinach (about ½ pound), all liquid squeezed out

4 tablespoons finely grated pecorino Romano or Parmesan cheese

Kosher salt

1½ cups Joan's Basic Tomato Sauce (page 119), pureed in a food processor

Grated pecorino Romano or Parmesan cheese for serving (optional)

TO PREPARE THE CREPES:

1. In a large bowl, beat the eggs until frothy. Beat in a small portion of the water, followed by a small portion of the flour. Continue adding water and flour, beating after each addition, to make a smooth batter. Season with salt.

recipe continued on next page

2. Line a baking sheet with waxed paper or plastic wrap and set aside. Brush an 8-inch crepe or nonstick pan with olive oil. Warm the pan over medium-high heat. Pour ¼ cup of the batter into the pan. Swirl the batter around the pan to evenly coat the bottom, and pour any excess batter back into the bowl. The batter should cover the bottom of the pan in a thin layer. Cook the crepe until bubbles appear, about 1 minute. Flip over the crepe and cook the other side for an additional minute.

3. Remove to the prepared baking sheet and continue cooking crepes, placing waxed paper or plastic wrap over each one on the baking sheet. (If the crepes begin to stick to the pan, brush it with more oil.) With this batter you will be able to make 24 crepes.

TO PREPARE THE FILLING:

1. In a large bowl, stir together the ricotta, mozzarella, egg, parsley, white sauce, and spinach. Stir in 1 tablespoon of the Romano cheese and season with salt.

2. Preheat the oven to 350° F. Divide ½ cup of the tomato sauce between two large baking dishes, and spread to cover the bottom with a thin layer.

3. Spread a rounded tablespoon of the filling across the bottom third of each crepe. Roll the crepe closed and place, seam side down, in one of the prepared baking dishes. Continue filling crepes and arranging them in the baking dishes, making sure that their sides do not touch. Spread a generous teaspoon of tomato sauce across the top of each crepe. Sprinkle with the remaining 3 tablespoons Romano cheese.

4. Cover the baking dishes with aluminum foil and bake until the crepes puff, about 20 minutes. Remove the foil and bake until lightly browned, about 5 minutes. Serve immediately, with remaining warm tomato sauce and grated Romano or Parmesan cheese if desired.

— MAKES 24 CREPES —

WINE PAIRING: Light red and medium red

polenta

polenta

There are many variations on this recipe, but I like to keep it simple. This is meant to be eaten with braised meat or stewed fish or with mushrooms. One of my favorite variations is "messy polenta." Mix ½ cup cooked white beans or kidney beans and ½ cup Gorgonzola cheese into the cooked polenta and serve immediately.

4 cups water	*2 tablespoons olive oil*
2½ teaspoons kosher salt	*1¼ cups finely ground yellow cornmeal*

1. Bring the water to a boil in a medium-size saucepan. Add the salt and olive oil, reduce the heat to a simmer, and gradually whisk in the cornmeal, a small amount at a time. Reduce the heat to low and cook the polenta, stirring occasionally, until tender, about 30 minutes.

2. Serve immediately, spooned onto serving plates, or pour into a 9 x 13-inch baking pan to cool. The cooled polenta may be sliced for grilling or pan-frying.

— SERVES 4 TO 6 —

WINE PAIRING: Medium red and full red

VARIATIONS: Add one or more of the following to the cooked polenta before serving:

2 tablespoons light cream

2 tablespoons softened butter

Freshly ground black pepper

1 tablespoon chopped fresh mixed herbs (such as rosemary, sage, thyme, or tarragon)

½ cup freshly grated Parmesan, Robiola, Gorgonzola, or Fontina cheese

½ pound sautéed sliced mushrooms

½ cup coarsely chopped walnuts

lasagna made with polenta and gorgonzola cheese

polenta pasticciata al gorgonzola

Lasagna is delicious as both a main course or as a pasta course served before grilled meat or fish. Look in your local cheese store for *dolce latte* (sweet milk) Gorgonzola, a sweet, mild cheese that doesn't have the hard bite of other Gorgonzolas. Brie, Jarlsberg, Gruyère, or Emmenthaler cheese may be substituted.

4 cups water

2½ tablespoons sea or kosher salt

2 tablespoons olive oil

1¼ cups finely ground yellow cornmeal

1½ cups Tomato Sauce with Mushrooms (page 129)

⅓ cup crumbled sweet Gorgonzola cheese

2 tablespoons finely grated Parmesan cheese

1. Bring the water to a boil in a medium-size saucepan. Add the salt and olive oil, reduce the heat to a simmer, and gradually whisk in the cornmeal, a small amount at a time. Reduce the heat to low and cook the polenta, stirring occasionally, until it is smooth and tender, about 30 minutes. Pour into an 8-inch square baking dish and allow to cool completely.

2. Preheat the oven to 350° F.

3. Turn the cooled polenta out onto a cutting surface. Cut the square in half to make two rectangles. Cut each half of the polenta, on the bias, into 8 slices, each about 1½ inches wide. Arrange the slices in a single tightly overlapping row in the baking dish. Spoon 1 tablespoon of the mushroom sauce between each pair of slices, and distribute the remaining sauce over the top of the polenta. Sprinkle with the Gorgonzola. Bake to warm through and melt the cheese, about 20 minutes. Sprinkle with the Parmesan and bake to brown, about 5 minutes. Serve immediately.

— SERVES 6 TO 8 —

WINE PAIRING: Medium red and full red

VARIATIONS: Other sauces, such as any of the ragù or marinara recipes in this book, may be substituted for the mushroom sauce.

vegetarian timpano

timpano di vegetali

When we were preparing this cookbook, Gianni offered this vegetarian variation on *timpano*. Despite its spectacular presentation, this dish is much simpler to prepare than you might think. All of the components may be prepared in advance: The eggplant may be broiled or baked one day ahead, and the sauce may be prepared one day in advance. Refrigerate the eggplant and sauce overnight and bring to room temperature before filling the timpano. In fact, the timpano maintains its shape best if it is baked earlier in the day and then reheated before serving.

4 medium-size eggplants (about 1½ pounds each), cut lengthwise into ½-inch-wide strips with the peel removed from every other piece

Kosher salt

3 tablespoons butter

½ cup plain dried bread crumbs

2 tablespoons all-purpose flour

1 cup cold milk

½ cup plus 2 tablespoons olive oil

1 cup diced onions

1 cup seeded and diced red bell pepper

1 cup seeded and diced green bell pepper

1 cup seeded and diced yellow bell pepper

Freshly ground black pepper

1 cup quartered and thinly sliced carrots

¾ cup thinly sliced tender celery

3 cups halved and thinly sliced zucchini

2 tablespoons chopped fresh basil leaves

2 tablespoons chopped fresh Italian, flat leafed parsley

2 cups canned whole plum tomatoes

1 cup fresh or frozen peas

¾ pound penne, ziti, or fusilli

2 cups diced mozzarella cheese

½ cup freshly grated Parmesan cheese

1. Generously sprinkle the eggplant slices with kosher salt, place them in a colander, and set aside to drain for 2 hours.

recipe continued on next page

2. Generously grease a 10-inch springform pan with 2 tablespoons of the butter. Sprinkle the bread crumbs on the bottom and sides of the pan. Do not knock out the excess crumbs. Set aside.

3. Melt the remaining 1 tablespoon butter in a small saucepan set over medium heat. Whisk in the flour, then gradually whisk in the milk. Bring to a simmer and cook this white sauce, whisking regularly, until it thickens, about 8 minutes. Remove from the heat and set aside.

4. Bring a large pot of salted water to a boil. Reduce the heat and hold at a low simmer until you are ready to cook the pasta.

5. Warm 2 tablespoons of the olive oil in a sauté pan set over medium-high heat. Add the onions and bell peppers and cook, stirring, until slightly softened but not browned, about 5 minutes. Season with salt and pepper. Add the carrots and celery and continue cooking, stirring frequently, until they have softened slightly, about another 10 minutes. Stir in the zucchini, basil, and parsley and cook to soften slightly, 2 to 3 minutes. Stir in the tomatoes, crushing them with your hand or the back of a slotted spoon as you add them to the pan. Bring to a boil, then reduce the heat to a simmer. Cook until the tomatoes have sweetened slightly, about 10 minutes. Stir in the peas and white sauce, and cook until the peas are tender, 5 minutes. Continue to gently cook the vegetables over low heat, stirring occasionally, while the pasta boils.

6. Return the water to a boil. Add the pasta and cook for 2 minutes longer than recommended on the package. Drain well and stir into the vegetable sauce. Remove from the heat and transfer to a wide bowl. Allow the sauce to cool at room temperature.

7. Preheat the oven broiler, or a gas or charcoal grill. Pat the eggplant slices dry with paper towels. Lightly brush the eggplant slices with the remaining ½ cup olive oil. Brown under the broiler or on the grill, about 5 minutes per side.

8. Preheat the oven to 350° F.

9. Line the prepared springform pan with overlapping slices of the eggplant, alternating the peeled and unpeeled slices, allowing each slice to overhang the edge of the pan by about 3 inches. Line the center of the pan with eggplant, alternating the peeled and unpeeled slices, overlapping the ends of the side pieces. There should be a few pieces of eggplant remaining to fill the top of the timpano.

10. Stir the mozzarella and Parmesan cheeses into the cooled vegetable sauce. Fill the eggplant shell with the pasta/vegetable mixture, pressing down with the back of a wooden spoon to compact it in the pan. Fold the eggplant slices that are hanging over the edge of the pan back over the filling. Patch the center of the timpano with a few remaining slices of eggplant. Cover with aluminum foil and bake for 15 minutes. Remove the foil, increase the oven temperature to 400° F, and continue baking until warmed through, another 15 minutes.

11. Remove from the oven and allow to rest for 10 minutes before removing the outer ring of the springform pan and placing on a serving platter. Serve immediately. (If you are baking it ahead of time, leave the timpano in the pan, cover, and store at room temperature. Reheat before serving.)

— SERVES 12 —

WINE PAIRING: Light red or medium red

VARIATIONS: This vegetable sauce may be tossed with fusilli, ziti, or penne and served as a pasta course. It also makes a nice filling for lasagna. Spoon ½ cup of the sauce onto the bottom of a baking dish. Top with 3 precooked lasagna noodles. Top with sauce and continue layering, using a total of 12 precooked lasagna noodles. Bake at 350° F until the sauce bubbles, about 35 minutes. You can also add 1 cup diced vegetables, such as string beans, artichokes, mushrooms, or asparagus to the sauce. And for a spicier version, add ½ teaspoon chopped jalapeño pepper or ¼ teaspoon red pepper flakes when cooking the onions and bell peppers.

Stanley and Stan assemble a timpano

drum of ziti and great stuff
timpano alla big night

One of the most impressive characters from the movie *Big Night* has no lines. It is the extravagant *timpano* that is created as the centerpiece of an excessive meal. Not only does this dish make a wonderful visual impression on dinner guests, it is intensely flavorful and well worth the process of preparing the components to fill the drum of pasta dough.

Timpano (as it is called in Calabrian dialect)—or *timballo*—has been prepared for feasts and festivals in Italy for centuries. It is generally believed to have entered the lexicon of traditional Italian cooking from Morocco through Sicily. The Tucci family recipe was brought to the United States by Apollonia Pisani, my father's maternal grandmother. She grew up in Serra San Bruno, a small hill town in Calabria.

I can't remember when we had the idea to use timpano as the centerpiece of the *Big Night* meal, but I'm glad we did. Structurally and creatively, it gave us a strong focus for the meal and had repercussions that we never anticipated. During the first screenings we were amazed at the audience's reactions to this dish. They were exactly those of the characters in the film—audible gasps of awe and wonder.

There is a fair amount of drama associated with creating a timpano. Lots of questioning: "Is there enough sauce?" "Is this the right amount of salami, or cheese, or egg?" "Is it done?" "Should we have used the other pan?" "Will it crack when we flip it over?" "Is it cool enough to slice?" "Is it as good as the last one we made?" "Next time . . ." I can imagine generations of Tuccis past, present, and future asking those same questions, and that adds to my enjoyment of timpano.

You may want to consider following my parents' example and make the preparation of the timpano into a family affair. They each take responsibility for different components. My mother cooks the Tucci Ragù Sauce, makes and fries the meatballs, and boils the eggs and pasta. My father slices the cheese and salami and prepares the dough.

Preparing the ingredients ahead of time will also make the process of assembling the timpano less time-consuming on the day you plan to serve it to your guests. The Tucci

recipe continued on next page

Ragù Sauce and the meatballs freeze well, so they may be prepared ahead or leftovers may be saved for future use. My family has frozen a whole timpano in the pan it will be baked in, with great success. A frozen timpano will take three days to fully defrost in the refrigerator before it can be covered with aluminum foil and baked as directed in the recipe.

The dough for timpano is rolled out into a thin round, the diameter of which is determined by the pan you are baking it in. Add the diameter of the bottom of the pan, the diameter of the top of the pan, and twice the height of the pan. The total will equal the approximate diameter needed. The dough may be kneaded in advance and set aside or refrigerated overnight. Return it to room temperature before rolling it out. It is important to generously grease the pan with butter and sprayed olive oil before lining the pan with the dough. Greasing and lining the pan with the dough may be done while the pasta is cooking.

The meat used in preparing the ragù sauce is generally served for dinner the night before the timpano is baked because no one has room for anything other than salad afterward.

FOR THE DOUGH:

4 cups all-purpose flour

4 large eggs

1 teaspoon kosher salt

3 tablespoons olive oil

½ cup water

TO PREPARE THE PAN:

Butter

Olive oil

FOR THE FILLING:

4 cups ¼ x ½-inch Genoa salami pieces

4 cups ¼ x ½-inch sharp provolone cheese cubes

12 hard-boiled eggs, shelled, quartered lengthwise, and each quarter cut in half to create chunks

4 cups small meatballs (made from one recipe Meatballs on page 252)

8 cups Tucci Ragù Sauce (page 122) prepared following recipe note

3 pounds ziti, cooked very al dente (about half the time recommended on the package) and drained (18 cups cooked)

2 tablespoons olive oil

1 cup finely grated pecorino Romano cheese

6 large eggs, beaten

1. Place the flour, eggs, salt, and olive oil in the bowl of a stand mixer fitted with a dough hook. (A large-capacity food processor may also be used.) Add 3 tablespoons of the water and process. Add more water, 1 tablespoon at a time, until the mixture comes together and forms a ball. Turn the dough out onto a lightly floured work surface and knead to make sure it is well mixed, about 10 minutes. Set aside to rest for 5 minutes.

2. To knead the dough by hand, mix the flour and salt together on a clean, dry work surface or pastry board. Form these dry ingredients into a mound and then make a well in the center. Break the eggs into the center of the well and lightly beat them with a fork. Stir in 3 tablespoons of the water. Use the fork to gradually incorporate some of the dry ingredients into the egg mixture. Continue mixing the dry ingredients into the eggs, adding the remaining water 1 tablespoon at a time. Knead the dough with your hands to make a well-mixed, smooth, dry dough. If the dough becomes too sticky, add more flour. Set aside to rest for 5 minutes.

3. Flatten the dough on a lightly floured work surface. Dust the top of the dough with flour and roll it out, dusting with flour and flipping the dough over from time to time, until it is about ¹⁄₁₆ inch thick and is the desired diameter.

TO PREPARE THE FILLING:

1. Grease the baking pan very generously with butter and olive oil so that it is well lubricated. Fold the dough in half and then in half again, to form a triangle, and place it in the pan. Open the dough and arrange it in the pan, gently pressing it against the bottom and the sides, draping the extra dough over the sides. Set aside.

2. Preheat the oven to 350° F.

3. Have the salami, provolone, hard-boiled eggs, meatballs, and ragù sauce at room temperature. Toss the drained pasta with the olive oil and allow to cool slightly before tossing with 2 cups of the ragù sauce. Distribute 4 generous cups of the pasta on the bottom of the timpano. Top with 1 cup of the salami, 1 cup of the provolone, 3 of the

recipe continued on next page

hard-boiled eggs, 1 cup of the meatballs, and ⅓ cup of the Romano cheese. Pour 2 cups of the sauce over these ingredients. Repeat this process to create additional layers using equal amount of the ingredients until they have come within 1 inch of the top of the pan, ending with 2 cups of ragù sauce. Pour the beaten eggs over the filling. Fold the pasta dough over the filling to seal completely. Trim away and discard any double layers of dough. Make sure that the timpano is tightly sealed. If you notice any small openings, cut a piece of the trimmed dough to fit over the opening. Use a small amount of water to moisten these scraps of dough to ensure that a tight seal has been made.

4. Bake until lightly browned, about 1 hour. Then cover with aluminum foil and continue baking until the timpano is cooked through (and reaches an internal temperature of 120°F) and the dough is golden brown, about 30 minutes. Remove from the oven and allow to rest for 30 or more minutes to allow the timpano to cool and contract before attempting to remove from the pan. The baked timpano should not adhere to the pan. To test, gently shake the pan to the left and then to the right. It should slightly spin in the pan. If any part is still attached, carefully detach with a knife.

5. To remove the timpano from the pan, place a baking sheet or thin cutting board that covers the entire diameter of the pan on top of the timpano. Grasp the baking sheet or cutting board and the rim of the pan firmly and invert the timpano. Remove the pan and allow the timpano to cool for 30 minutes. Using a long, sharp knife, cut a circle about 3 inches in diameter in the center of the timpano, making sure to cut all the way through to the bottom. Then slice the timpano as you would a pie into individual portions, leaving the center circle as a support for the remaining pieces. The cut pieces should hold together, revealing the built-up layers of great stuff.

— SERVES 16 —

WINE PAIRING: Light red or medium red

NOTE: The traditional Tucci timpano is baked in a round enamelware pan that is wider on top than it is on the bottom. Finding such a pan might be difficult. For this cookbook we tested several 6-quart containers, the size pan this recipe is written for, and found one that we recommend here. Chantal Cookware Corporation manufactures an enamelware 8-quart lidded casserole. The principal drawbacks to this casserole are its depth and its straight sides, which make it difficult to remove the baked timpano without its breaking. Chantal's products are widely available or can be ordered online or by calling (800) 365-4354. This recipe will serve 12 to 16 people. The proportions may be adapted to fit a smaller or larger container.

rice and risotto

riso e risotto

There are three types of rice recipes in this section—those prepared with long-grain or basmati rice, and risottos prepared with Arborio rice. Basmati rice isn't typically Italian but it is flavorful, especially as prepared in the recipe my mother created and that I share here. Though risotto is now quite popular in this country, this was not true in the 1950s, the period in which *Big Night* is set. That is why in one of the first scenes in *Big Night* we choose to use risotto metaphorically, as it effectively represented a prejudicial preconception for what "Italian" food really is. Because it is northern Italian in origin and most of the Italians who emigrated to America were from the poorer south, few Americans were familiar with risotto back then.

My introduction to risotto was my mother's risotto Milanese that she would often make when I was young. But I have Gianni Scappin to thank for showing me the finer points of the art of making risotto, beginning with shopping for the correct rice. I look for brands marked superfine Carnaroli. If that is not available, I buy a superfine Arborio rice or Vialone Nano rice, both of which may be found in most supermarkets. The rice you buy is important because different varieties absorb liquid at different rates. If the rice is still tough after you've added all the liquid called for in the recipe, you'll need to add more, so I recommend having excess hot liquid available. The following risotto recipes call for more liquid than you will most likely use.

There are two important steps to remember when cooking risotto. First, before adding any liquid make sure to heat the rice well with the onions that are cooked until softened as the first step in these risotto recipes. This will seal the rice grains and helps to keep them from overcooking. Second, test the rice for the desired texture after it has cooked for twelve to fifteen minutes. Risotto may be served al dente, with a slight crispness to the bite, or with a softer consistency—the choice is yours. In Italy they call a risotto of perfect consistency *all'onda*, which means "on the wave," and describes the movement the rice should make as you spoon it onto a plate. Just don't overcook risotto or it will turn into paste.

Preparing risotto requires your focused attention for about twenty minutes, so I like to open a bottle of wine and gather my family and friends around the stove to keep me company while I stir.

rice salad

insalata di riso

The year my family lived in Florence, my mother shopped at a local *tavola calda* (specialty food store), which carried a number of prepared salads. This was one of my favorites. My mother asked the owner for his recipe so she could make it at home herself. It has long been one of our standard lunch dishes.

1 cup long-grain white or brown rice

2½ cups cold water

3 tablespoons freshly squeezed lemon juice
  (from about 1 lemon)

2 tablespoons red wine vinegar

Kosher salt and freshly ground black pepper

¼ cup olive oil

1 cup frozen peas

2 tablespoons chopped fresh Italian, flat leafed parsley

1. Place the rice and water in a small saucepan over medium-high heat. Cover and bring to a boil. Reduce the heat to low and simmer until the rice is tender and most, if not all, of the water has been absorbed, about 20 minutes. If water remains, drain the rice before placing it in the serving bowl.

2. In a small bowl, whisk the lemon juice and vinegar, and season with salt and pepper. Gradually whisk in the olive oil. Pour a small portion of this dressing onto the rice and toss. Set the rice aside to cool.

3. Place the peas in a colander. Pour 3 to 4 cups of hot water over them to defrost and cook slightly. Drain, then stir the peas and parsley into the cooled rice. Whisk the remaining dressing before pouring it over the rice and tossing to coat evenly. Serve at room temperature.

— SERVES 4 —

WINE PAIRING: Medium white and light red

rice with tomato sauce

r i s o   c o n   p o m o d o r o

This is a dish my grandmother served as a quick no-meat supper on Friday evenings. It has a creamy texture and is quite filling. It was not enough of a meal for my grandfather, however, so he would follow it with some my grandmother's fresh baked bread, olives, slices of provolone, and a salad.

1 cup long-grain rice

2½ cups cold water

1½ cups Joan's Basic Tomato Sauce (page 119) prepared with green bell peppers

Freshly grated Parmesan or pecorino Romano cheese for garnish (optional)

Place the rice and water in a small saucepan over medium-high heat. Cover and bring to a boil. Reduce the heat to low and simmer the rice until it is tender and all of the water has been absorbed, about 20 minutes. Stir the tomato sauce into the cooked rice. Cook the rice mixture over low heat to blend the flavors, about 5 minutes. Serve hot, topped with cheese if desired.

— SERVES 6 —

WINE PAIRING: Light red and medium red

rice with zucchini

riso con zucchini

The zucchini adds nice flavor to this simple dish, which I serve with grilled chicken or fish. The rice may be cooked and mixed with the onion and zucchini several hours in advance. Add the cheese just before baking.

1 cup brown basmati rice

2½ cups cold water

2 tablespoons olive oil

½ cup coarsely chopped onions

2 cups coarsely chopped zucchini

Kosher salt and freshly ground black pepper

½ cup grated Jarlsberg cheese

¼ cup finely grated Parmesan cheese

1. Place the rice and water in a small saucepan over medium-high heat. Cover and bring to a boil. Reduce the heat to low and simmer the rice until it is tender, about 20 minutes. If there is water left in the pan, do not drain it off.

2. Preheat the oven to 350° F.

3. Warm the olive oil in a medium-size sauté pan set over medium heat. Add the onions and cook, stirring, until softened, about 5 minutes. Add the zucchini and season with salt and pepper. Cook until the white portion of the zucchini has softened but the green rind remains firm, about 5 minutes.

4. In a small casserole, mix the cooked rice, zucchini, and grated cheeses. Cover and bake until the cheeses have melted, 15 to 20 minutes. Serve immediately.

—SERVES 4—

WINE PAIRING: Medium white

VARIATIONS: Asiago, Gruyère, or Monterey Jack cheese may be substituted for the Jarlsberg.

rice with sage

riso alla salvia

Most Americans use Arborio rice only when preparing risotto. However, it is also very delicious if you cook it as you would conventional rice and blend it with herbs and butter. It makes a tasty side dish in place of potatoes or beans. For a simple and delicious dinner, cook rice according to this recipe and add a drained 3.5-ounce can of Italian tuna and 2 teaspoons rinsed capers. Drizzle with a little extra virgin olive oil and serve.

2 cups Arborio rice

2 tablespoons butter or olive oil

12 fresh sage leaves

½ cup freshly grated Parmesan cheese

1. Bring a medium-size saucepan of salted water to a boil. Add the rice and cook, uncovered, until tender, about 15 minutes.

2. Melt the butter in a small sauté pan set over low heat. Remove from the heat and add the sage leaves. Set aside.

3. Reserve ¼ cup of the cooking water before draining the rice. Return the drained rice to the saucepan. Stir in the reserved water, melted butter with sage, and cheese. Blend well and serve.

— SERVES 6 —

WINE PAIRING: Medium white

VARIATIONS: Other soft-leaved herbs such as basil, parsley, or marjoram may be substituted for the sage. Boiled Arborio rice may be used in place of pasta in any of the pasta salad recipes found in this book. Cook the rice, run it under cold water, and toss with the recipe of your choice.

rice with milk

riso e latte di "bertilla"

Gianni named this dish for his mother, Maria-Bertilla, who would make it for him as an after-school snack. "I savored each bite," Gianni recalls, "spooning around the edges of the bowl toward the center until each morsel was eaten."

4 cups milk

1½ cups water

2 cups arborio rice

Kosher salt

1 tablespoon butter or olive oil

1. Bring the milk and water to boil in a large saucepan set over medium-high heat. Stir in the rice and salt to taste. Simmer until the rice has absorbed most of the liquid, about 20 minutes. Remove from the heat and allow to cool for 2 minutes. The rice should be creamy and, when poured into bowls, should be *all'onda*, which means "wavy." Top each portion with a little butter or olive oil. Serve immediately.

—SERVES 4 TO 6—

WINE PAIRING: Sparkling or full-bodied white

milanese risotto

risotto alla milanese

In Italy they sell small paper packages of powdered saffron, but in the United States it is more typical to find saffron threads sold in small vials, which may be used to prepare this dish. It is traditional to serve *Risotto alla Milanese* with osso buco. It may also be served as a first course before chicken or other veal dishes.

With the leftover risotto, make risotto cakes to serve for lunch on top of a green salad or for brunch with fried eggs. Just add an egg to the leftover risotto and enough bread crumbs to form a soft dough. Shape the risotto into patties about 3 inches in diameter and ½ inch thick. Heat 3 tablespoons olive oil in a sauté pan set over medium-high heat. When the oil is hot but not smoking, add the risotto cakes. Cook until warmed through and golden brown on both sides, about 8 minutes altogether. Serve immediately.

8 cups hot chicken broth

½ teaspoon powdered saffron or 20 saffron
  threads

4 tablespoons butter

2 tablespoons olive oil

½ cup coarsely chopped onions

2 cups Arborio rice

½ cup dry white wine

¼ cup finely grated Parmesan cheese

1. Measure out ½ cup of the hot broth, stir in the saffron, and set aside. Keep the remaining broth warm in a medium-size saucepan set over medium-low heat.

2. Melt 2 tablespoons of the butter in the olive oil in a large saucepan set over medium heat. Add the onions and cook, stirring, until they have softened but not browned, about 5 minutes. Add the rice and stir to coat with the butter, oil, and onions. Add the wine and cook, stirring continuously, until the wine evaporates, about 1 minute. Stir in the saffron broth and cook, allowing the rice to absorb it, about 2 minutes. Add the

remaining broth, ½ cup at a time, stirring after each addition and allowing the rice to absorb the broth before adding more. Cook until the rice is tender but al dente, about 15 to 20 minutes. You may have broth left over. Remove from the burner and stir in the remaining 2 tablespoons of butter and ¼ cup of Parmesan cheese. Serve immediately.

— SERVES 6 —

WINE PAIRING: Medium red

VARIATION: Dried porcini mushrooms make a nice addition to this risotto. Soak 1 cup chopped dried porcini in 1 cup warm water. After the saffron broth has been added to the rice, strain the mushrooms through a fine-mesh sieve, reserving the liquid. Stir the mushrooms and the strained liquid into the risotto, allowing the rice to absorb the liquid before proceeding with the recipe.

asparagus risotto
risotto con asparagi

Canned asparagus may sound gross, but it provides lots of flavor and makes the rice very creamy. This dish can also be prepared using canned peas or crushed plum tomatoes. Of course, this risotto may also be prepared using fresh ingredients. But it also makes for a great "lazy" risotto with ingredients we usually have on hand—rice, onion, canned vegetables, Parmesan cheese, olive oil, chicken broth (or just water), and sometimes parsley.

2 tablespoons olive oil

1 small onion, coarsely chopped

2 tablespoons chopped fresh Italian, flat leafed parsley

2 cups Arborio rice

One 15-ounce can asparagus (do not drain)

6 cups hot chicken or vegetable broth

Tips from 8 fresh asparagus stalks (optional)

Kosher salt and freshly ground black pepper

1 tablespoon butter (optional)

1 tablespoon extra virgin olive oil

⅓ cup finely grated Parmesan cheese

1. Warm the olive oil in a medium-size saucepan set over a medium heat. When the oil is hot but not smoking, stir in the onions and cook, stirring frequently, until soft but not browned, about 5 minutes. Stir in 1 tablespoon of the parsley and all of the rice. Stir to toast lightly and coat the rice with oil. Stir in the canned asparagus with its liquid, plus 2 cups of the chicken broth. Bring to a boil, then reduce the heat to simmer. Add more chicken broth, ½ cup at a time, stirring frequently and allowing the rice to absorb the liquid after each addition, until the rice is al dente, about 15 minutes. (If you use fresh asparagus tips, add them with the last ladleful of broth.) The rice should have a slight resistance to the bite. If it seems too hard, add a little bit more liquid and continue cooking for another minute or two.

2. Remove from the heat and season with salt and pepper. Add the remaining 1 table-spoon parsley, the butter, if using, olive oil, and Parmesan. Whip with a wooden spoon to bring out the creaminess of the rice and to incorporate all the ingredients. Adjust the seasoning with salt and pepper if necessary. Serve immediately.

— SERVES 4 —

WINE PAIRING: Medium white

VARIATIONS: White canned asparagus may be used in place of green asparagus. Also, 2 teaspoons chopped fresh tarragon leaves stirred in at the end of the recipe makes a nice addition to this risotto.

If using fresh asparagus, chop the tips off 1 pound asparagus and set aside. Coarsely chop the remaining portion of the asparagus, discarding any woody stems. Stir the chopped asparagus into the risotto along with the first 2 cups of broth, and proceed with the recipe as written. Add the asparagus tips along with the parsley, butter, if using, olive oil, and Parmesan.

You can make an even simpler version of this recipe: Cook the onion and parsley in olive oil, add the rice, and gradually stir in 6 cups of warm chicken stock. After seasoning with salt and pepper, stir in ½ cup grated or crumbled Fontina, Gorgonzola, or Gruyère cheese. These creamy cheeses add texture and flavor to this one-dish meal.

risotto with vegetables and fine herbs

risotto di vegetali alle erbette fini

This dish is visually stunning and in every bite you will find a little something different. Although the types and quantities of vegetables used in this recipe vary, I would not use strong-flavored vegetables such as fennel, broccoli, cauliflower, cabbage, garlic, or even mushrooms, which would overpower the other flavors.

2 teaspoons chopped fresh basil leaves

2 teaspoons chopped fresh Italian, flat leafed parsley

½ teaspoon chopped fresh thyme leaves

½ teaspoon chopped fresh sage leaves

1 tablespoon plus 2 teaspoons butter

2 tablespoons olive oil

½ cup diced shallots or onions

12 small artichoke hearts, cut in half (frozen hearts or canned artichoke bottoms may be used)

4 string beans, ends trimmed and cut into 2-inch pieces

2 tablespoons finely diced tender celery

1¼ cups halved and thinly sliced zucchini (about 1 small zucchini)

1¼ cups halved and thinly sliced carrots (about 2 medium-size carrots)

¼ cup fresh or frozen peas

½ cup 1-inch-length asparagus (about 3 stalks)

½ cup chopped fresh or canned plum tomatoes (about 2 tomatoes)

2 cups Arborio rice

6 cups hot chicken or vegetable broth

Kosher salt and freshly ground black pepper

1 tablespoon extra virgin olive oil

⅓ cup freshly grated Parmesan cheese

1. In a small bowl, mix together the chopped herbs and set aside.

2. In a large saucepan set over medium-high heat, melt 2 teaspoons of the butter in the olive oil. Add the shallots, cover, and cook until they are soft but not browned, about 5 minutes. Add all of the vegetables and half of the herb mixture, stirring to combine. Add the rice, stirring to toast lightly and coat with the oil. Add 2 cups of the chicken broth.

Bring to a rapid boil, then reduce the heat to a gentle boil. Add the remaining broth, ½ cup at a time, stirring frequently and allowing the rice to absorb the liquid after each addition, until the rice is al dente, about 15 minutes. The rice should have a slight resistance to the bite. If it seems too hard, add a little more liquid and continue cooking for another minute or two.

3. Remove from the heat and season with salt and pepper. Stir in the remaining herbs, the remaining 1 tablespoon butter, the extra virgin olive oil, and the Parmesan. Whip with a wooden spoon to bring out the creaminess of the rice and to incorporate all of the ingredients.

— SERVES 4 —

WINE PAIRING: Medium white, light red, and rosé

risotto with butternut squash, lobster, and sage

risotto di zucca con aragosta e salvia

This was the first dish Gianni ever cooked for me while I was doing research for *Big Night* at Le Madri. I knew then I was in the hands of a master.

Naturally sweet butternut squash and seafood create the unique flavor of this beautiful, creamy risotto. Adding pumpkin puree to enrich the chicken broth saves the time of preparing a vegetable broth, and the small amount of seafood called for makes this dish a relatively inexpensive way to serve lobster to a group. Serve this risotto with a green salad, a loaf of bread, and a dry white wine.

6 cups chicken or vegetable broth

¼ cup canned pumpkin puree

3 tablespoons olive oil

½ cup diced onions

1 pound butternut squash, peeled, seeded, and diced into ¼-inch cubes (about 3 cups)

2 cups Arborio rice

1 teaspoon chopped fresh sage leaves

½ pound cooked lobster meat, cut into small bite-size pieces (about 1 cup)

Kosher salt and freshly ground black pepper

2 tablespoons brandy or cognac

1 tablespoon chopped fresh Italian, flat leafed parsley

2 tablespoons butter

1. In a large saucepan, whisk the chicken broth and pumpkin puree. Bring to a boil, then reduce the heat to medium-low and leave the broth at a gentle simmer.

2. In a large high-sided sauté pan, warm 1 tablespoon of the olive oil over medium heat. Stir in the onions and cook until softened but not browned, about 5 minutes. Stir in the squash and cook to flavor with the onions, about 2 minutes. Stir in the rice, sage, and 2 cups of the simmering broth. Bring to a boil, stirring frequently, then reduce the heat to a simmer.

3. When the rice has absorbed the liquid, add half the lobster meat and ½ cup of the simmering broth. Stir the rice until the liquid is absorbed. Continue adding the remaining broth, ½ cup at a time, stirring after each addition and allowing the rice to absorb the liquid before adding more. After 15 minutes, taste a grain of rice. It should have a slight resistance to the bite. If it seems too hard, add a little more broth and continue cooking for another minute or two. When the rice has absorbed the last of the broth, add the remaining lobster. Remove from the heat.

4. Season with salt and pepper. Stir in the brandy, parsley, butter, and remaining 2 tablespoons olive oil. Whip with a wooden spoon to bring out the creaminess of the rice and to incorporate all the ingredients. Cover and allow to rest for 5 minutes before serving.

— SERVES 4 TO 6 —

WINE PAIRING: Medium white or full white

VARIATIONS: Culls (lobsters without claws) or single lobster tails may be used for this recipe—you will need about 1½ pounds lobster in the shell. An additional ¼ pound chopped butternut squash may be substituted for the pumpkin puree, and crabmeat or shrimp may be substituted for the lobster. Parmesan cheese may be served as a garnish.

risotto with shrimp

risotto con gamberetti

My father's family emigrated from Italy to Vermont, where they would gather wild mushrooms to use when preparing risotto. That recipe became a family staple that has now been passed down through three generations of Tuccis. My mother created this variation using delicate shrimp, which beautifully accent the pearly white Arborio rice.

1 pound medium-size shrimp, peeled and deveined, shells reserved	1 clove garlic, chopped
1 medium-size onion, quartered	2 tablespoons butter
1 celery stalk, cut into thirds	¼ cup chopped onions
1 carrot (optional), peeled and cut into thirds	1 cup Arborio rice
4 sprigs fresh Italian, flat leafed parsley	½ cup dry white wine
Kosher salt	1 fresh or canned plum tomato, peeled, seeded, and diced
5 cups water	¼ cup finely grated Parmesan cheese
4 tablespoons olive oil	(optional)

1. In a large saucepan, combine the shrimp shells, quartered onion, celery, carrot, if using, parsley, salt to taste, and water. Bring to a boil, then simmer gently, with the lid slightly askew, for 15 to 20 minutes. Strain through a fine-mesh sieve. Discard the shells and vegetables. When you are ready to prepare the risotto, warm the broth to a gentle simmer.

2. Warm 2 tablespoons of the olive oil in a large high-sided sauté pan set over medium heat. Add the garlic and sauté lightly but do not brown, about 1 minute. Add the shrimp and cook until they turn light pink, about 4 minutes. Remove the shrimp from the pan to a plate and set aside.

3. Add the remaining 2 tablespoons olive oil, 1 tablespoon of the butter, and the chopped onions to the sauté pan. Cook over medium-high heat until the onions have softened but not browned, about 5 minutes. Add the rice, stirring to coat it with the olive oil. Stir in 1 cup of the simmering broth. When the rice has absorbed the broth, add the wine and tomato and stir until the wine has been absorbed by the rice. Add the remaining broth, ½ cup at a time, stirring frequently and allowing the rice to absorb the liquid after each addition, until the rice is al dente, 15 to 20 minutes. Add the reserved shrimp along with the last ladleful of broth and any juices that may have accumulated on the plate.

4. The rice should have a slight resistance to the bite. If it seems too hard, add a little more liquid and continue cooking for another minute or two. Remove the rice from the heat and briskly stir in the remaining 1 tablespoon butter and the Parmesan, if using. Serve immediately.

— S E R V E S 4 —

WINE PAIRING: Medium white

VARIATIONS: The shrimp may be peeled and the broth prepared several hours ahead of time. Chicken stock may be substituted for the shrimp broth, although this will alter the flavor slightly.

NOTE: Leftover shrimp broth may be frozen in an airtight container for up to 3 months.

recipe pictured on page 186

vegetables and side dishes

vegetali e contorni

Gardening was a way of life for my grandparents. At their house on the Point in Verplanck, New York, they cultivated a wide variety of fruits and vegetables—there was always something growing year-round. Pole beans, cucumbers, peppers, zucchini, eggplant, tomatoes, escarole, and more—I have fond memories of helping Nonno Tropiano in the garden when I was very little. He also had a root cellar for the garlic, onions, potatoes, and celery he grew. With all of this bounty, it was rare for my mother's family to eat a vegetable they hadn't grown.

The great thing about these vegetable and side dish recipes is that even children will eat them. For a young boy to look forward to eggplant sandwiches is a rare thing. But I did. For children to beg for stuffed mushrooms seems an impossibility, but it's not—mine do. You will find these dishes to be more than something that "goes with." Instead, you may end up looking for dishes to "go with" them. Enjoy.

puree of white beans, rosemary, and garlic

purè di fagioli, rosmarino, e aglio

These pureed beans are made especially flavorful by the addition of olive oil that has been infused with rosemary. To create a pungent oil, it must first be heated with the rosemary for at least twenty minutes. Simply warming the oil on top of a stove is not as effective as the method Gianni devised for this recipe: Place the oil and the rosemary in a jar that is then set in the pot along with the simmering beans. This is an efficient way of preparing the small amount of oil called for.

You do not need to presoak the dried cannellini beans called for in this recipe. Canned beans may also be substituted for dried. They don't need to be cooked, so you can begin the recipe at the point where they are processed in the olive oil. (Reserve 3 tablespoons of the canned bean liquid to use in place of the cooking water called for.) Serve this as a side dish with lamb or seafood, or spread it on top of bruschetta.

*1 cup dried cannellini beans, picked over and
   rinsed*

½ medium-size onion

1 teaspoon kosher salt, plus more as needed

6 tablespoons extra virgin olive oil

Four 5-inch sprigs fresh rosemary

3 cloves fresh garlic

¼ teaspoon ground cumin

2 tablespoons freshly squeezed lemon juice

*1 teaspoon chopped fresh Italian, flat leafed
   parsley*

Freshly ground black pepper

1. Place the beans in a large pot. Fill the pot with water to a level 2 inches above the beans. Add the onion and 1 teaspoon salt, and bring to a boil. Cover, reduce the heat to a simmer, and cook until the beans are tender, about 1½ hours.

2. Meanwhile, place the olive oil in a heat-resistant jar (such as a canning jar). Strip the rosemary leaves from the sprigs and add to the oil. When the beans have cooked for 1 hour and 10 minutes, place the jar in the pot of simmering beans and let it heat for

the last 20 minutes of cooking time. This will infuse the oil with the flavor of the rosemary. (If using canned beans, place the jar in a pot of boiling water and simmer for 20 minutes.)

3. Remove the oil-filled jar from the beans and set it aside. Discard the onion and drain the beans, reserving 3 tablespoons of the cooking water. Place the beans in a food processor or blender along with the reserved water, garlic, cumin, and lemon juice. Strain the olive oil, discarding the rosemary leaves, and add the oil to the beans. Process until all of the ingredients are blended and the beans are smooth. Stir in the parsley, and season with salt and pepper.

— SERVES 8 —

WINE PAIRING: Medium white, light red, and rosé

VARIATION: Shrimp may be served with these beans to make a delicious appetizer. Shell and devein 8 jumbo shrimp. Warm 2 tablespoons olive oil and 1 clove garlic, chopped, in a small sauté pan set over medium-high heat. When the oil is hot but not smoking, add the shrimp and cook until pink and cooked through, about 7 minutes. Distribute equal portions of the bean puree onto eight small plates. Top each plate with one of the cooked shrimp. In a small bowl, whisk together 1 tablespoon balsamic vinegar and 1 tablespoon extra virgin olive oil. Drizzle some of this dressing over each plate and serve.

stewed beans tuscan style

fagioli stufati all'uccelletto

Serve these beans as a side dish with pork, stewed meat, lamb, or grilled fish. They are also delightful pureed and served on bruschetta for lunch or as an appetizer. The advantage of using great Northern or navy beans is that they do not require any presoaking. If you use other dried beans, such as cannellini, they may be cooked, drained, and set aside several hours before you add them to the sautéed vegetables.

1 pound dried navy or great Northern beans

8 cups water

2 cloves garlic, lightly crushed

6 large fresh sage leaves

Two 5-inch sprigs fresh rosemary

5 tablespoons olive oil

⅓ cup diced pancetta or bacon (optional)

1 cup chopped onions

¾ cup diced carrots

¾ cup diced celery

5 fresh or canned whole plum tomatoes, peeled, seeded, and chopped

2 tablespoons chopped fresh Italian, flat leafed parsley

Kosher salt and freshly ground black pepper

1. Rinse the beans, removing any oddly colored ones or stones. Place the beans in a large flameproof casserole set over low heat. Add the water and bring to a gentle simmer. Add the garlic, 3 of the sage leaves, 1 sprig of rosemary, and 1 tablespoon of the olive oil. Simmer until the beans are tender but not mushy, about 45 minutes. Strain, discarding the garlic and sage, and set aside.

2. Add the remaining 4 tablespoons olive oil to a sauté pan set over medium-high heat. When the oil is hot but not smoking, add the pancetta or bacon, if using, stirring briskly. Stir in the onions, carrots, and celery and cook, stirring to soften slightly, about 5 minutes. Chop the remaining 3 sage leaves and the leaves from the remaining rosemary sprig, and add to the vegetables along with the tomatoes and parsley. Then season with

salt and pepper. Cook to warm the tomatoes, about 5 minutes more. Stir in the beans and reduce the heat to medium. Cook to warm the beans and to flavor them with the tomatoes, about 10 minutes. Season with additional salt and pepper if desired, and serve.

— SERVES 6 TO 8 —

WINE PAIRING: Medium red

VARIATION: Thyme or marjoram may be substituted for or added to the sage and rosemary. A terrific way to use any leftover beans is to puree them in a blender or food processor until smooth. Add a small amount of olive oil (or a small quantity of the water the beans cooked in) and process until the beans reach a spreadable consistency. Serve at room temperature on toasted bread or crackers as an appetizer or as a lunch dish. Pureed beans may be stored in the refrigerator for up to 3 days or frozen in an airtight container for up to 1 month.

braised lentils

lenticchie brasate

Inspiration for recipes can come from many sources. For this recipe, Gianni was inspired by one of his restaurant patrons. "One day at Le Madri, a very well dressed elderly woman came to the restaurant and ordered this dish. When it was served she asked the waiter if she could speak with me. She explained that she was originally from Morocco, where lentils are a staple. She suggested that the next time I cooked this dish I should add a little fennel at the last moment. I followed her advice and the flavor was amazing. I have prepared it this way ever since."

Serve these lentils as a side dish with grilled fish or lamb or as a topping for bruschetta.

1½ cups dried green lentils, picked over and
    rinsed

¼ cup extra virgin olive oil

⅓ cup finely chopped shallots

⅓ cup finely chopped carrots

⅓ cup finely chopped celery

¼ cup chopped fresh Italian, flat leafed
    parsley

1 bay leaf

¼ cup peeled and crushed tomatoes (about 2
    fresh or canned)

4 cups chicken broth

Kosher salt and freshly ground black pepper

½ bulb fresh fennel, very finely chopped or
    thinly sliced

1. Place the lentils in a medium-size saucepan and cover with water to a level 1 inch above the lentils. Bring to a boil and cook to parboil the lentils, about 5 minutes. Drain, rinse in cold water to cool, and set aside.

2. Warm the olive oil in a medium-size saucepan set over medium heat. Add the shallots, carrots, and celery and cook, stirring occasionally, until the vegetables are golden, about 8 minutes. Stir in the parsley, bay leaf, and lentils and cook to flavor with the

vegetables, about 2 minutes. Stir in the tomatoes, then pour in 3 cups of the chicken broth. Season with salt and pepper. Bring to a boil, then reduce the heat to a simmer. Cook until the lentils are tender, adding more broth as necessary to keep the liquid just above the lentils, about 15 minutes. Stir in the fennel and cook to flavor the broth, about 5 minutes. Remove from the heat and allow to rest at least 10 minutes before removing the bay leaf and serving.

— SERVES 6 —

WINE PAIRING: Medium red and full red

VARIATIONS: To add a smoky taste to the basic lentil recipe, add 2 strips bacon, diced, and cook with the shallots, carrots, and celery. And 2 tablespoons freshly squeezed lemon juice may be stirred into the lentils just before serving to brighten the flavors.

This recipe may also be used to make a delicious lentil soup. Follow the basic recipe, adding 1 peeled and cubed Idaho potato when you add the tomatoes. Increase the broth by 2 cups (for a total of 6 cups). Proceed with recipe as written.

string beans with tomatoes

fagiolini al pomodoro

My mother grew up with a large garden that came right up to the edge of the house. "My parents cultivated a wide variety of fresh fruits and vegetables," she remembers. "Everyone helped in the garden, turning the soil and planting in the spring, harvesting and canning in the fall. In fact I have pictures of Stanley as a baby helping Pop in the garden." Among the vegetables my grandfather grew were wide, flat Italian pole beans. He would pick a basket of beans, a few tomatoes, and a small zucchini. My grandmother would cook them all together to create a light dish for lunch or dinner, followed by chicken or meat.

1 cup water

1 pound string beans, ends trimmed

1 small zucchini, cut in quarters lengthwise and chopped into ½-inch-wide chunks

1 medium-size all-purpose potato, peeled and quartered

½ cup chopped and seeded ripe tomatoes or canned whole plum tomatoes, crushed

2 tablespoons olive oil

Kosher salt and freshly ground black pepper

1 clove garlic, cut in half

Place the water in a medium-size pot set over medium-high heat. Add the string beans, zucchini, potato, and tomatoes. Stir in the olive oil and season with salt and pepper. Add the garlic, bring to a boil, then cover, reduce the heat to medium-low, and simmer until the vegetables are tender, about 25 minutes. Remove the vegetables to a serving dish with a slotted spoon. Spoon some of the sauce on top and serve.

— SERVES 4 —

WINE PAIRING: Light red, medium red, and medium white

concetta's stuffed artichokes

carciofi alla concetta

When we began work on this book project, it was before my grandmother had passed away at the age of eighty-seven, and we were very excited about preserving so many of her recipes. One day my mother went to visit my grandmother in the hospital. She told her that we didn't have her recipe for stuffed artichokes and we wanted to include it in the book. Without hesitation my grandmother began to tell her how she prepared them. The nurse who was attending her said, "Only an Italian could come out of surgery and start discussing food."

But the telling of a recipe is very different from the actual process of making a dish with its creator. So this recipe, which is named for my grandmother, is based on memories of her stuffed artichokes.

4 medium-size or 2 extra-large artichokes, stems and top ¼ inch sliced off and discarded, sharp outer leaf points snipped off and discarded

2 teaspoons chopped fresh Italian, flat leafed parsley

5 teaspoons finely grated pecorino Romano cheese

2 cloves garlic, minced

1 cup coarsely grated day-old bread or 1 cup plain dried bread crumbs, or a combination of both

4 tablespoons olive oil

1. Preheat the oven to 350° F.

2. Snugly fit the artichokes in a small saucepan and add water to a depth ¼ inch below the tops of the artichokes. Cover, bring to a boil, and simmer until an outside leaf pulls away easily, about 20 minutes. Do not overcook or the artichokes will fall apart. Remove from the water, turn upside down to drain, and set aside to cool.

3. In a small bowl, mix the parsley, Romano cheese, garlic, and bread. Sprinkle teaspoons of the filling between the leaves, working from the outer leaves toward the center of the

artichoke, spreading the inner leaves slightly if necessary. Place the artichokes in a glass baking pan. Drizzle 1 tablespoon of the olive oil over each artichoke (2 tablespoons if using extra-large ones). Fill the pan with water to a depth of 1 inch. Cover with aluminum foil and bake for 30 minutes. Remove the foil, add more water to the pan if necessary, and continue baking until the artichokes are tender and lightly browned, about 15 minutes more. Serve hot or at room temperature.

— SERVES 4 —

WINE PAIRING: Light white and medium white

VARIATIONS: When serving steamed or boiled artichokes that have not been stuffed, I like to whisk 1 teaspoon freshly squeezed lemon juice and ¼ cup melted butter to dip the tender leaves into before eating. One steamed artichoke may be served as part of an antipasto with drinks before dinner. Separate the leaves and arrange them on a platter. Serve along with a small dish of Basic Vinaigrette (page 48).

broccoli rabe tucci style

broccoli di rape alla tucci

My father's family prepared broccoli rabe differently than my mother, so when they got married my mother learned to prepare it this way. The basic difference is that the Tuccis sauté their broccoli rabe and the Tropianos boil theirs. Serve as a side dish with meat, chicken, or fish. It may also be served between slices of Italian bread as a sandwich or as a topping on pizza or focaccia.

2 pounds broccoli rabe (about 2 bunches)

½ cup olive oil

3 cloves garlic, chopped

Kosher salt

¼ cup water

1 lemon, quartered (optional)

1. Snap off the flowered stems and leaves of the broccoli rabe, discarding the tough stems. Coarsely chop the remaining stems, leaving the buds whole, and set aside.

2. Warm the olive oil in a large sauté pan set over medium-high heat. Add the garlic and cook, stirring, until lightly colored, about 2 minutes. Add the broccoli rabe. Season with salt, add the water, and cover. Reduce the heat to a simmer and stir occasionally until tender, 8 to 10 minutes. (More water may be added, ¼ cup at a time, if the broccoli rabe begins to stick to the pan.) Serve with the lemon quarters if desired.

— SERVES 4 —

WINE PAIRING: Medium white and light red

broccoli rabe tropiano style
broccoli di rape alla tropiano

Many of the recipes in this book call for reserving some of the cooking water before draining vegetables or pasta. This flavorful water is used in place of tap water to achieve the right consistency in a finished dish. If you refrigerate or freeze cooked broccoli rabe, store it in an airtight container filled with cooking water.

2 pounds broccoli rabe (about 2 bunches)   *1 clove garlic, cut in half*
¼ cup olive oil

1. Snap off the flowered stems and leaves of the broccoli rabe, discarding the tough stems. Coarsely chop the remaining stems, leaving the buds whole, and set aside.

2. Bring a large pot of salted water to a boil. Add the broccoli rabe and cook until tender, about 5 minutes. Remove to a bowl with a slotted spoon. Add ½ cup of the cooking water to the broccoli rabe and set aside. (This may be done several hours in advance.)

3. Warm the olive oil in a sauté pan set over medium-high heat. Add the garlic and cook to flavor the oil but do not brown the garlic, about 2 minutes. Add the broccoli rabe along with 2 tablespoons of the cooking water. (More water may be added, 2 tablespoons at a time, if the broccoli rabe begins to stick to the pan.) Cover and simmer to flavor the broccoli rabe with the garlic, about 3 minutes.

— SERVES 4 —

WINE PAIRING: Medium white and light red

VARIATION: Stir 1 cup drained and rinsed canned cannellini beans into the broccoli rabe along with the water. Serve drizzled with extra virgin olive oil.

escarole

scarola

My mother's father grew escarole in his garden every year. If the winter was mild, it could survive into late November or early December. She remembers him covering the plants with a bushel basket at night to protect them from frost. We serve escarole prepared this way on top of pizza and as a side dish. It freezes well in small batches, packed in containers filled with some of the cooking water.

1 pound escarole (about 1 large head), leaves   *3 tablespoons olive oil*
    coarsely chopped   *2 cloves garlic, cut in half*

1. Bring a large pot of salted water to a rapid boil. Add the escarole and cook until tender but firm, about 10 minutes after the water returns to a boil. Remove the escarole with a slotted spoon, place in a bowl, and set aside. Reserve ½ cup of the cooking water. Set aside. (The escarole may be parboiled and set aside several hours before proceeding with the recipe.)

2. Warm the olive oil in a large sauté pan set over medium heat. Add the garlic and cook to flavor the oil but do not let it brown, about 2 minutes. Add the escarole and the reserved cooking water. Cook, stirring occasionally, to warm through and bring the flavor of the garlic and escarole together, about 4 minutes. Serve immediately.

— SERVES 4 —

WINE PAIRING: Light white and rosé

VARIATIONS: Kale, Swiss chard, and mustard greens may also be prepared this way. They may need to be sautéed for an additional 5 minutes to soften and absorb the garlic flavor. Cannellini or other white beans make a tasty addition to this recipe. Warm one 19-ounce can cannellini beans, drained and rinsed, with the reserved cooking water. Add the beans and water to the escarole as it warms through with the garlic. Cannellini beans may also be warmed in ¾ cup of Joan's Basic Tomato Sauce (page 119). Stir the tomato-bean mixture into the escarole in place of the cooking water as it warms with the garlic.

roasted potatoes with rosemary

patate arrosto

Nonno Tropiano stored the potatoes he grew over the summer in the cold, dry cellar of his house along with the salami he was curing and the wine he was aging. This simple recipe for roasting potatoes with rosemary is very flavorful and has been popular with everyone I have served it to. Serve as a side dish with meat, fish, or chicken.

10 large Yukon Gold or baking potatoes, peeled and quartered, or red potatoes, left unpeeled and quartered

4 cloves garlic, cut in half

1 tablespoon chopped fresh rosemary leaves

2 teaspoons chopped fresh oregano leaves or ½ teaspoon dried

Kosher salt and freshly ground black pepper

¼ cup olive oil

1. Preheat the oven to 375° F.

2. Place the potatoes in a large baking dish or casserole. Add the garlic, rosemary, and oregano and season with salt and pepper. Drizzle the olive oil over the potatoes and toss to coat evenly. Bake, stirring occasionally, until the potatoes are browned and cooked through, about 1½ hours. Serve immediately.

— SERVES 4 —

WINE PAIRING: Sparkling and medium white

VARIATION: Two medium-size carrots, cut into 2-inch pieces, may be roasted with the potatoes.

cauliflower, herb, and anchovy timbale

timballo di cavolfiore, erbette fresche, e acciuga

In this recipe the anchovies complement the cauliflower perfectly without giving the dish a fishy flavor. And similar to a potato gratin, it may be prepared ahead of time and reheated in the oven. Timbale is very nice served as a side dish with roasted chicken, or it may be served as a lunch dish with crunchy bread and a tossed green salad.

Here is a tip I learned from Gianni: When boiling the cauliflower, always add a little flour and lemon juice as you prepare the cooking water. This helps the cauliflower to retain its white color. In this recipe he adds a slice of onion to flavor the water. You may also add herbs, carrots, or celery to make a broth for the cauliflower to cook in. Follow this same procedure when you cook artichokes.

3 tablespoons butter

¼ cup plain dried bread crumbs

1 medium-size head cauliflower, rinsed and separated into florets

4 tablespoons all-purpose flour

2 tablespoons freshly squeezed lemon juice

One ½-inch-thick slice onion

2 tablespoons extra virgin olive oil

¾ cup diced onions

1 tablespoon chopped fresh Italian, flat leafed parsley

1 tablespoon chopped fresh marjoram leaves

⅛ tablespoon ground nutmeg

Kosher salt and freshly ground black pepper

1¼ cups milk

2 tablespoons chopped anchovy fillets

½ cup finely grated Parmesan cheese

1. Preheat the oven to 350° F. Grease a 9-inch round casserole or baking pan with 1 tablespoon of the butter. Sprinkle the bread crumbs on the bottom and sides of the pan and set aside.

2. Bring a large pot of salted water to a rapid boil. Add the cauliflower florets, 1 tablespoon of the flour, the lemon juice, and the onion slice. Simmer until the florets are easily pierced with a fork, about 10 minutes. Drain, discarding the onion slice, and set aside.

3. Warm the olive oil in a large sauté pan set over medium-high heat. When the oil is hot but not smoking, add the diced onions and drained cauliflower. Stir in the parsley, marjoram, and nutmeg and season with salt and pepper. Cook until the florets start sticking to the pan a bit, about 5 minutes. Reduce the heat to medium-low and coarsely mash the cauliflower with the back of a wooden spoon or with a potato masher. Add the remaining 2 tablespoons butter. Sprinkle in the remaining 3 tablespoons flour. Mix well, then stir in the milk. Continue cooking and stirring until the mixture thickens and the milk has been absorbed, about 8 minutes.

4. Remove from the heat and stir in the anchovies. Stir in ¼ cup of the Parmesan cheese. Pour the mixture into the prepared baking pan. Sprinkle the remaining ¼ cup Parmesan on top. Bake until heated through and golden brown on top, about 25 minutes.

— SERVES 4 —

WINE PAIRING: Sparkling and medium white

VARIATION: Once the cauliflower has finished baking, arrange ¼-inch-thick slices fresh tomatoes on top. Set aside for a few moments to allow the cauliflower to warm the tomatoes through before serving.

For a rich version of this dish, heavy cream may be substituted for the milk. For a lighter version of this dish, olive oil may be substituted for the butter.

Four hard-boiled eggs may be sliced and arranged between the layers of the cooked cauliflower before baking.

Other cheeses such as Fontina, Gruyère, or Asiago may be substituted for the Parmesan.

This cauliflower mixture is terrific served over cooked penne. Eliminate the baking dish and follow the basic recipe. After adding the milk to the cauliflower, cook 1 pound of penne in rapidly boiling salted water until al dente, following the package instructions. Complete the cauliflower recipe, reserving the final ¼ cup of the Parmesan cheese. Add the cooked drained penne to the pan with the cauliflower mixture and toss. Serve immediately, garnished with the remaining ¼ cup Parmesan.

mashed potato and artichokes

purè di patate ai carciofini

Fresh artichokes are very popular in Italy, and at many farm stands you will see older women making quick work of stripping away the spiky leaves, rubbing the hearts with lemon juice, and packing them into small bags for those without the time or inclination to start from scratch. I have rarely seen freshly peeled artichoke bottoms for sale in the United States, so you may need to purchase whole artichokes for this recipe and peel them down to the heart yourself. Reserve some of the tender leaves to use as a garnish. Canned artichoke bottoms or frozen artichoke hearts may be substituted for the fresh. The artichokes may be prepared several hours ahead and mixed into the mashed potatoes just before serving.

2 tablespoons olive oil	*½ teaspoon chopped fresh thyme leaves*
½ cup chopped shallots	*Kosher salt and freshly ground black pepper*
1 clove garlic, chopped	*2 cups water*
1 tablespoon chopped fresh Italian, flat leafed parsley	*2½ pounds Idaho potatoes, peeled*
	1 clove garlic, peeled
½ pound artichoke bottoms or hearts, cut into ½-inch pieces	*¾ cup milk, warmed*
	6 tablespoons (¾ stick) butter, softened

1. Warm the olive oil in a small sauté pan set over medium-high heat. Add the shallots, chopped garlic, and parsley and cook, stirring, until the shallots soften, about 5 minutes. Stir in the artichokes and thyme, then season with salt and pepper. Add the water and bring to a boil. Reduce the heat to medium-low and simmer until all of the liquid has been absorbed and the artichokes are tender, about 12 minutes. Remove from the heat and set aside.

2. Place the potatoes in a large pot of salted water. Add the whole garlic clove and bring to a boil. Reduce the heat to medium and simmer the potatoes until tender when pierced with a fork, about 20 minutes. Drain the potatoes, discard the garlic, and return the potatoes to the pot. Heat over low heat to remove any excess moisture, about 1 minute. Remove from the heat and add the milk and butter. Use a potato masher or electric mixer set on low to incorporate all of the ingredients, leaving the mixture slightly chunky. Stir in the artichokes. Season with salt and pepper and serve.

— SERVES 4 —

WINE PAIRING: **Medium white**

eggplant and zucchini casserole with potatoes

casseruola di melanzane con patate

My family refers to this casserole as Nonno's dish. As my mother explains, "It was Stan's father who originally prepared this recipe. I remember enjoying it on a cold, rainy day when we were camping in upstate New York. Stan's sister Rosalinda lived near our campsite so she and her husband, Lee, brought Nonno's dish, still warm from the oven, over for lunch. It was just what we needed to cheer up an otherwise dreary day."

This casserole may be assembled one day in advance, refrigerated overnight, and baked the next day. Or it may be assembled and frozen for up to one month. Allow the casserole to defrost before baking, or bake the frozen casserole for an additional thirty minutes. It is an excellent complement to meat or chicken.

1 medium-size eggplant, cut into ½-inch-thick slices

2 medium-size zucchini, cut into ½-inch-thick slices

½ cup olive oil

2 medium-size all-purpose potatoes, peeled and cut into ¼-inch-thick slices

1 red bell pepper, seeded and cut into ½-inch-thick slices

2 cups Sailor's-Style Sauce (page 120) or your own favorite marinara sauce

½ cup finely grated pecorino Romano cheese

1. Preheat the oven broiler.

2. Lightly brush both sides of the eggplant and zucchini slices with some of the olive oil, and place on a baking sheet. Place under the broiler and brown lightly on each side, about 2 minutes per side. Remove from the oven and set aside.

3. Place about one third of the remaining olive oil in a large sauté pan set over medium-high heat. Sauté the potatoes, then the bell pepper, adding more oil as necessary and cooking each vegetable until slightly cooked but still firm, 3 minutes on each side.

4. Preheat oven to 350° F.

5. Cover the bottom of a large shallow dish with about ½ cup of the marinara sauce. Arrange a layer of eggplant slices on top of the sauce. Top the eggplant with a thin layer of marinara sauce and a sprinkling of the Romano cheese. Layer the zucchini on top of the eggplant, followed by a layer of potato, and finally a layer of bell pepper. Top with the remaining marinara sauce and Romano cheese.

6. Cover and bake until the mixture is bubbling and the vegetables are tender, about 40 minutes. Remove the cover and continue baking until the vegetables are soft when pierced with a fork, about another 10 minutes. Allow the casserole to stand for 10 minutes before serving.

— SERVES 4 —

WINE PAIRING: Medium white

VARIATIONS: To make a great cold sandwich, place a leftover portion of this casserole between slices of Italian bread.

Some of the recommended alternative ingredients for this dish include substituting a green or yellow bell pepper for the red pepper and substituting yellow squash for the zucchini.

A smaller, deeper casserole may be substituted for the large shallow one called for here. Arrange alternating layers of the vegetables as you would when preparing lasagna, and proceed with the recipe as written, cooking the covered casserole for approximately 15 additional minutes until the mixture is bubbling before removing the cover. Continue to bake until vegetables are soft when pierced with a fork, about another 10 minutes.

mushroom and potato casserole

funghi e patate al forno

This recipe is a great example of learning to trust your instincts and not being afraid to try things. The first version we tested didn't come out well at all. We tried again, all working together, and finally arrived at this version. Serve this dish as a side dish with simply prepared fish, meat, or chicken.

1 pound porcini, portobello, or cremini mushrooms, stems removed and reserved and caps cut into ¼-inch-thick slices

1 cup finely chopped onions

2 cloves garlic, minced

1 teaspoon finely chopped fresh oregano leaves

2 tablespoons chopped fresh Italian, flat leafed parsley

4 tablespoons extra virgin olive oil

3 large baking potatoes, peeled, halved, and cut into ½-inch-thick slices

2½ teaspoons kosher salt

Freshly ground black pepper

1 cup chicken broth

1. Preheat the oven to 375° F.

2. Coarsely chop the mushroom stems. Set aside.

3. In a small bowl, toss the onions, garlic, oregano, and parsley. Set aside.

4. Drizzle 1 tablespoon of the olive oil over the bottom of a small casserole. Spread ⅓ cup of the onion mixture on top of the olive oil. Arrange the potato slices on top of the onion mixture, overlapping them to form a single dense layer. Season with salt and pepper, and top with ⅓ cup of the onion mixture. Sprinkle the chopped mushroom stems on top. Season with salt and pepper. Sprinkle ⅓ cup of the onion mixture on top. Top the casserole with a dense, single overlapping layer of mushroom slices. Distribute the remaining 3 tablespoons olive oil on top. Pour the chicken broth into the casserole, cover with aluminum foil, and bake until the potatoes are tender and the mushrooms have softened, about 50 minutes. Serve immediately.

— SERVES 8 —

WINE PAIRING: Light red and rosé

vegetable casserole
parmigiana di melanzane

My mother's father maintained a large vegetable garden. Consequently my grandmother would experiment with different ways to prepare the harvest. When eggplant were in season she would pickle some of them and others she would use in recipes similar to this one. In this dish the vegetables are sautéed individually before being baked together in a casserole. This is done to maintain the distinct flavor of each vegetable.

½ cup plus 2 tablespoons olive oil

1 medium-size eggplant, coarsely chopped

1 medium-size zucchini, coarsely chopped

½ pound cremini or white mushrooms, stems discarded and caps coarsely chopped

½ cup coarsely chopped onions

Kosher salt and freshly ground black pepper

1 cup Sailor's-Style Sauce (page 120) or your own favorite marinara sauce

¼ cup freshly grated Parmesan or pecorino Romano cheese

1. Preheat the oven to 350° F.

2. Warm ¼ cup of the olive oil in a medium-size sauté pan set over medium heat. Add the eggplant and cook, stirring, until softened, about 5 minutes. Use a slotted spoon to transfer the eggplant to a medium-size casserole dish and set aside. Add 2 more tablespoons of the olive oil and the zucchini to the sauté pan and cook until the center is softened and the rind still firm, about 3 minutes. Transfer the zucchini to the casserole with a slotted spoon and set aside. Finally, add the remaining 2 tablespoons olive oil and the onions to the sauté pan and cook until softened, about 3 minutes. Transfer to the casserole with a slotted spoon.

3. Season the vegetables with salt and pepper. Add the marinara sauce and toss to distribute the sauce evenly among the vegetables. Sprinkle with the cheese. Bake until the vegetables are cooked through, about 25 minutes. Serve immediately.

— SERVES 6 —

WINE PAIRING: Medium white and light red

roasted vegetables
vegetali arrostito

My mother created this recipe a few years ago after noticing that almost every cooking show and food magazine was featuring recipes for roasted vegetables. "I decided to try my own version," says Joan. "I mixed together my favorite vegetables—potatoes, butternut squash, zucchini, carrots—and cooked the firm ones first, adding the softer ones later so they retained their shapes and fresh flavors. The marinara sauce and balsamic vinegar nicely accent this dish." Serve with grilled chicken or fish.

1 tablespoon coarsely chopped fresh basil leaves

1 tablespoon chopped fresh rosemary leaves

1 tablespoon chopped fresh Italian, flat leafed parsley

1 tablespoon chopped fresh thyme leaves

2 large Yukon Gold or Red Bliss potatoes, peeled, cut in half, and then into 2-inch pieces

2 large carrots, peeled, cut in half, and then into 1-inch pieces

4 cloves garlic, cut in half

Kosher salt and freshly ground black pepper

3 tablespoons Sailor's-Style Sauce (page 120) or your own favorite marinara sauce (optional)

½ cup olive oil

1 large yellow or green zucchini, cut in half, and then into 1-inch pieces

1 large sweet potato, peeled, cut in half, and then into 1-inch pieces

1 medium-size butternut squash, peeled, cut in half, seeded, and then cut into 1-inch pieces

1 tablespoon balsamic vinegar

1 tablespoon extra virgin olive oil

1. Preheat the oven to 350° F.

2. In small bowl, combine the chopped herbs. Set aside.

3. In a large casserole or baking dish, toss the potatoes and carrots with half of the herb mixture. Stir in the garlic and season with salt and pepper. Stir in the marinara sauce, if using, and ¼ cup of the olive oil. Bake, stirring occasionally, until the potatoes begin to brown and soften, about 30 minutes.

4. Add the zucchini, sweet potato, butternut squash, the remaining herbs, and ¼ cup olive oil. Toss to coat evenly. Continue baking, stirring occasionally, until all of the vegetables are browned but firm and cooked through, about 1 hour. Drizzle the vinegar and extra virgin olive oil over the vegetables and toss. Serve immediately.

— SERVES 8 —

WINE PAIRING: Medium white and light red

VARIATION: Turnips may be added to this casserole and cooked along with the potatoes. Different fresh herbs, such as marjoram, sage, and oregano, may be substituted for the rosemary and thyme.

recipe pictured on page 204

fresh tomato salad

insalata di pomodoro

My mother remembers her father growing wonderful tomatoes in his garden. "When they were in season, we ate this salad almost every day. My mother didn't eat raw tomatoes," recalls Joan. "Instead, she would use a piece of fresh or grilled bread (*biscotto*, as we called it) to soak up the juice and the dressing, a move the Italians call *la scarpetta*, meaning 'little shoe.'"

3 large ripe tomatoes

¼ cup extra virgin olive oil

3 fresh basil leaves, torn in half

1 clove garlic, quartered

Kosher salt and freshly ground black pepper

Cut the tomatoes in half and then into ½-inch-wide wedges. Cut these wedges in half to create chunks. Place in a medium-size serving bowl and toss with the olive oil, basil, and garlic. Season with salt and pepper just before serving.

— SERVES 4 —

WINE PAIRING: Light white, light red, and rosé

VARIATIONS: For an excellent luncheon salad, add a 6-ounce can Italian tuna, drained and flaked apart with a fork, and substitute ¼ cup thinly sliced red onions for the garlic.

Another way to vary the basic recipe is to add a cucumber that has been peeled, cut in half lengthwise, and then cut into ¼-inch-thick slices. Toss with 1 tablespoon red wine vinegar and a pinch of chopped fresh oregano leaves in addition to the ingredients in the basic recipe.

ricotta balls
palline di ricotta

Nonna Tucci would prepare these delicate ricotta balls to serve as a side dish with chicken or veal in place of potatoes or rice. They may be served plain or with a light sauce: Warm 3 tablespoons butter with 6 fresh sage leaves over low heat. Spoon this simple sauce over the cooked ricotta balls before serving.

1 cup ricotta cheese (about ½ pound)

1 large egg, lightly beaten

1 tablespoon finely chopped fresh Italian, flat leafed parsley

1 cup plain dried bread crumbs

Kosher salt and freshly ground black pepper

1 tablespoon butter, cut into thirds

1. Mix the cheese, egg, parsley, bread crumbs, and salt and pepper to taste to form a soft dough that holds together, adding a small amount of additional bread crumbs if necessary. Set aside.

2. Grease a large sauté pan with one piece of the butter. Fill the sauté pan with water to a depth of 1½ inches. Add the remaining butter and bring to a simmer.

3. Scoop out tablespoons of the dough and shape them into compact balls. Add the balls to the simmering water and cook to warm through, about 3 minutes. Remove from the water with a slotted spoon and serve immediately.

— SERVES 6 —

WINE PAIRING: Medium white

string bean salad

insalata di fagiolini

This is a recipe my mother learned from my father's family and it is best made when tender white or pale yellow beans are available in the market. It is a wonderful salad that is delicious served cold or at room temperature to accompany grilled meats or fish. The beans may be cooked, then cooled and refrigerated one day in advance. Refrigerate in an airtight container overnight. Return to room temperature before proceeding with the recipe.

1 pound string, wax, or haricot vert beans,
   ends trimmed
1 clove garlic, chopped

Kosher salt and freshly ground black pepper
2 tablespoons red wine vinegar
¼ cup olive oil

Bring a large pot of salted water to a boil. Add the beans and cook until al dente, about 7 minutes (haricots verts will cook in about 4 minutes). Remove the beans to a serving plate and allow to cool. In a small bowl, mix the garlic, salt, and pepper to taste, and the vinegar. Gradually whisk in the olive oil. Pour over the cooled beans and toss.

— SERVES 4 —

WINE PAIRING: Light white and medium white

carrot salad

insalata di carote

When my family was living in Florence my parents would on occasion eat out at local trattorias. They would frequent neighborhood spots that they could easily walk to from the apartment where we were staying. At one restaurant they were greeted by a long table set up near the entrance where an array of colorful salads was on display. "One of the salads was this simple carrot dish," my mother remembers. "I ordered it and loved its taste and texture so I decided to try it at home." This recipe has been a part of our family repertoire ever since.

Dress this salad just before serving so the flavor and texture stay crisp. I often serve this dish at lunch, and sometimes when I'm serving it for dinner I will add ¼ cup soft, plump raisins.

2 large carrots, peeled

¼ cup extra virgin olive oil

1 tablespoon freshly squeezed lemon juice

Kosher salt and freshly ground black pepper

Use a vegetable peeler to cut the carrots into long thin strips. There should be about 2½ cups of carrot strips. Place in a bowl and toss with the olive oil and lemon juice. Season with salt and pepper and serve.

— SERVES 4 —

WINE PAIRING: Light white

VARIATION: To the traditional recipe add the following ingredients to create a colorful, refreshing salad: 1 peeled, cored, grated Granny Smith apple; 1 cup thinly sliced radicchio; 1 cup thinly sliced endive; and 2 cups thinly sliced tender cabbage.

potato salad
insalata di patate

Potatoes prepared this way make a great lunch dish served along with roasted peppers, a green salad, and an assortment of olives and cheeses. I also serve this salad with grilled meat or as part of a buffet. Serve it warm, at room temperature, or chilled.

6 large all-purpose, red, or Yukon Gold potatoes (about 2 pounds), scrubbed

1 clove garlic, crushed in a press

1 teaspoon Dijon mustard

2 tablespoons red wine vinegar

Kosher salt and freshly ground black pepper

¼ cup olive oil

1 tablespoon chopped fresh Italian, flat leafed parsley

2 tablespoons chopped onions or shallots

1. Place the potatoes in a large pot. Cover with water to about 1 inch above the potatoes. Add salt and bring to a boil. Continue to boil until tender when pierced with a knife, about 15 minutes. Drain, run under cold water to cool and cut into 2-inch pieces. (If using all-purpose potatoes, peel and discard the skins.) Place in a large serving bowl.

2. In a small bowl, whisk the garlic, mustard, vinegar, and salt and pepper to taste. Gradually whisk in the olive oil. Pour over the potatoes and toss to coat evenly. Add the parsley and onions, toss gently, and serve.

— SERVES 4 —

WINE PAIRING: Sparkling and rosé

beet salad

insalata di barbabietole rosse

In the summer and fall my father's family prepared this salad with beets from their garden. In the winter they would substitute canned whole beets. Fresh beets may be cooked one day ahead of time. Leave whole, cover, and store in the refrigerator. Return to room temperature before slicing, dressing, and serving. I serve this salad as part of a summer buffet.

6 medium-size beets, tops removed

1 teaspoon chopped fresh oregano leaves or
 ½ teaspoon dried

2 tablespoons red wine vinegar

1 clove garlic, chopped

2 tablespoons olive oil

Trim each beet to remove any roots and the tougher skin on the top and bottom. Place in a pot and cover with cold water. Bring to a boil and cook until the beets are tender when pierced with a knife, about 20 minutes. Drain and set aside to cool slightly. Peel the beets while they are still warm to the touch, and cut into ¼-inch-thick slices. Toss with the oregano, vinegar, garlic, and olive oil. Serve at room temperature.

— SERVES 4 —

WINE PAIRING: Medium white and rosé

VARIATION: Beet greens may be cooked and served as a side dish. Follow the recipe for Escarole (page 218).

FOR AN ALTERNATIVE SALAD: Substitute balsamic vinegar for the red wine vinegar and add ½ cup thinly sliced red onions, 1 tablespoon finely grated orange zest, 2 teaspoons chopped fresh chives, and 2 teaspoons chopped fresh Italian, flat leafed parsley to the basic recipe.

mediterranean lentil salad

insalata di lenticchie alla mediterranea

Lentils are traditionally eaten in Italy at the end of the year because people say, "Eat lentils and it will bring you money in the new year." This salad may be served to accompany fish, meat, or chicken and also makes a great lunch dish. Chickpeas, borlotti (pinto or cranberry), or cannellini beans may be substituted for the lentils.

1 pound dried green lentils, picked over

1 bay leaf

1 cup diced red onions

1 clove garlic, chopped

1 tablespoon chopped fresh Italian, flat leafed parsley

⅛ teaspoon ground cumin

1 teaspoon chopped fresh mint leaves

3 tablespoons freshly squeezed lemon juice (from about 1 lemon)

2 tablespoons red or sherry wine vinegar

3 tablespoons extra virgin olive oil

Kosher salt and freshly ground black pepper

1. Place the lentils in a large pot and add water to a level 2 inches above them. Add the bay leaf and set over medium-high heat. Bring to a boil, then simmer gently over medium-low heat until the lentils are tender, about 1 hour. Drain the lentils and allow to cool.

2. In a large serving bowl, toss the lentils with the onions, garlic, parsley, cumin, and mint. In a separate bowl, whisk the lemon juice, vinegar, olive oil, and salt and pepper to taste. Pour the dressing over the lentils and toss to coat evenly. Serve immediately.

— SERVES 8 —

WINE PAIRING: Light red and medium red

VARIATIONS: Any good-quality lentil may be substituted for the green lentils.

meat

carne

The Italian futurists believed in the abolition of pasta because they said it "slowed down" the Italian people. They believed in a diet consisting mostly of meat. Some of their bizarre recipes called for a variety of meats cooked and served together. They felt this high-protein diet would propel them to be more aggressive and therefore successful in every way. Fortunately, while the futurists' art had great impact culturally, their dietary regimen did not. What would Italian cuisine be without the tradition of lingering over multiple, perfectly proportioned courses?

One of the distinguishing features of dining around an Italian table is the pacing of the meal. Beginning with a pasta dish, the meat course follows—the portion only large enough to satisfy, complementing what came before but saving room for the following course. This is one of the reasons Italians live long and healthy lives. That and the daily consumption of red wine.

beef tenderloin with prosciutto

filetto di bue al prosciutto

This dish is very good when served with Mashed Potatoes and Artichokes (page 224). Domestically cured prosciutto may be purchased for this recipe; because it will be roasted along with the meat, there is no need to purchase an imported brand. You may even use pancetta or American bacon instead.

2 tablespoons canola or vegetable oil

1 large carrot, halved lengthwise and cut into 2-inch pieces

1 medium-size onion, quartered

2 celery stalks, halved lengthwise and cut into 2-inch pieces

One 2½- to 3-pound beef tenderloin or Chateaubriand

2 tablespoons Dijon mustard

1 tablespoon coarsely chopped fresh rosemary leaves

1 tablespoon coarsely chopped fresh sage leaves

Kosher salt and freshly ground black pepper

12 very thin slices prosciutto

1 tablespoon all-purpose flour

½ cup dry red wine

1 cup chicken broth

1. Preheat oven to 500° F. Grease a small roasting or baking pan—one that will hold the beef snugly—with the oil.

2. Arrange the carrot, onion, and celery on the bottom of the prepared pan. Place a wire rack in the pan and set aside.

3. Rub the beef all over with the mustard. Sprinkle the rosemary, sage, and salt and pepper to taste all over the beef. Place 6 to 8 slices of the prosciutto, slightly overlapping, on a clean work surface. Place the beef on top of the prosciutto. Wrap the prosciutto up and over, and use the remaining slices of prosciutto to completely enclose the beef. Secure the prosciutto around the beef by gently tying the roast with butcher's string.

4. Place the roast on the rack and cook in the oven until browned on top, about 15 minutes. Turn the roast and continue cooking until browned and medium-rare, about 15 minutes more. (An internal thermometer should register about 130° F for medium-rare beef.) Transfer the meat to a platter and set aside to rest for 10 minutes before removing and discarding the string. Carve into 1-inch-thick slices.

5. Meanwhile, set the roasting pan over high heat (or transfer the contents to a wide saucepan). Stir in the flour, wine, and broth, bring to a boil, and cook, stirring constantly, to slightly thicken the juices in the pan, about 5 minutes. Strain through a fine-mesh sieve and spoon over the sliced roast.

— SERVES 6 TO 8 —

WINE PAIRING: Medium red and full red

stuffed beef rolls

braciole

There are many variations on this basic recipe, and it seems that every southern Italian family has its own version. My mother prefers to stuff several pieces of beef round pounded to ⅛-inch thickness, brown them, and then add them to a simple tomato sauce.

The tomato sauce is served over pasta as a first course, and the meat is sliced and served as a second course, followed by salad. This entire recipe may be prepared in advance. Cover and refrigerate for up to three days or freeze for up to one month.

6 pieces beef round for braciola (about 1½ pounds total)	¼ cup olive oil
	½ cup finely chopped onions
Kosher salt and freshly ground black pepper	½ cup dry red wine
6 cloves garlic, minced	4 cups canned whole plum tomatoes (about
½ cup freshly grated pecorino Romano cheese	one 35-ounce can), pureed in a blender
½ cup finely chopped fresh Italian, flat leafed parsley	

1. Place each piece of meat between two sheets of waxed paper and pound until it is about ⅛ inch thick. Season with salt and pepper. Sprinkle the pieces evenly with equal portions of the garlic, cheese, and parsley. Gently roll up the meat, pressing the filling into it, to make a tight roll. Tuck in the ends and secure the rolls with butcher's string. Set aside.

2. Warm the olive oil in a wide, deep saucepan set over medium heat. When the oil is hot but not smoking, add the onions. Cook until softened but not browned, about 4 minutes. Remove the onions from the pan with a slotted spoon. Add the beef rolls to the pan and cook until browned on all sides, about 8 minutes. Return the onions to the

pan. Add the wine and cook, scraping to loosen any meat that has stuck to the bottom of the pan. When the wine has reduced slightly, about 1 minute, remove the meat rolls from the pan to a plate and set aside.

3. Add the tomatoes to the saucepan. Season with salt and pepper and simmer to warm through, about 10 minutes. Return the meat rolls to the pan, along with any juices that have accumulated on the plate. The meat should be completely submerged in the sauce. Simmer gently, with the cover of the pan slightly askew, until the meat is tender and the sauce has thickened, about 1½ hours.

— SERVES 6 —

WINE PAIRING: Medium red and full red

VARIATION: Add ½ cup whole pine nuts to the stuffing for added texture.

milanese casserole

casseruola lombarda

Gianni generally considers most variations of this type of stew to be too heavy, and that is what inspired him to create a recipe that is rich in flavor and won't leave you feeling overly full. Be sure to tightly pack all of the ingredients into a heavy-bottomed casserole so the broth is absorbed by the meat and vegetables and does not just boil away. Serve this one-dish meal with polenta or crusty bread to dip into the sauce. It may be prepared a day in advance and reheated before serving.

2 tablespoons olive oil

1 cup coarsely chopped onions

¾ cup coarsely chopped shallots

⅓ pound slab bacon, cut into ½-inch chunks

½ cup coarsely chopped fresh Italian, flat leafed parsley

2 teaspoons sweet paprika

2 bay leaves

1 pound cabbage, trimmed, cored, and coarsely chopped

3 medium-size carrots, peeled and cut into ½-inch-thick slices

Kosher salt and freshly ground black pepper

6 lean beef short ribs

6 links sweet sausage

3 cups chicken broth

2 cups water or 1 cup water and 1 cup dry white wine

2 Idaho potatoes, peeled, halved, and each half cut into 6 pieces.

1. Warm the olive oil in a flameproof casserole set over medium-high heat. Stir in the bacon and continue cooking until it has softened and begun to brown, about 3 minutes. Add the onions and shallots and cook, stirring, until softened, about 8 minutes. Stir in the parsley, paprika, bay leaves, cabbage, and carrots, and season with salt and pepper.

2. Season the short ribs with salt and pepper, then add them to the casserole. Add the sausage, pressing down on the meat to tightly compact all the ingredients into the pan. Pour in the broth and water. Cover and bring to a boil. Reduce the heat to a low boil and

recipe continued on next page

cook, skimming off any fat that accumulates on top of the stew, until the meat begins to become tender, 1 to 1½ hours. Then add the potatoes and continue cooking until they are soft and the meat is cooked through, about another hour.

— SERVES 6 —

WINE PAIRING: Medium red and full red

VARIATIONS: Country-style pork spareribs may be used in place of beef ribs. They will take about half as long to cook through. Also, parsnips or turnips may be cut in the same manner as the potatoes and added to the stew, or in place of them.

steak oreganato
bistecca origanata

Nonna Tucci cooked steak this simple, quick, flavorful way. We don't serve meat "American style"—with a vegetable and potato on the side. Instead we begin with pasta, followed by meat accompanied by a simply cooked vegetable. We finish with a green salad followed by nuts and fresh fruit. This has long been the tradition in my family, one that I continue to maintain today as I find that pacing the meal this way leaves me feeling less full.

1 top round beef steak (2½ to 3 pounds)   *Kosher salt and freshly ground black pepper*
2 tablespoons butter   *½ cup dry red wine*
2 tablespoons olive oil   *½ teaspoon dried oregano*

1. The steak should be ½ inch thick. If necessary, pound it between two sheets of waxed paper to achieve this thickness.

2. Warm the butter and olive oil in a large sauté pan set over medium-high heat. When the butter is foaming rapidly, add the steak and fry to brown on one side, about 3 minutes. (If the steak is larger than your sauté pan, cut it in half.) Turn, and season with salt and pepper. Brown the other side, about 3 minutes. Remove from the pan to a warm platter and set aside.

3. Add the wine and oregano to the pan, scraping up any meat that may have stuck to the bottom. Simmer to sweeten the wine, about 1 minute. Meanwhile, cut the meat into six equal portions. When the wine sauce is ready, pour it over the meat and serve immediately.

—SERVES 6—

WINE PAIRING: Medium red and full red

recipe pictured on page 242

meatballs
polpette

My father recalls that on occasion his mother would not feel like cooking a large meal. "Then we would have one of our favorite dishes: freshly fried *polpette*." She would serve them with salad and lots of crusty Italian bread with butter. This was the only time that butter ever appeared at the table.

These meatballs may be eaten as a main meal, freshly fried and served with salad and lots of crusty Italian bread with butter, or they may be lightly sautéed and added to the recipe for Tucci Ragù Sauce (page 122). They are also an important ingredient in Drum of Ziti and Great Stuff (*timpano,* page 181). Dried bread is an essential ingredient in this recipe. I purchase long, thin loaves of unseeded Italian white bread. Set aside leftover bread for 2 or 3 days out of the wrapper before you plan to prepare these meatballs.

Ten 1-inch thick slices of dry Italian bread

1 cup warm water

1 pound ground beef chuck

2 tablespoons chopped fresh Italian, flat leafed parsley

2 cloves garlic, finely chopped

1 large egg

5 tablespoons finely grated pecorino Romano cheese

Kosher salt and freshly ground black pepper to taste

2 tablespoons olive oil

1. Place 6 slices of the dried bread in a bowl and cover with the warm water. Set aside until the bread softens, about 5 minutes.

2. In another bowl, combine the meat, parsley, garlic, egg, Romano cheese, and salt and pepper to taste, using your hands to mix the ingredients. Remove and discard the crust from each slice of bread. Squeeze the water out of the bread, and breaking it into small pieces, add it to the meat. Work the bread into the meat until they are equally combined

and the mixture holds together like a soft dough. Moisten the remaining slices of dried bread and add as needed.

3. Warm the olive oil in a large frying pan set over medium-high heat. Scoop out a heaping tablespoon of the meat mixture. Roll it between the palms of your hands to form a ball about 1½ inches in diameter. (Meatballs that are being prepared for Drum of Ziti should be very small. Use a ½ teaspoon to scoop out the dough and form it into ¾-inch balls.) Cook one meatball until well browned on all sides, about 8 minutes. (A meatball that sticks to the pan is not ready to be turned.)

4. Taste the meatball, and if needed, adjust the seasoning of the remaining mixture by adding more garlic, parsley, cheese, and salt and pepper. Proceed to cook the meatballs in small batches. As each batch is completed, remove it to a warmed serving plate. Serve when all the meatballs are cooked.

— SERVES 4 —

WINE PAIRING: Medium red and full red

VARIATION: Meatballs that will be added to Tucci Ragù Sauce should be slightly undercooked (about 6 minutes), as they will finish cooking in the sauce. Add them during the last half hour of cooking.

Some of the pan juices from cooking the meatballs may be used to flavor the ragù sauce: Discard half of the oil and cooking juices left in the pan. Pour the remaining half of the pan juices into the sauce. Add 2 tablespoons water to the pan and stir with a wooden spoon to remove any meat that may have stuck to the bottom of the pan. Pour this into the ragù sauce as well.

stuffed peppers

peperoni ripieni

These stuffed peppers make a hearty main course, preceded by pasta and followed by salad. It is important that dry Italian bread be used in this recipe. We have bread with almost every meal. If there is any left over, I place it in a basket and let it dry for a day or two until it is hard. I then either use it in recipes such as this one or grind it in the food processor to make bread crumbs.

1 long loaf Italian bread (not seeded), cut
    into 1-inch-thick slices

2 tablespoons olive oil

1 pound ground beef chuck

2 cloves garlic, diced

1 large egg

¼ cup finely grated pecorino Romano cheese

Kosher salt and freshly ground black pepper

2 tablespoons chopped fresh Italian, flat
    leafed parsley

2 cups Joan's Basic Tomato Sauce (page
    119) or your own favorite tomato sauce

3 large green bell peppers, cut in half
    lengthwise and stems and seeds discarded

¼ cup water

1. Arrange the bread on a baking sheet and allow it to dry out, uncovered, for about 3 days or place on a baking sheet and bake in an oven preheated to 300° F, stirring occasionally, until dry but not brown, about 20 minutes.

2. Preheat the oven to 400° F.

3. Place the dry bread in a large bowl and cover with warm water. Set aside to soak until the bread softens, about 5 minutes.

4. Use olive oil to grease a baking dish that is large enough to hold the pepper halves in one layer.

5. In a large bowl, combine the meat, garlic, egg, cheese, salt and pepper to taste, and parsley, using your hands to mix the ingredients. Remove and discard the crust from

each slice of bread. Squeeze the water out of the bread, and breaking it into small pieces, add it to the meat. Use your hands to work the bread into the meat until they are equally combined and the mixture holds together like a soft, moist dough.

6. Add ½ cup of the tomato sauce to the meat mixture. Mix well. The original meat mixture will now have doubled in size. Divide the filling equally among the pepper halves, mounding it high, and place each filled pepper in the prepared baking dish. Top each pepper with 1 tablespoon of the tomato sauce. Pour the water and ¼ cup of the tomato sauce around the peppers. Cover with aluminum foil and bake until the peppers soften slightly, about 15 minutes.

7. Remove the foil and baste the peppers with additional tomato sauce throughout the remainder of the cooking time. Continue to bake, uncovered, adding sauce and basting occasionally, until the peppers are soft and the meat has browned, 1½ to 2 hours.

— SERVES 6 —

WINE PAIRING: Medium red and full red

VARIATIONS: The peppers may be placed in a baking dish and cooked in a microwave oven for 5 minutes to soften slightly before stuffing. This will shorten the baking time by 20 to 30 minutes. Red bell peppers may be used instead of green. However, they will bake more quickly. After the initial 15-minute baking period, uncover and cook until softened, about 1 hour.

To make a lower-fat version of this dish, substitute ground turkey breast for the ground chuck and 2 egg whites for the whole egg.

Sometimes I will make additional stuffing and use it to prepare a *polpettone,* or meat loaf. To this basic mixture add enough marinara or Bolognese sauce to make a very moist mixture. Place in a covered casserole and bake in a preheated oven at 375° F for 1 hour. It makes a fine meat dish for dinner, but we like it best cooled and sliced for sandwiches.

veal chops stuffed
with fontina and prosciutto

costolette farcite al prosciutto e fontina

This is a great dish to serve when you are celebrating a special occasion. It is generous, rich, and will leave your guests happy and full. It has the added advantage of not requiring too much time in the kitchen on the day of the special event. The chops can be stuffed, breaded, and refrigerated several hours in advance and the veal cooks quickly.

Thickly sliced pork chops or boneless chicken breast may also be stuffed and cooked this way. Serve with asparagus, steamed artichokes, spinach, or an arugula salad with sliced tomato as a side dish.

4 veal chops cut from the rack, bone in
  (about ½ pound each)

4 fresh sage leaves

3½ ounces Fontina cheese, cut into 4 equal
  pieces

8 very thin slices prosciutto

2 tablespoons extra virgin olive oil

½ cup all-purpose flour

3 large eggs, beaten

About 1½ cups plain dried bread crumbs

3 tablespoons butter

3 tablespoons canola oil

Kosher salt and freshly ground black pepper

1 lemon, quartered

1. Have the butcher cut each chop in half horizontally, leaving it still joined by the bone, to form a pocket. Place each chop between two layers of plastic wrap and pound to a ¼-inch thickness. Open the pocket and place a single sage leaf on the bottom portion of each chop. Layer 1 slice of Fontina between 2 slices of prosciutto inside each chop. Drizzle the top slice of prosciutto with ½ tablespoon of the olive oil. Close the pocket by gently pulling the top section of meat slightly over the bottom section.

2. Dredge the chops in flour, shaking off any excess. Dip the chops into the beaten eggs and then into the bread crumbs, coating well. Arrange the chops on a baking sheet and press the pocket of each chop firmly closed with the side of a wide knife. Allow the

chops to sit for at least 5 minutes before cooking. (Refrigerate if it will be more than 30 minutes before cooking. Bring to room temperature before proceeding with the recipe.)

3. In a large sauté pan set over medium-high heat, warm the butter and the canola oil. When the butter is hot and foaming, add the chops. Cook until well browned, about 5 minutes, and then turn. Season with salt and pepper, and reduce the heat to medium. Continue cooking until the other side is well browned, about 7 minutes. Remove the chops from the pan and drain on paper towels before serving each chop with one of the lemon quarters.

— SERVES 4 —

WINE PAIRING: Medium white or light red

VARIATION: Truffle oil may be substituted for the olive oil drizzled inside the chops.

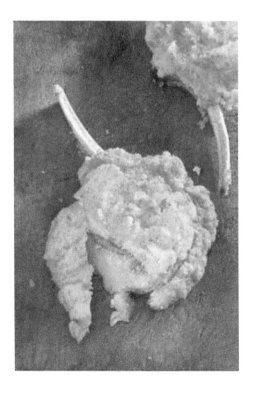

stewed veal shanks with mushrooms

ossobuco con verdurine e funghi

Excellent stews and braised meats require patience, so cooking them in the oven, where it is easier to maintain uniform heat, is the preferred method in our family. The oven heat allows the meat to simmer very gently, so it holds to the bone and does not fall apart. For a truly rich flavor, prepare this *ossobuco* a day ahead, refrigerate it overnight, and reheat in the oven the next day.

When shopping for veal shanks, request ones cut from the center. These have more meat and less bone. Ask the butcher to securely tie the meat so it does not fall off the bone. Serve accompanied by Milanese Risotto (page 194), Risotto with Vegetables and Fine Herbs (page 198), gnocchi (potato or semolina), or mashed potatoes.

6 pieces center-cut veal shank (8 to 10 ounces each, 1 to 1½ inches thick)

3 tablespoons all-purpose flour, plus additional for dusting

Kosher salt and freshly ground black pepper

4 tablespoons canola oil

1 tablespoon butter

½ cup finely sliced celery

½ cup finely diced carrots

1 cup finely diced onions

1 cup dry white wine

1 cup dried porcini mushrooms, soaked for at least 15 minutes in 1 cup warm water

1 teaspoon plus 1 tablespoon finely chopped sage leaves

1 teaspoon plus 1 tablespoon finely chopped fresh rosemary leaves

2 cups drained and chopped canned whole plum tomatoes

3 cups chicken broth or water

1 tablespoon finely chopped lemon zest

1. Preheat the oven to 350° F.

2. Dust the veal with flour, shaking off any excess. Season with salt and pepper. Warm 2 tablespoons of the oil in a large flameproof casserole or sauté pan set over medium-high heat. Cook the veal, browning it evenly on both sides, about 5 minutes per side. Transfer the meat to a platter and set aside.

3. Drain off any juices remaining in the pan. Place the pan over medium-high heat and melt the butter in the remaining 2 tablespoons oil. When the butter begins to foam, add the celery, carrots, and onions. Cook, stirring occasionally, until the vegetables have softened but not browned, about 5 minutes.

4. Return the veal to the pan, along with any juices that have accumulated on the plate. Stir in the 3 tablespoons flour, then add the wine. Remove the mushrooms from the water, reserving the water. Squeeze the mushrooms gently to remove excess moisture, coarsely chop them, and add them to the pan. Bring to a boil and cook to sweeten the wine, about 1 minute.

5. Reduce the heat to a simmer and add 1 teaspoon of the sage, 1 teaspoon of the rosemary, the chopped tomatoes, and the chicken broth. Strain the mushroom water through a fine-mesh sieve or coffee filter and add to the pan. Season with salt and pepper. Slowly return the liquid to a boil, shaking the pan to combine all the ingredients. Transfer to the oven and cook until the meat feels soft when gently probed, about 1½ hours.

6. Just before serving, combine the remaining tablespoon each sage and rosemary and the lemon zest. Sprinkle this mixture over the individual portions of the veal shank.

— SERVES 6 —

WINE PAIRING: Medium red and full red

veal stew

spezzatino di vitello

My mother created this stew, which is a perfect dish to serve on cold autumn and winter evenings. Double the recipe when you need to feed a large group or if you want to have some on reserve in the freezer where it will keep, stored in an airtight container, for up to three months. Like most stews, this recipe is best when cooked a day in advance, then warmed up slowly before serving. Polenta, plain fettuccine, or egg noodles make a good bed for the stew.

2½ pounds lean veal stew meat

¼ cup all-purpose flour

⅓ cup olive oil

½ cup sliced onions

1 clove garlic

2 cups dry white wine

2 cups Sailor's-Style Sauce (page 120) or
    your own favorite marinara sauce

3 small yellow onions, peeled and left whole,
    or 3 medium-size yellow onions,
    quartered

1 teaspoon chopped fresh thyme leaves

2 tablespoons chopped fresh rosemary leaves

3 large fresh sage leaves, torn in half

1 fresh or dried bay leaf

Kosher salt and freshly ground
    black pepper

4 medium-size all-purpose potatoes, peeled
    and cut into eighths

4 large carrots, peeled and cut into ¾-inch-
    thick slices

1 cup fresh or frozen peas

1. Place the veal and flour in a large bowl or sealable plastic bag. Shake to coat the veal lightly with the flour. Toss the meat in a strainer to remove any excess flour. In a deep flameproof casserole, warm the olive oil over medium heat. Cook the veal in the oil, a few pieces at a time, browning on all sides, about 5 minutes per batch. Remove the cooked pieces to a plate and reserve.

recipe continued on next page

2. When all the veal has been browned and removed from the casserole, reduce the heat to medium-low and add the sliced onions and the garlic. Cook, stirring frequently, until softened but not browned, about 1 minute. Add 1 cup of the wine and stir, scraping the bottom of the pan clean.

3. Return the veal to the pan, along with any juices that have accumulated on the plate. Add the remaining 1 cup wine, the marinara sauce, onions, thyme, rosemary, sage, and bay leaf. Season with salt and pepper. The veal should be immersed in liquid; add more wine if necessary. Cover the pan and simmer the stew over low heat, stirring frequently, about 30 to 45 minutes.

4. Add the potatoes and carrots, cover, and continue simmering until the vegetables are tender but not mushy, about 50 minutes. Stir the stew frequently, making sure that none of the meat is sticking to the bottom of the pan. Remove the cover and stir in the peas. Simmer until they are tender, 5 to 7 minutes. (The stew may be set aside before adding the peas. Refrigerate overnight. Reheat slowly, stirring frequently, before adding the peas.)

— SERVES 6 —

WINE PAIRING: Medium red

VARIATION: One pound mushrooms, quartered and sautéed in olive oil until browned but still firm, may be added to the stew along with the peas.

roman-style meat loaf

polpettone alla romana

Enjoy this meat loaf thickly sliced for dinner or thinly sliced on a sandwich the following day. This meat is also delicious cooked as individual hamburger patties. I like to form the mixture into two small loaves so the meat holds together when sliced. One large loaf may require 20 minutes additional baking time. This meat loaf may also be prepared using ground pork, adding 1 tablespoon of fennel seeds to the mixture along with the fresh herbs.

¼ pound day-old crustless white bread

1 cup warm water

1½ pounds ground veal

1 cup ricotta cheese

3 tablespoons finely grated Parmesan cheese

3 large eggs

¼ teaspoon ground nutmeg

2 tablespoons chopped fresh Italian, flat leafed parsley

2 tablespoons chopped fresh sage leaves

2 tablespoons chopped fresh rosemary leaves

Kosher salt and freshly ground black pepper

2 tablespoons butter, melted

2 tablespoons canola oil

1 cup dry white wine

Three 5-inch sprigs fresh rosemary

1. Preheat the oven to 350° F.

2. Cut the bread into 1-inch cubes. Place in a bowl and cover with the water. Allow the bread to absorb the water and become very soft, about 5 minutes. Gently squeeze all the water out of the bread. Place the bread in a large bowl (discard the water).

3. Add the veal to the bread and use a wooden spoon to blend them together to form an even mixture. Stir in the ricotta and Parmesan cheese and mix well. Add the eggs and mix well. Add the nutmeg, parsley, sage, rosemary, salt to taste, and generous grindings of pepper. Mix well.

recipe continued on next page

4. Divide the mixture in half, and shape each half into a loaf measuring approximately 10 inches long by 3 inches wide. Pour the melted butter, canola oil, and wine into a large baking dish. Place the meat loaves in the baking dish, leaving at least an inch between them. Distribute the rosemary sprigs in the dish. Bake until browned and cooked through, about 40 minutes.

5. Remove the loaves to a warm platter, cover with aluminum foil, and set aside. Strain the liquid left in the baking dish through a fine-mesh sieve into a saucepan. Bring to a boil over medium-high heat and cook to reduce by half, 6 to 8 minutes.

6. Cut the meat loaf into 1-inch-thick slices and arrange on a platter or dinner plates. Spoon some of the sauce over each portion and serve immediately.

— SERVES 6 TO 8 —

WINE PAIRING: Medium red and full red

stewed lamb with artichokes

agnello con carciofini

The use of lean meat from the leg of lamb gives this stew a light and subtle flavor. It may be prepared two days in advance up to the point where the lemon juice and eggs are added. Simply reheat and then complete the recipe. Spoon this stew over a wide pasta noodle such as pappardelle. It may also be served preceded by Asparagus Risotto (page 196) and accompanied with Escarole (page 218).

10 medium-size to small artichokes, or 9 ounces thawed frozen artichoke hearts, or one 15-ounce can artichoke bottoms, quartered

1 tablespoon plus 1 teaspoon freshly squeezed lemon juice

3 tablespoons olive oil

3 cloves garlic, crushed

2 pounds boneless leg of lamb, trimmed of fat and cut into 1½-inch cubes

½ cup chopped fresh Italian, flat leafed parsley

Leaves from two 5-inch sprigs of fresh thyme

¾ cup dry white wine

1½ cups warm chicken broth

2½ teaspoons kosher salt

Freshly ground black pepper

2 large egg yolks

1. Remove the tough outer leaves of the artichokes. Trim ¼ inch off the tops of the artichokes and discard. Cut the artichokes in half. Remove any of the fine choke from the center and discard. Slice each half lengthwise into ¼-inch-thick slices. Place in a bowl of cold water mixed with 1 tablespoon of the lemon juice. Set aside. (Skip this section if using frozen or canned artichokes.)

2. Warm the olive oil in a large flameproof casserole set over medium-high heat. Add the garlic and cook until lightly browned, about 2 minutes. Remove and discard the garlic. Adjust the heat to high and add the lamb. Cook until browned on all sides, about

recipe continued on next page

5 minutes. Stir in ¼ cup of the parsley and all of the thyme. Add the wine and allow it to evaporate, about 2 minutes. Remove the artichokes from the water, pat dry, and stir into the stew. Cover and cook to soften slightly, about 3 minutes. Pour in the warm broth and cover. Reduce the heat to medium-low and simmer until the lamb is tender, about 1 hour. Season with the salt and pepper to taste.

3. In a small bowl, whisk the egg yolks and remaining 1 teaspoon lemon juice. Remove ¼ cup of the broth from the stew and gradually whisk it into the egg mixture. Gradually add the egg mixture to the stew, stirring constantly. Stir in the remaining ¼ cup parsley, and serve immediately.

— SERVES 4 —

WINE PAIRING: Medium red and full red

VARIATIONS: Five shallots, quartered, may be browned with the meat, as may 1 cup quartered cremini mushroom caps.

pork tenderloin with fennel and rosemary

arista di maiale alla fiorentina

In this recipe, the pork absorbs the finely diced fennel's sweet, pungent flavor while mellowing its natural licorice zest. Either pork tenderloin or boneless loin of pork may be used. Serve it with roasted potatoes and a simply prepared winter green, such as escarole or broccoli rabe.

1 tablespoon chopped fresh rosemary leaves

2 cloves garlic, finely chopped

1 bulb fresh fennel, finely diced

3 tablespoons canola oil

2 pork tenderloins (1½ pounds each)

1 sprig fresh rosemary

Kosher salt and freshly ground black pepper

½ cup finely diced carrots

½ cup finely diced celery

½ cup coarsely chopped onions

1½ cups chicken broth or water

1. Preheat the oven to 375° F.

2. Toss the rosemary in a bowl with the garlic, fennel, and 1 tablespoon of the oil, stirring to make a paste. Spread half the mixture on top of one of the pork tenderloins. Place the second tenderloin on top. Firmly tie the two tenderloins together with butcher's string. With a sharp knife, make several large holes or angled incisions in the tenderloins and stuff the remaining fennel mixture into these incisions. Cut the rosemary sprig into thirds and tuck under the string. Season the tenderloin with salt and pepper on all sides.

3. Warm the remaining 2 tablespoons oil in a large flameproof casserole set over medium-high heat. Sear the tenderloin until browned on all sides, 6 to 8 minutes. Distribute the carrots, celery, and onions around the meat. Place the casserole in the oven and bake until the meat reaches an internal temperature of 155° F on a meat thermometer, about 30 minutes.

recipe continued on next page

4. Remove the tenderloin from the casserole to a warm plate, wrap in aluminum foil, and set aside.

5. Set the casserole over medium-high heat. Stir the chicken broth into the vegetables and bring to a boil. Boil, stirring frequently, to loosen any meat that has stuck to the bottom of the casserole. Allow the sauce to reduce slightly, about 5 minutes. Strain the sauce through a fine-mesh sieve into a bowl. Press firmly on the vegetables with the back of a spoon to extract their flavor. Discard the vegetables and reserve the sauce. Remove the butcher's string and thinly slice the pork.

6. Arrange the pork on a platter or individual plates. Spoon the sauce over the slices of pork, and serve immediately.

— SERVES 6 —

WINE PAIRING: Light red and medium red

NOTE: Here are a few other ideas for cooking with fennel:

- The leafy part of the fennel bulb may be used as an herb in place of dill; it is a flavorful addition to marinades for fish or meat.
- To make a simple salad, thinly slice a fennel bulb and toss it with orange sections, thinly sliced red onion, arugula, and a mild vinaigrette.
- Pureed fennel is an excellent accompaniment to fish. Warm 2 tablespoons olive oil in a small sauté pan set over medium-high heat. Add 1 fennel bulb, cut into wedges, 1 shallot, diced, and 1 teaspoon fresh thyme leaves. Cover and cook until tender, about 15 minutes. Puree these ingredients in a blender or processor. Stir in the grated zest of 1 orange and 2 tablespoons extra virgin olive oil. Place a dollop in the center of each diner's plate, and top with a portion of grilled fish. Use a vegetable peeler to shave a few slices of raw fennel over the fish, and garnish with a few fennel leaves.

braised italian-style pot roast

brasato al barolo

In Italy it is possible to find inexpensive Barolo wines that are perfect to cook with. Unfortunately, that is not the case in America. Because you don't want to pour a fifteen-dollar bottle of wine over a four-dollar piece of meat, I recommend cooking with a flavorful inexpensive red wine and reserving the Barolo to serve with dinner. For tender, flavorful meat, it is best to prepare this dish several hours or, even better, a full day ahead of time. Reheat it in the oven before serving with mashed potatoes or polenta.

I begin this recipe by preparing a *sacchétto di spezie,* a little bag of herbs and spices.

recipe continued on next page

One 5-inch sprig fresh thyme

5 fresh Italian, flat leafed parsley stems

2 dried bay leaves or 1 fresh bay leaf

One 5-inch sprig fresh rosemary

2 juniper berries, crushed

FOR THE POT ROAST:

One 2-pound piece shoulder of beef, bottom round, or pot roast

Kosher salt and freshly ground black pepper

All-purpose flour for dusting

5 tablespoons butter

1 cup coarsely chopped celery (about 2 stalks)

1¼ cups coarsely chopped onion (1 medium-size onion)

½ cup coarsely chopped carrot (1 medium-size carrot)

1 bottle (750ml) dry red wine

½ cup dried porcini mushrooms, coarsely chopped and soaked in 1 cup warm water

1 tablespoon tomato paste

2 cups canned whole or crushed plum tomatoes

Chicken broth or water as needed

2 tablespoons arrowroot or cornstarch

¼ cup dry red or white wine

TO PREPARE THE SACCHÉTTO DI SPEZIE:

Combine all the ingredients in the center of a piece of cheesecloth that is large enough to hold the herb sprigs, and tie in a bundle with butcher's string.

TO PREPARE THE POT ROAST:

1. Preheat the oven to 350° F.

2. Season the beef with salt and pepper, then lightly dust with flour. Melt the butter in a large (6-quart) flameproof casserole set over medium-high heat. When it is foaming, add the beef and brown it on all sides, 5 minutes. Add the celery, onions, carrots, and sacchétto di spezie. Cook, stirring occasionally, until the vegetables soften slightly, about 2 minutes. Raise the heat to high and add the bottle of wine. Cook until

the wine begins to boil, about 2 more minutes, skimming off any fat that rises to the surface.

3. Strain the porcini mushrooms through a fine-mesh sieve, reserving the liquid. Rinse the mushrooms under cold running water to remove any grit, and add them to the casserole along with the strained mushroom liquid, tomato paste, and tomatoes. The liquid should just cover the meat. If it does not, add chicken broth or water. Cover the casserole and bake it in the oven until the meat is cooked through and tender, about 2 hours. Remove the meat from the casserole to a cutting board, cover with aluminum foil, and set aside.

4. Strain the broth through a fine-mesh sieve and discard the vegetables and herb bag. Pour the broth back into the casserole and set it over high heat. Bring to a boil and add the arrowroot and the ¼ cup wine. Cook to reduce and thicken the liquid, about 5 minutes. Carve the meat into ¼-inch-thick slices. Serve immediately, spooning some of the broth over each portion.

— SERVES 4 —

WINE PAIRING: Medium red and full red

VARIATION: If you have any leftover meat, shred it and stir it into any remaining sauce. Heat through and serve as a savory pasta sauce over cooked penne.

stuffed roasted rabbit

arrosto di coniglio ripieno

Rabbit is eaten in Italy almost as often as chicken. If you cannot find it at your local grocers, I have found that most American butchers can order rabbit with a few days' notice. Ask the butcher to remove the bones or, using a sharp knife, cut the meat away by following the shape of the bones. (Reserve the bones to make a sauce.) The meat is then pounded into a neat rectangle, stuffed, and roasted. Because rabbit stays very tender, it may be cooked one day ahead of time and reheated before serving.

Serve this dish with roasted potatoes or vegetables, or with sautéed vegetables such as broccoli rabe or escarole. Butterflied loin of pork pounded to a thickness of about ¼ inch is also delicious prepared this way. Cook the pork until it reaches an internal temperature of 155° F on a meat thermometer, about 1½ hours.

Butter to grease aluminum foil

1 boned rabbit, bones reserved and skin removed

1 tablespoon chopped fresh sage leaves

2 tablespoons chopped fresh Italian, flat leafed parsley

1 tablespoon chopped fresh rosemary leaves

Kosher salt and freshly ground black pepper

½ boneless, skinless chicken breast, cut lengthwise into 1-inch-wide strips

½ cup pitted prunes

2 tablespoons olive oil

1 carrot, coarsely chopped

1 celery stalk, coarsely chopped

1 tablespoon all-purpose flour

½ cup dry white wine

1 cup chicken broth

1. Preheat the oven to 325° F. Generously grease a long sheet of aluminum foil with butter. Set aside.

2. Place the rabbit between two sheets of waxed paper or plastic wrap. Pound the meat into a large thin rectangle. Transfer the meat to the center of the aluminum foil, with the

long end facing you. In a small bowl, mix the sage, parsley, and rosemary. Sprinkle half the herb mixture on the rabbit. Season with salt and pepper.

3. Arrange the strips of chicken breast in a single long line down the center of the rabbit. Arrange the prunes on top of the chicken. Sprinkle with the remaining herb mixture. Roll the rabbit into a neat, tight log. Fold the foil tightly around the rabbit, and twist the foil closed at both ends. Place in a roasting pan.

4. In a large bowl, toss the rabbit bones with the olive oil, carrot, and celery. Distribute this around the rabbit in the roasting pan. Bake until the rabbit is cooked through and reaches an internal temperature of 160° F on a meat thermometer, about 1½ hours. Remove from the oven, transfer the rabbit in foil to a cutting board, and set aside.

5. Set the roasting pan over high heat (or transfer the contents to a wide saucepan). Stir in the flour, wine, and broth. Bring to a boil and cook, stirring constantly, to slightly thicken the juices in the pan, about 5 minutes. Strain through a fine-mesh sieve and set aside.

6. Slice the rabbit into 1½-inch-wide portions. Spoon the sauce over the sliced meat, and serve.

—SERVES 6—

WINE PAIRING: Medium red

VARIATIONS: Six to eight thin slices prosciutto may be placed on the aluminum foil and wrapped around the rabbit as you roll the stuffed meat. And cubes of apple or pear may be substituted for the prunes in the stuffing.

grilled butterflied leg of lamb

cosciotto di agnello

When serving a meat dish as a main course I follow the Italian tradition of beginning the meal with a pasta dish, followed by the meat course accompanied by a simply cooked vegetable. We finish with a green salad followed by nuts and fresh fruit. I find that pacing the meal in this way leaves me feeling less full.

1 boneless butterflied leg of lamb (about 4 pounds off the bone)

¼ cup olive oil

2 cloves garlic, crushed

2 fresh sage leaves

Two 5-inch sprigs fresh rosemary, cut in half

Two 5-inch sprigs fresh oregano, torn into pieces, or ¼ teaspoon dried

½ cup dry red wine

1 medium-size onion, cut into 1-inch-thick slices

1 tablespoon balsamic vinegar

½ lemon, quartered

1. Place the lamb in a large glass baking dish or sealable plastic bag. In a medium-size bowl, mix the olive oil, garlic, sage, rosemary, oregano, wine, onion, and vinegar. Add the lemon sections, squeezing them gently to release some of the juice. Pour this over the lamb, cover, and refrigerate for at least 2 hours, basting the meat occasionally. Allow the meat to return to room temperature before grilling.

2. Prepare a grill that has a cover. Cook the meat on the grill, covered, basting once or twice with the marinade, until well browned on one side, about 12 minutes. Turn the meat over and baste once. Cover the grill and cook the meat for 12 minutes more for medium to medium-rare, and 15 minutes for medium-well to well-done meat. (Rare lamb registers 160° F on a meat thermometer; well done is 175° F. If the fire flares

around the meat, remove the cover and spray the fire with water to prevent charring.) Remove from the grill, cover with a sheet of aluminum foil, and allow to rest for 5 to 10 minutes before carving.

— SERVES 6 TO 8 —

WINE PAIRING: Medium red and full red

NOTE: Marinade that has been in contact with raw meat may be used if the heat of the fire will have time to cook it along with the meat. That is why we do not advise basting again during the last half of grilling time.

poultry

pollame

Many years ago, my sisters and I cooked a surprise meal for our mother's birthday, the main course being duck that was stuffed with sausages and apples. Though we were not experienced cooks, the meal was a success. That experience made me realize how versatile and relatively simple cooking poultry can be. This is especially true with chicken, which we eat in our house at least three times a week.

The following recipes are fairly inexpensive, easy to make, and can help you turn what is rather ordinary meat into something special. My mother also recommends improvising, depending on the ingredients you have on hand, how many people you are serving, the time of year, and personal taste. Start with Gianni's Chicken on a Brick with Lemon and Rosemary and then try my mother's *Pollo alla Cacciatora,* and you'll see what I mean.

chicken cutlets

cotolette di pollo

My grandmother prepared this recipe using veal cutlets. Today I prefer to use chicken cutlets because they are so easy to purchase and are a healthier choice. I serve it accompanied by Milanese Risotto (page 194) or Rice with Zucchini (page 191), sautéed broccoli rabe, or sautéed escarole. If you have any leftover chicken cutlets, they make a delicious sandwich on slices of country bread.

6 boneless skinless chicken breast halves

2 large eggs

1 tablespoon water

1 cup plain dried bread crumbs

1 tablespoon freshly grated Parmesan cheese
  (optional)

Kosher salt

¼ cup olive oil, plus more as needed

1 lemon, cut into 6 wedges

1. Remove the white tendons from the chicken breasts and discard. Cut off the tender chicken pieces (the fillets) that are not part of the whole breasts and set them aside.

2. Pound each piece of chicken breast between sheets of waxed paper or plastic wrap until it is uniformly ¼ inch thick. Pound the fillet pieces as well.

3. In a shallow bowl, beat the eggs and water. In another shallow bowl, toss the bread crumbs, cheese if desired, and salt to taste. Dip the individual chicken pieces into the egg mixture, letting the excess drip off, and then into the bread crumb mixture. Coat the chicken thoroughly with the bread crumbs. Place the coated pieces of chicken on a cookie sheet and set aside for at least 5 minutes to allow the bread crumbs to dry and adhere.

4. In a large sauté pan, heat the olive oil over medium-high heat. When the oil is hot but not smoking, add as many pieces of chicken as will fit comfortably in the pan. Cook, turning once, until the breasts are no longer pink in the center but still tender, about 6 minutes per side. (Reduce the heat if the bread crumbs begin to brown too quickly.) Remove to a platter lined with paper towels to drain. Add more oil to the pan as needed to cook the remaining chicken pieces. Serve immediately, garnished with the lemon wedges.

— SERVES 6 —

WINE PAIRING: Medium white and light red

VARIATION: Veal or chicken prepared this way may be used for a Parmesan casserole. This dish is, I believe, a purely American creation. Although the ingredients would suggest southern Italian origins, I've never seen it served in Italy. I'm especially confused by the Parmesan cheese called for in several of the recipes I've seen, since southern Italians mostly use pecorino Romano. This has become a classic dish that is easy to prepare in advance and then bake just before serving.

Arrange the cooked cutlets in a casserole, slightly overlapping. Spoon about 2 cups of Joan's Basic Tomato Sauce (page 119) over the cutlets. Sprinkle 1 cup grated mozzarella cheese and ¼ cup grated pecorino Romano on top. Bake in a preheated oven at 350° F to warm the cutlets through and melt the cheese, about 20 minutes. Serve with a salad and bread.

chicken with rosemary

pollo al rosmarino

When my mother decided to eat food that is lower in fat and cholesterol, she created this simple and healthful chicken dish that can be prepared in under thirty minutes. This tasty recipe calls for sautéed chicken breasts flavored with lemon, lime, and rosemary—her favorite herb. Serve with a crisp, dry white wine, a tossed salad, and some warm Italian bread.

4 boneless, skinless chicken breast halves

¼ cup olive oil

2 cloves garlic, thinly sliced

1 cup dry white wine

1 tablespoon chopped fresh rosemary leaves

Kosher salt and freshly ground black pepper

3 tablespoons freshly squeezed lemon juice

2 tablespoons freshly squeezed lime juice

2 tablespoons butter or margarine (optional)

1. Preheat the oven to 300° F. Place a serving platter in the oven.

2. Remove the white tendons from the chicken meat and discard. Remove the tender chicken pieces (the fillets) that are not part of the whole breast, and freeze them for Chicken Cutlets (page 278) or other recipes.

3. Place each piece of chicken between two sheets of waxed paper or plastic wrap. Lightly pound the breasts until they are uniformly about ¼ inch thick. Set aside.

4. Warm the olive oil in a large sauté pan set over medium heat. Add the garlic and cook until it is slightly colored, about 2 minutes. Remove the garlic and set aside.

5. Place the chicken breasts in the pan and brown them, about 3 minutes per side. Remove the cooked chicken to the warmed platter in the oven. Drain off any oil in the sauté pan. Reduce the heat to medium-low and add the wine, stirring and scraping the bottom of the pan. Add the rosemary and return the garlic to the pan. Cook, stirring

frequently, to flavor the wine, about 1 minute. Season with salt and pepper. Return the chicken to the pan, along with any juices that have accumulated on the platter. Add the lemon and lime juices and cook to flavor the chicken, turning frequently, about 1 minute. Transfer the chicken back to the warm platter.

6. Increase the heat to high and add the butter to the pan. Briskly stir the butter to emulsify the sauce. Spoon the sauce over the chicken and serve immediately.

— SERVES 4 —

WINE PAIRING: Medium white and light red

VARIATION: Half a pound any variety of mushrooms may be thinly sliced and cooked in 2 tablespoons olive oil before preparing the chicken. Set aside and add to the pan with the butter to warm through before spooning over the chicken.

baked chicken wings

alette di pollo al forno

This recipe, created by my mother, is a good example of how she and I typically cook. She had some chicken wings and no recipe to follow. So she began to mix a little of this and a little of that—garlic, olive oil, rosemary. "At the last moment I decided to add some wine and tomato sauce," says Joan. "I have since tried this recipe without the sauce and the dish was not as good."

16 chicken wings, rinsed, patted dry, and
   wing tips removed

3 tablespoons olive oil

Kosher salt and freshly ground black pepper

6 cloves garlic, cut in half

1 small shallot, chopped

1 medium-size onion, quartered and
   separated into layers

Two 5-inch sprigs fresh rosemary

4 large fresh sage leaves

1 teaspoon dried thyme

1 teaspoon dried oregano

½ cup dry white wine

½ cup Sailor's-Style Sauce (page 120) or
   Joan's Basic Tomato Sauce (page 119) or
   your own favorite tomato sauce

1. Preheat the oven to 350° F.

2. Split the wings into two pieces at the joint. Place the split wings in a roasting or baking dish large enough to hold them in a single layer. Drizzle the olive oil on top and season with salt and pepper. Add the garlic, shallot, onion, rosemary, sage, thyme, and oregano, and toss to coat evenly. Bake, stirring once or twice, until lightly browned, about 15 minutes. Stir in the wine and bake for about 5 minutes.

3. Stir in the tomato sauce and bake, stirring once or twice, until the wings are browned and cooked through, about another 10 minutes. Serve immediately.

— SERVES 4 —

WINE PAIRING: Medium white and light red

chicken rolled and stuffed with smoked mozzarella, spinach, and prosciutto

rollatina di pollo con mozzarella affumicata, spinaci, e prosciutto

This recipe calls for smoked mozzarella, although any cheese of a similar tender consistency may be substituted. The breasts may be stuffed, rolled in aluminum foil, and refrigerated for several hours before baking, making this a quick and simple dish to serve. It was inspired by Gianni's aunt Angela, who relied on this practical recipe to make a satisfying meal for him and his siblings while his parents were cooking and serving guests at the Scappin family trattoria in Mason Vicentino.

1 pound spinach, washed well and tough stems removed

8 thin slices prosciutto, cut into short ½-inch-wide strips

¼ pound smoked mozzarella, cut into small dice

Kosher salt and freshly ground black pepper

4 whole boneless, skinless chicken breasts

4 teaspoons olive oil

4 teaspoons mixed chopped fresh herbs, such as parsley, rosemary, and/or sage

3 tablespoons butter

1 tablespoon diced shallots

1 cup Marsala wine

1 cup dry white wine

1. Preheat the oven to 400° F.

2. Place the spinach in a medium-size saucepan over medium-high heat with a small amount of water. Cover and cook to wilt, about 5 minutes. Drain the spinach and squeeze out all of the water. Coarsely chop and place in a small bowl. Add the prosciutto and mozzarella, season with salt and pepper, and toss to combine. Set aside.

recipe continued on next page

3. Trim off any fat on the chicken breasts. Remove the white tendon and discard. Spread one whole breast flat on a sheet of waxed paper or plastic wrap, slightly overlapping the halves of the breast in the center. Cover with another sheet of waxed paper or plastic wrap, and pound the breast to flatten into a circular shape that is about doubled in size.

4. Spread one quarter of the spinach filling on one half of the breast. Fold the other half on top, sandwich style. Firmly roll the chicken into a sausage shape. Brush the top lightly with 1 teaspoon of the olive oil. Sprinkle 1 teaspoon of the fresh herbs over the chicken. Wrap snugly in a single layer of aluminum foil. Repeat this procedure with the remaining three whole breasts.

5. Place the wrapped rolls in a baking dish and bake until cooked through, about 30 minutes. Remove from the oven and allow to rest for 5 minutes before unwrapping.

6. While the chicken is resting, melt 1 tablespoon of the butter in a medium-size sauté pan set over medium-high heat. Add the shallots and cook until softened, about 2 minutes. Increase the heat to high and add the wines. Cook, stirring occasionally, until the liquid is reduced to ½ cup. Whisk the remaining 2 tablespoons butter into the sauce to thicken it slightly. Remove from the heat and set aside.

7. Slice each cooked breast on the diagonal into 6 to 8 pieces. Arrange several slices in a fan shape on each plate. Spoon some of the sauce on top, and serve immediately.

— SERVES 6 TO 8 —

WINE PAIRING: Medium white and light red

VARIATIONS: Several different stuffings may be used to prepare this dish:

In a small sauté pan, warm 1 tablespoon olive oil over medium heat. Add ½ cup each diced artichoke hearts, potatoes, and onions and cook until softened, about 10 minutes. Season with 1 teaspoon chopped fresh mint or parsley leaves. Stuff the breasts with equal portions of this mixture, topping with fresh herbs.

Crumble ½ cup goat's milk cheese into a bowl. Toss with ¼ cup diced sun-dried tomatoes, ¼ cup coarsely chopped pine nuts, and 2 tablespoons plain dried bread crumbs. Stuff the breasts with equal portions of this mixture, topping with fresh herbs.

In a small sauté pan, warm 1 tablespoon olive oil over medium heat. Add ½ cup thinly sliced onions, 1 finely diced clove garlic, and ½ cup thinly sliced mushrooms. Cook, stirring, until softened, about 10 minutes. Transfer to a bowl and allow to cool. Add ½ cup finely diced Asiago or Fontina cheese, 1 tablespoon chopped fresh Italian, flat leafed parsley, and 2 tablespoons plain dried bread crumbs. Toss to combine. Stuff the breasts with equal portions of this mixture, topping with fresh herbs.

chicken with sausage and peppers
spezzato di pollo "scappinello"

Serve a soup, such as minestrone, or a traditional *antipasti* platter of cheeses, olives, and salami as a first course before this hearty dish. Transfer the roasted meats and vegetables to a large serving platter, place in the center of the table along with a loaf of country bread, and allow everyone to serve himself. The chicken, sausages, onions, and peppers may be prepared several hours in advance. Toss with the potatoes and herbs just before baking.

½ cup canola or peanut oil

One 4-pound free-range chicken, cut into 16 serving pieces (reserve the back and gizzards for broth)

Kosher salt and freshly ground black pepper

1 pound sweet or hot sausage, cut into ½-inch-thick slices

2 medium-size onions, each cut into 6 wedges

1 large green bell pepper, seeded and cut into 8 to 10 pieces

10 cloves garlic, cut in half

3 large Idaho or all-purpose potatoes, peeled, quartered lengthwise, and cut into ½-inch dice

Six 5-inch sprigs fresh rosemary

8 fresh sage leaves

1 teaspoon red pepper flakes or ½ fresh jalapeño pepper, seeded and diced

1. Preheat the oven to 450° F.

2. Heat the oil in a large skillet set over medium-high heat. Add the chicken, skin side down, in a single layer (cook the chicken in batches if necessary). Season with salt and pepper and brown well on one side, about 5 minutes. Turn and brown lightly on the other side, about 3 minutes. Transfer to a roasting pan that will hold all of the ingredients in a single layer.

3. Drain off all but 1 tablespoon of the fat in the skillet. Add the sausage, onions, bell pepper, and garlic to the skillet. Cook, stirring frequently, until the sausage is lightly browned, about 3 minutes. Transfer to the roasting pan. Stir the potatoes, rosemary, sage, and red pepper flakes into the roasting pan. Toss well and bake, stirring occasionally, until the chicken is cooked through and the potatoes are browned, about 35 minutes. Remove from the oven and serve immediately.

—SERVES 8 TO 10—

WINE PAIRING: Medium white and light red

chicken cacciatore

pollo alla cacciatora

Each Italian family seems to have its own variation on this classic dish. My father notes that this recipe, from the Tropiano family, is very similar to the Tucci family version. "The only difference is that we didn't add tomatoes or marinara sauce."

¼ cup olive oil

2 red or green bell peppers, seeded and cut into 1-inch-wide strips

½ pound mushrooms, cut into ¼-inch-thick slices

One 3-pound free-range chicken, cut into serving-size pieces

Kosher salt and freshly ground black pepper

½ cup dry white wine

2 cloves garlic, coarsely chopped

2½ cups coarsely chopped onions (about 2 medium-size onions)

1 cup canned whole plum tomatoes, Sailor's-Style Sauce (page 120), or your own favorite marinara sauce

1. Warm the olive oil in a large sauté pan set over medium-high heat. Add the peppers and cook, stirring, until slightly softened, about 10 minutes. Remove from the pan and set aside.

2. Stir the mushrooms into the pan and cook, stirring, until slightly softened, about 8 minutes. Remove from the pan and set aside.

3. Season the chicken with salt and pepper. Add to the pan and brown lightly on both sides, about 15 minutes in all. Remove the chicken from the pan to a platter and set aside. Pour the wine into the pan and stir to incorporate any cooking juices. Add the garlic and onions and cook until the onions are slightly softened, about 3 minutes. Stir in the tomatoes, crushing them with your hand or the back of a slotted spoon as you add

them to the pan. Return the chicken to the pan, along with any juices that have accumulated on the plate. Bring to a boil, then reduce the heat to a simmer. Cover and cook, stirring occasionally, until the chicken is cooked through, about 30 minutes.

4. Stir the peppers and mushrooms into the chicken. Return to a simmer, cover, and cook to blend in the flavor of these ingredients, about 10 minutes. The cacciatore may be set aside at this point for several hours before reheating and serving with bread to dip into the sauce.

— SERVES 4 —

WINE PAIRING: Medium white and light red

VARIATION: Rabbit cut into serving portions may be substituted for the chicken. Omit the peppers. Quarter rather than slice the mushrooms. To the basic recipe add 2 all-purpose potatoes, peeled, halved, and each half quartered. Stir these into the pan along with the rabbit.

simple chicken breast with sage

petto di pollo semplice alla salvia

This is an easy and tasty recipe to prepare. The secret is to control the heat of the pan so the chicken breast does not brown too quickly and the meat remains tender and moist. Serve this dish with a tossed green salad, sautéed broccoli rabe (pages 216, 217), Roasted Vegetables (page 230), or a simple Carrot Salad (page 236).

2 boneless, skinless chicken breast halves

Kosher salt and freshly ground black pepper

1 tablespoon butter, cut into thirds

2 teaspoons canola or olive oil

4 fresh sage leaves

¼ cup dry white wine

1. Remove the white tendons from the chicken meat and the tender chicken pieces (the fillets) that are not part of the whole breast and discard. The chicken breasts should be evenly thick, about 1 inch. If necessary, place each breast between two sheets of waxed paper or plastic wrap and pound slightly to achieve an even thickness.

2. Season the chicken breasts on both sides with salt and pepper. In a large skillet set over medium-low heat, warm two thirds of the butter with the oil. Add the sage to the pan. When the butter begins to foam, add the chicken breasts, smooth side down.

3. Cook slowly, lightly browning the breasts, about 6 minutes. Turn the breasts and continue cooking to lightly brown the other side, about 6 minutes. Add the wine and the remaining butter to the pan. Increase the heat to medium-high and reduce the liquid until slightly thickened, about 1 minute. Transfer the chicken to a plate, pour the sauce over the top, and serve immediately.

— SERVES 2 —

WINE PAIRING: Medium white and light red

VARIATIONS: One of the following ingredients may be added to the sauce along with the wine: 2 tablespoons freshly squeezed lemon juice, 3 tablespoons freshly squeezed orange juice, or 2 tablespoons Marsala wine.

chicken on a brick
with lemon and rosemary

pollo al mattone con limone e rosmarino

In Italy it is customary for kitchens to include an indoor grill, where poultry and meat are prepared. To cook a whole chicken easily, it is butterflied and held down on the grill by a brick or a heavy pot. In this way the chicken cooks quickly and the meat stays tender and juicy. To butterfly a chicken, follow the simple instructions provided here, or ask the butcher to butterfly it for you.

To accompany the chicken, I recommend serving roasted potatoes or roasted vegetables and sautéed broccoli rabe or escarole.

One 3-pound free-range chicken, washed and patted dry, giblets discarded

1 tablespoon very thinly sliced lemon zest

1 cup white wine

3 tablespoons olive oil

1 tablespoon red wine vinegar

Kosher salt and freshly ground black pepper

1 tablespoon chopped fresh sage leaves

2 tablespoons chopped fresh rosemary leaves

1 clove garlic, finely chopped

¼ teaspoon red pepper flakes

1. To butterfly the chicken, trim the wings at the second joint (reserve for making stock). Place the chicken, breast side down, on a cutting board. Use a sharp knife or poultry shears to cut along either side of the backbone. Remove the bone and reserve it for making stock.

2. With scissors or kitchen shears, cut away and discard any small, sharp protruding bones. Use both hands to press down, breaking the ribs and flattening the chicken. Turn the chicken skin side up. Make a small incision just below the breast near the leg, where the meat thins out. Insert the bone end of the drumstick into the incision. Make a small incision in the thickest part of each chicken leg.

recipe continued on next page

3. Place the chicken between two pieces of plastic wrap. Pound until the chicken is uniformly ½ inch thick. The chicken is now ready to cook.

4. In a large casserole or baking dish, whisk the lemon zest, wine, olive oil, and vinegar. Add the chicken, skin side down. Season with salt and pepper. Sprinkle with the sage, rosemary, garlic, and red pepper flakes. Turn the chicken over and season with salt and red pepper. Turn the chicken several times in the casserole to coat it evenly with the marinade. Cover and marinate in the refrigerator for at least 1 hour or for up to 24 hours. (Note: If you are going to marinate the chicken overnight, do not add any salt until just before cooking. The salt will cure the chicken and make the meat tough.)

5. Prepare a charcoal or gas grill. Wrap a brick or heavy rock in aluminum foil and set aside.

6. Remove the chicken from the marinade, reserving the marinade. Place the chicken, skin side down, on the grill. Sear the skin for about 5 minutes, then rotate the chicken on the grill to make cross-hatched grill marks. Continue searing for another 5 minutes.

7. Turn the chicken over and baste with some of the reserved marinade. Place the brick on top of the chicken. Cover the grill and cook the chicken, basting from time to time with the marinade, until golden brown, about 30 minutes.

8. Remove from the heat, cover with aluminum foil, and allow to rest for 5 minutes before serving.

— SERVES 4 —

WINE PAIRING: Medium white and light red

VARIATIONS: This chicken is equally delicious baked in a preheated oven at 375° F. Heat 2 tablespoons olive oil in a wide cast-iron pan. Remove the marinade from the chicken and reserve. Sear the chicken, skin side down, placing a heavy pan or aluminum-foil-covered brick on top to hold it firmly in the pan. Cook until golden brown, about 7 minutes. Turn the chicken over. Pour the marinade into the pan. Place the brick on top and bake in the oven, uncovered, basting occasionally during the first 35 minutes of cooking time. Bake until the chicken is golden brown and cooked through, a total of about 45 minutes.

Individual Cornish game hens may be prepared in this same way. Bake or grill for about 20 minutes.

NOTE: Do not baste with the marinade during the last 15 minutes of cooking. Because it was in contact with the raw chicken, any unused marinade should be discarded and not served.

roasted chicken with vegetables

pollo arrosto

My grandfather Tropiano made wine. My mother says: "There was no science to his method, and whatever didn't work one year would be changed the next. If the wine wasn't drinkable, we had lots of vinegar." My father claims, "The year your grandfather made his best batch of wine was the year your mother and I became engaged."

My grandmother often liked to serve this one-dish meal accompanied by a glass of homemade wine. To her basic recipe my mother has added rosemary.

One 3-pound free-range chicken, giblets removed

Kosher salt and freshly ground black pepper

1 cup coarsely chopped onions (about 1 medium-size onion)

Four 5-inch sprigs fresh rosemary

Four 5-inch sprigs fresh thyme

½ cup plus 1 tablespoon olive oil

2 large carrots, peeled and cut into 2-inch pieces

3 medium-size red or Yukon Gold potatoes, peeled and quartered

3 cloves garlic

½ cup dry white wine

1. Preheat the oven to 350° F.

2. Rinse the chicken and pat it dry. Salt and pepper the inside of the cavity, and fill it with half the chopped onions, 2 sprigs of the rosemary, and 2 sprigs of the thyme. Truss the chicken and rub all over with 1 tablespoon of the olive oil. Place in a roasting pan or a large baking dish.

3. In a bowl, toss the remaining 2 sprigs each rosemary and thyme, the remaining onions and the carrots, potatoes, garlic, and ½ cup olive oil. Season with salt and pepper. Surround the chicken with the vegetables. Pour the wine over the vegetables and bake, stirring the vegetables occasionally, until the chicken juices run clear and the vegetables are roasted, about 1¼ hours.

4. Remove the chicken from the oven and transfer it to a cutting board. Allow to rest for 5 minutes before carving and arranging on a platter. Remove the vegetables from the roasting pan with a slotted spoon and arrange around the chicken. Serve immediately with the pan juices.

— SERVES 4 —

WINE PAIRING: Medium white, light red, and rosé

roast duck with fresh figs

anitra arrosta con fichi freschi

Figs grow in both northern and southern Italy and thus are a delicacy enjoyed by both the Tucci and Scappin families. The fruit was in abundance on the day Gianni created this sauce that makes a happy pairing of port and figs. To balance the sweetness of the figs, consider serving a mixed salad of bitter greens, such as arugula, topped with thin slices of fennel bulb and tossed with a simple vinaigrette.

One 4-pound duck	*½ cup coarsely chopped carrots*
Two 5-inch sprigs fresh rosemary	*½ cup coarsely chopped celery*
6 fresh sage leaves	*3 cloves garlic, cut in half*
4 cloves garlic, crushed	*One 5-inch sprig fresh thyme*
½ medium-size onion	*⅓ cup honey*
2 tablespoons olive oil	*1 tablespoon butter*
Kosher salt and freshly ground black pepper	*6 large fresh figs, quartered*
½ cup coarsely chopped onions	*1 cup port*

1. Preheat the oven to 400° F.

2. Wash the duck inside and out, reserving the giblets. Pat dry. If there is a long flap of neck skin, cut it off and discard it. Cut the wing tips at the joints and place in a large roasting pan along with the giblets. Set aside. Fill the duck cavity with one of the rosemary sprigs, the sage, and the garlic. Add the onion half, positioning it so that it holds the herbs inside the duck.

3. Warm the olive oil in a large sauté pan set over medium-high heat. Add the duck and sear it, browning it evenly on all sides, 6 to 8 minutes. Remove from the pan and season all over with salt and pepper. Place the duck, breast side down, in the roasting pan. Roast, turning once, to render the fat, about 30 minutes.

4. Add the chopped onions, carrots, celery, and halved garlic to the roasting pan, distributing them evenly around the duck. Cook to soften the vegetables, about 15 minutes. Add the remaining rosemary sprig and the thyme sprig. Continue cooking to begin to brown the vegetables, about 15 minutes.

5. Reduce the oven to 350° F. Brush one third of the honey over the duck. Continue roasting until the duck is golden brown and cooked through, about 30 minutes. During this time, brush the duck twice with additional honey and stir the vegetables.

6. Remove the duck from the oven. Place it on a cutting board and cover with aluminum foil. Set aside.

7. Remove the giblets and wing tips from the vegetables and discard. Discard the sprigs of herbs. Drain off the fat, reserving about ½ cup of the cooking juices. Place the reserved cooking juices and the vegetables in a blender, puree until smooth, and set aside.

8. Melt the butter in a sauté pan set over medium-high heat. Stir in the figs and cook until softened and lightly browned, about 5 minutes. Pour in the port. Allow to simmer until reduced by half, about 8 minutes. Stir in the pureed vegetables and simmer gently to warm through, about 2 minutes. Cut the duck into portions and serve, topping each portion with some of the sauce.

— SERVES 4 —

WINE PAIRING: Light to medium red

VARIATIONS: Plums, quartered and pitted, may be substituted for the figs and cooked in the same way.

Four Granny Smith apples or 4 firm, ripe pears may be substituted for the figs. Peel, core, and coarsely chop 2 of the apples or pears. Cook these with the vegetables around the duck. Peel and core the other 2 apples or pears. Cut into ½-inch-thick slices and cook in the butter until softened and lightly browned before adding the port and pureed vegetables.

fish and shellfish

pesce

Although I love to eat fish, I haven't had much luck catching them, despite many expeditions with my father to the numerous reservoirs and streams near our town. One day we went to a bridge overlooking a reservoir where, we had been told, even small children were known to catch fish. As usual, we caught nothing. I suggested that we try our luck under the bridge, but again, no fish. As I gazed at the water in frustration I noticed what looked like a silver ladle resting on the bottom of the stream. I took off my shoes and socks, rolled up my pants, and pulled it out. It was a sterling silver ladle marked Black/Gorham/1890. My father polished it and now it is mounted like a trophy on a piece of cherrywood cut in the shape of a fish.

We all know the benefits of eating fish—it's an excellent source of low-calorie protein and it can be cooked so many different ways: poached, steamed, grilled, baked, or broiled. Here you will discover how to prepare seafood in healthy, simple, and extraordinary ways, all of which are unforgettable. Two of my favorites are Gianni's baked whole fish and my father's bluefish. Give them a try!

baked whole fish

pesce al forno intero

This dish is not complicated to prepare and it makes for an impressive presentation. Red snapper, sea bass, striped bass, pompano, and salmon are all good whole fish to bake. When a fish is baked whole, it is flavorful and juicy. This is especially true for smaller fish that can be dry when cooked as fillets, such as Mediterranean sea bass (branzino) and sea bream (dorado). Whatever type of fish you select be sure it is fresh, with bright gills and no fishy smell.

One 3-pound fish, cleaned and scaled (head and tail left on)

Kosher salt and freshly ground black pepper

4 cloves garlic, crushed

Five 5-inch sprigs fresh rosemary

One 5-inch sprig fresh thyme

5 fresh Italian, flat leafed parsley stems

2 tablespoons chopped fresh fennel leaves

½ lemon, cut into wedges

4 celery stalks

4 tablespoons extra virgin olive oil

1 cup dry white wine

¼ cup water

2 tablespoons freshly squeezed lemon juice

1. Preheat the oven broiler

2. Season the cavity of the fish with salt and pepper. Tuck the garlic, rosemary, thyme, parsley, fennel, and lemon wedges into the cavity. Place the celery stalks on the bottom of a roasting pan large enough to hold the fish, and lay the fish on top. Brush 2 table-spoons of the olive oil over the fish. Broil the fish about 3 inches below the heat source until the skin colors slightly, about 3 minutes.

3. Remove from the oven and reduce the oven temperature to 375° F. Roast the fish until the flesh is firm and flakes away when a small knife is inserted near the spine, about 35 minutes. Remove from the oven. Transfer the fish to a warm serving platter, cover with aluminum foil, and set aside.

4. Remove the celery from the pan and discard it. Place the pan over medium heat and add the wine, water, and lemon juice. Whisk in the remaining 2 tablespoons olive oil and simmer to thicken slightly, about 1 minute. Pour the sauce over the fish and serve immediately.

— SERVES 4 —

WINE PAIRING: Light white, medium white, and rosé

VARIATION: Carrots may be used instead of celery under the fish.

baked whole fish in an aromatic salt crust

pesce al sale aromatizzato

If you want to impress your guests, this is the dish to prepare. It's perfect for large parties, makes an unforgettable centerpiece for a buffet, and is always tender and moist. I would use red snapper, striped bass, or sea bass. Garnish it with lemon slices and sprinkle with olive oil. Simple vegetables, such as roasted potatoes and sautéed spinach, make good side dishes.

5 pounds sea salt or kosher salt

2 large egg whites

2 cups water

One 4-pound fish, cleaned and scaled, fins removed (head and tail left on)

Kosher salt and freshly ground black pepper

4 tablespoons chopped fresh fennel leaves

1 lemon, cut into 6 wedges

Eight 5-inch sprigs fresh rosemary

2 bay leaves

5 fresh Italian, flat leafed parsley stems

4 cloves garlic, crushed

1 tablespoon finely chopped fresh sage leaves

1 lemon, thinly sliced

1. Preheat the oven to 400° F.

2. In a large bowl, combine the salt, egg whites, and water. The salt should be moist but not wet. Set aside.

3. Line a large roasting or baking pan with two layers of aluminum foil. Fold up the edges of the foil to make a boat shape. Spread one quarter of the salt mixture on top of the foil. Place the whole fish on top of the salt. Season the cavity of the fish with salt and pepper. Place 2 tablespoons of the fennel leaves, the lemon wedges, 4 of the rosemary sprigs, and the bay leaves, parsley stems, and garlic in the cavity. Place the remaining 4 rosemary sprigs, the chopped sage, and the remaining 2 tablespoons fennel leaves on top of the fish. Arrange the lemon slices down the center of the fish.

4. Cover the fish with the remaining salt mixture, patting it into place to completely enclose the fish. (If the head and tail protrude from the baking dish, wrap them in aluminum foil.) Bake until the fish reaches an internal temperature of 145° F (use an instant-read thermometer to check this), about 45 minutes. Remove from the oven and set aside to rest for 20 minutes.

5. When ready to serve, crack the salt shell with a hammer. (If you want to impress your family and friends, do this at the table.) Lift the solid salt away from the dish. Discard the lemon and herbs and gently separate the skin of the dish from the meat. Transfer portions of the fish to each dinner plate, and serve immediately.

— SERVES 4 TO 6 —

WINE PAIRING: Light white, medium white, and sparkling

fillets of fish in a basil tomato sauce with crostini

filetti di pesce in guazzetto di pomodoro e basilico con crostini

The simple preparation of this dish makes an elegant meal that is perfect for family and company alike. Select fresh whitefish such as halibut, grouper, snapper, or sea bass. The fresh herbs, tomatoes, potatoes, and onions may be sautéed in an ovenproof casserole in advance and set aside at room temperature. As the family gathers for dinner, lay the fish fillets on top of the vegetables and bake in the short time it will take to set the table and open some wine.

5 tablespoons olive oil

1 small onion or 2 shallots, thinly sliced

5 fresh or canned whole plum tomatoes, peeled and diced

8 large fresh basil leaves, chopped

½ cup dry white wine

3 tablespoons water

2 cloves garlic, thinly sliced

Kosher salt and freshly ground black pepper

4 fish fillets about 1 inch thick (7 ounces each)

4 large red potatoes, unpeeled

4 to 8 slices day-old country-style bread

1 clove garlic, cut in half

1 tablespoon chopped fresh Italian, flat leafed parsley

1. Preheat the oven to 375° F.

2. In a large ovenproof sauté pan, heat 3 tablespoons of the olive oil over medium-low heat. Add the onion and cook, stirring, until softened and translucent, about 6 minutes. Add the tomatoes, basil, wine, water, and the 2 sliced garlic cloves. Season with salt and pepper and stir to combine. Add the fish, and spoon some of the tomato mixture on top. Cover and place in the oven. Bake for 10 to 15 minutes for thin fillets (snapper or sea

bass) and 20 to 25 minutes for thicker fillets (halibut or cod). The fish is done when it is firm and flakes away when tested with a fork.

3. Meanwhile, bring a large saucepan filled with salted water to a boil. Add the potatoes and cook until tender when pierced with a fork, 15 to 20 minutes. Cut each potato into ½-inch-thick slices. Set aside and keep warm.

4. During the last 5 minutes of cooking time for the fish, toast the bread slices until lightly browned. Rub each slice with the garlic clove, then brush each slice with some of the remaining 2 tablespoons olive oil.

5. In the center of four deep plates or shallow soup bowls, arrange equal portions of the sliced potatoes. Top each portion with a fish fillet, and spoon some of the onion-and-tomato sauce over the fish. Garnish with the parsley and serve immediately with the toasted bread.

— SERVES 4 —

WINE PAIRING: Light white and light red

VARIATIONS: One teaspoon capers, rinsed and patted dry, and a dozen pitted niçoise olives or Calabrese olives may be added to the sauce as a garnish with the parsley. Polenta makes an excellent side dish in the place of the potatoes.

broiled bluefish

pesce azzurro alla griglia

As a kid, I found it exhausting to eat around the bones in fish. However, this recipe for bluefish was so tasty it was impossible to resist. In this recipe the bluefish is butterflied—meaning it is left whole, sliced in half lengthwise, and opened up flat on the baking or broiling pan. This way the fish cooks quite quickly and does not require turning to brown evenly. I serve pasta with sauce, such as Tomato Sauce with Mushrooms (page 129) or Spaghetti with Tomato and Tuna (page 150), before the bluefish. Sautéed mushrooms and a crisp salad make excellent side dishes for this main course.

One 3-pound bluefish, cleaned and scaled (fins, head, and tail removed), and butterflied

2 tablespoons freshly squeezed lemon juice

1 cup plain bread crumbs

3 cloves garlic, finely chopped

2 tablespoons finely chopped fresh Italian, flat leafed parsley

½ cup olive oil

1 lemon, cut into ¼-inch-thick slices

Lemon wedges for garnish (optional)

1. Preheat the oven to 350° F.

2. Line a broiling pan with aluminum foil. Place the fish on the foil and sprinkle with the lemon juice. In a small bowl, mix the bread crumbs, garlic, and parsley. Gradually add the olive oil, stirring with a fork, until the ingredients stick together. Evenly spread the bread crumb mixture over the fish. Arrange the lemon slices in a slightly overlapping line down the middle of the bluefish, on top of the bread crumb mixture. Bake until the fish flakes away from the bone, about 30 minutes.

3. Remove from the oven. Set the oven on broil and return the fish to the oven. Broil for about 2 minutes or until the bread crumbs are lightly toasted. Remove from the oven and serve immediately, garnished with lemon wedges if you like.

—SERVES 6—

WINE PAIRING: Light white and light red

VARIATION: Sea trout or sea bass is also luscious prepared this way.

grilled swordfish

pesce spada alla griglia

I think of fish as a summertime meal. I enjoy preparing this swordfish dish on my gas grill. It may also be cooked on a charcoal barbecue, or baked and then finished under the broiler. Serve it with grilled vegetables and a tomato salad.

¼ cup olive oil

6 tablespoons freshly squeezed lemon juice (from about 2 lemons)

Two 3¼-inch-thick swordfish steaks (about 2 pounds in all)

1 lemon, cut into quarters

Stir the olive oil and 3 tablespoons of the lemon juice in a glass baking dish. Add the swordfish and marinate for 10 minutes, turning the steaks over once. Place the fish on a lightly oiled cooking rack, or oil the rack of the grill. Grill the fish on one side to sear and warm through, about 5 minutes. Turn, and drizzle the remaining 3 tablespoons lemon juice on the swordfish. Grill until the fish is cooked through and easily breaks into sections, about 5 minutes more. Serve immediately, garnished with the lemon quarters.

—SERVES 4—

WINE PAIRING: Medium white and full white

sweet-and-sour swordfish

pesce spada in agrodolce

The type of capers used in this recipe makes a big difference in the flavor. Salt-packed capers are preferable. They have a sweet taste and will not overwhelm the sauce.

Six 1-inch-thick swordfish steaks (about 6 ounces each)

Kosher salt and freshly ground black pepper

½ cup plus ½ teaspoon all-purpose flour

¼ cup vegetable oil

2 teaspoons olive oil

1 cup dry white wine

½ cup balsamic vinegar

3 tablespoons salted capers, well rinsed, drained, and patted dry

1 tablespoon chopped fresh Italian, flat leafed parsley

1. Slice off and discard any dark skin along the edges of the swordfish steaks. Pat the steaks dry with paper towels, and season with salt and pepper. Dredge lightly in the ½ cup flour, shaking off any excess.

2. Heat the vegetable oil in a large nonstick pan over medium-high heat. When the oil is hot but not smoking, add the fish. Cook until browned, about 5 minutes, and then turn. Continue to cook until the fish is firm and browned, about another 5 minutes. Transfer the fish to a warm platter and set aside.

3. Discard any oil left in the pan and wipe it clean. Add the olive oil and warm over medium-high heat. Add the remaining ½ teaspoon flour and stir, allowing the flour to brown. Add the wine and vinegar and bring to a boil. Continue cooking, shaking the pan and stirring occasionally, until the sauce thickens into a light syrup, about 6 minutes. Stir in the capers and parsley. Remove from the heat. Arrange each swordfish steak on a plate, and spoon some sauce over each portion. Serve immediately.

— SERVES 4 —

WINE PAIRING: Medium white and full white

grilled salmon

salmone alla griglia

Ask your local fishmonger to butterfly the salmon, slicing it in half lengthwise so it can be opened up flat but stays in one piece. The salmon may also be baked in the oven and finished under the broiler. Serve with pesto, or with Spaghetti with Fresh Tomatoes (page 130) before the salmon. Grilled vegetables make a nice side dish.

One 3-pound salmon, cleaned and scaled
  (fins, head, and tail removed), and
  butterflied

¼ cup olive oil

2 tablespoons freshly squeezed lime juice
  (from about 1 lime)

Place the butterflied salmon on a large sheet of aluminum foil. Brush the salmon with the olive oil and drizzle with the lime juice. Place the fish, still on the foil, on the grill. Close the grill's cover. Cook until the fish develops a white coating and the inside of the thickest part of the salmon is firm and resembles tuna fish, about 25 minutes.

— SERVES 6 —

WINE PAIRING: Medium white and light red

VARIATION: Salmon steaks may also be prepared this way. They do not need to be placed in aluminum foil.

grilled tuna

tonno alla griglia

I think tuna is best served rare to medium-rare for maximum flavor. This is delicious served with grilled zucchini and portobello mushrooms.

Four 1-inch-thick tuna steaks (about 7
　　ounces each)

¼ cup olive oil

3 tablespoons freshly squeezed lime juice
　　(from about 2 limes)

1 tablespoon balsamic vinegar

Prepare a charcoal or gas grill. When the fire is ready, brush each tuna steak with the olive oil and lime juice. Grill the tuna for 5 minutes, turning once. Remove from the grill, sprinkle with the vinegar, and serve.

—SERVES 4—

WINE PAIRING: **Light red**

seared tuna with tomato bread salad

tonno alla piastra con insalata di pomodoro e pane

This is a wonderful dish to make in the summertime when the tomatoes are exceptionally flavorful and juicy. The fish does not need to be marinated for very long—just about the same amount of time as it will take to make the bread salad. This recipe calls for Gaeta or kalamata olives. Brine-cured Gaeta (as opposed to the wrinkly salt-cured ones) are very similar to kalamata, although they are generally smaller in size. You may choose whichever is most readily available at your local gourmet store or supermarket.

FOR THE TUNA:

3 tablespoons freshly squeezed lemon juice (from about 1 lemon)

1 sprig fresh thyme

2 sprigs fresh rosemary, broken in half

1 clove garlic, crushed

¼ cup plus 1 teaspoon olive oil

2 tablespoons sherry vinegar or mild white vinegar

Freshly ground black pepper

Four 1-inch-thick tuna steaks (about 7 ounces each)

FOR THE TOMATO BREAD SALAD:

Three ½-inch-thick slices country bread, cut into ¼-inch cubes

2 cups ½-inch wedges ripe tomatoes (about 3 large tomatoes)

1 cup peeled, seeded, and cubed cucumbers

Kosher salt and freshly ground black pepper

2 tablespoons chopped fresh basil leaves

¼ teaspoon chopped fresh oregano leaves

2 tablespoons extra virgin olive oil

½ red onion, diced

2 tablespoons balsamic vinegar

12 Gaeta or kalamata olives, pitted

1. In a shallow dish large enough to hold all the tuna steaks in a single layer, mix the lemon juice, thyme, rosemary, garlic, ¼ cup of the olive oil, vinegar, and pepper to taste. Add the tuna and coat with the marinade on both sides. Marinate the tuna at room temperature for at least 30 minutes but no more than 2 hours.

recipe continued on next page

2. To make the salad, preheat the oven to 300° F. Place the bread cubes on a baking sheet and bake, stirring occasionally, until dry, about 8 minutes. Do not brown. Set aside.

3. In a large bowl, stir the tomato wedges, cucumbers, and salt and pepper to taste, basil, oregano, extra virgin olive oil, and onion. Set aside for 30 minutes.

4. Wipe a large cast-iron or nonstick skillet with the remaining 1 teaspoon olive oil and set over medium-high heat. When the skillet is hot, add the tuna and sear on both sides, about 1 minute per side for rare or 2 minutes per side for medium-rare.

5. Add the bread cubes, vinegar, and olives to the tomato salad. Toss, and serve immediately with the tuna.

— SERVES 4 —

WINE PAIRING: Light red and rosé

VARIATIONS: This recipe may be prepared with swordfish. The remaining half of the red onion may be cut into ½-inch-thick slices. Warm 2 tablespoons olive oil in a small skillet set over medium-high heat. Add the onion slices and cook, stirring frequently, until browned, about 8 minutes. Serve on top of the bread salad.

Here is an Asian inspired recipe for a marinade that is less traditionally Italian but is also very good with tuna or swordfish:

> ½ tablespoon chopped fresh ginger
> 2 cloves garlic, crushed or sliced
> 3 tablespoons teriyaki sauce
> 1 teaspoon coarsely ground black pepper
> 2 sprigs rosemary, broken in half
> 2 tablespoons canola oil
> Kosher salt to taste

Whisk all of the ingredients in a shallow dish. Add the tuna to coat with marinade on both sides. Cover and set aside to marinate at room temperature for at least 30 minutes but not more than 2 hours. Cook following the instructions for the basic tuna recipe.

tuna tiepido in the chianti cucina style

tonno tiepido alla chianti cucina

I like to serve pan-seared tuna on a bed of arugula. Here is my recipe, which is an homage to the *tonno tiepido* served at Chianti Cucina in Los Angeles.

1 tablespoon balsamic vinegar

1 tablespoon extra virgin olive oil

5 tablespoons olive oil

Kosher salt and freshly ground black pepper

2 bunches arugula, stemmed

Four 1-inch-thick tuna steaks (about 7 ounces each)

16 long shavings Parmesan cheese (about 3 ounces)

1. In a small bowl, whisk the vinegar, extra virgin olive oil, 3 tablespoons of the olive oil, and salt and pepper to taste. Pour this dressing over the arugula and toss to distribute evenly. Arrange the arugula on a serving platter and set aside.

2. Season the tuna steaks with salt and pepper. Heat the remaining 2 tablespoons olive oil in a large cast-iron or heavy-bottomed skillet set over medium-high heat. When the oil is hot but not smoking, add the tuna and cook to sear each side, about 1 minute per side.

3. Remove to a cutting board and cut the tuna on the bias into ½-inch-thick slices. Arrange the tuna slices on top of the arugula. Lay the Parmesan shavings on top, and serve immediately.

— SERVES 4 —

WINE PAIRING: Light red and rosé

shellfish and bean casserole

fagioli e pesce in casseruola

This recipe is tasty and economical—with inexpensive beans adding flavor and volume to the other more costly main ingredients, shrimp and squid. It may be served for lunch or as a light supper. Allow guests to help themselves from the casserole, placed in the center of the table along with a basket filled with toasted country bread that has been rubbed with garlic. It is also terrific served as an appetizer in shallow soup bowls with extra virgin olive oil drizzled on top, or tossed with cooked fettuccine as a pasta course.

3 tablespoons extra virgin olive oil

2 cloves garlic, thinly sliced

¼ teaspoon red pepper flakes or ½ jalapeño
　　pepper, seeded and diced

½ pound medium-size shrimp, shelled and
　　deveined

¾ pound cleaned baby squid, sliced ½ inch
　　thick

Kosher salt and freshly ground black pepper

2 tablespoons chopped fresh Italian, flat
　　leafed parsley

½ cup dry white wine

3 cups drained cooked white beans (such as
　　cannellini or navy)

½ cup bean-cooking liquid

2 cups peeled and diced fresh or canned
　　whole plum tomatoes (about 4 tomatoes)

½ cup chicken or vegetable broth

6 fresh basil leaves

1. Warm the olive oil in a flameproof casserole set over high heat. Stir in the garlic. When the garlic begins to color, stir in the red pepper flakes, shrimp, squid, salt and pepper to taste, and 1 tablespoon of the parsley. Cook, stirring occasionally, until the shrimp turns light pink, about 2 minutes. Add the wine and continue cooking until it evaporates, about 1 minute.

2. Stir in the beans along with the bean-cooking liquid. Add the tomatoes and broth, and season with salt. Bring the mixture to a boil and cook to slightly thicken the sauce, about 1 minute. Remove from the heat and stir in the remaining 1 tablespoon parsley and basil. Serve immediately.

— SERVES 4 —

WINE PAIRING: Medium white and sparkling

VARIATIONS:

- Canned beans that have been drained and rinsed may be used in place of cooked beans. Add ½ cup more broth to the recipe instead of the bean-cooking liquid, and proceed with the recipe as written.
- ½ pound sea or bay scallops may be used in place of the shrimp. Quarter large scallops before cooking.
- ¾ pound red snapper or striped bass fillet may be used in place of the squid. Cut into four chunks before cooking.

mussels with white wine

cozze in bianco

The first time my mother made this dish was on a visit to Cape Cod with my father, her sister Grace, and her sister's husband, Tony. They went to a protected cove on the ocean side of the Cape. "As the tide went out, thousands of mussels appeared," my mother recalls, "clinging to the rocks in the shallow water. We gathered up a bucketful of the shiny black mollusks, scrubbed them clean, and steamed them in a delicate wine sauce with delicious results."

Cockles can be substituted for mussels in this dish, which I recommend as a main course at lunch or as an appetizer before a special meal. Be sure to have focaccia or crusty bread on hand to soak up the sauce. This dish may also be served over cooked linguine.

¼ cup olive oil

2 cloves garlic, chopped

½ cup dry white wine

2 pounds mussels, scrubbed and debearded

2 tablespoons chopped fresh Italian, flat leafed parsley.

Warm the olive oil and garlic in a large pot set over medium heat. When the oil is warm but not smoking and the garlic is still pale, not browned, add the wine and mussels. Cover and cook until the mussels open, about 5 minutes. Stir once or twice during the cooking time, bringing the mussels on the bottom of the pan up to the top. Add the parsley halfway through the cooking time. Spoon the cooked mussels into four soup bowls, discarding any unopened ones. Distribute the sauce among the bowls and serve immediately.

— SERVES 4 —

WINE PAIRING: Light white and medium white

VARIATIONS: My mother's sister Grace cooks mussels in beer. In a large saucepan, combine 1 tablespoon olive oil, 2 cloves garlic, chopped, 4 sprigs fresh parsley, and 1 can beer. Add the cleaned 2 pounds of mussels and toss. Cover the pot and bring to a boil. Simmer until the mussels open, about 5 minutes. Discard any unopened mussels and serve immediately as a first course.

Mussels cooked in marinara are excellent served over linguine. Follow Grace's recipe above, substituting 1 cup Sailor's-Style Sauce (page 120) for the beer.

recipe pictured on page 298

desserts

dolci

As we were growing up, our meals traditionally ended with a dish of seasonal fresh fruits, dried figs, and nuts in their shells. This type of dessert is as good for conversation as it is for digestion. I believe dessert exists so we might stave off the inevitable postprandial depression. A rush of sugar will do this, at least for a time. It is also the one part of the meal, as we showed in *Big Night,* that has no real time constraints.

And no holiday meal is complete without dessert. Similar to the American tradition of fruitcake at Christmastime, Italians have *panettone.* Classic panettone is made with raisins and candied fruit, although it may also be baked with chocolate or cream inside. Fresh panettone is served with a bottle of spumante, a sweeter, less expensive version of champagne. And leftover panettone is eaten over the next few mornings with *caffè latte.*

The *dolci* that follow present the perfect way to end a meal, the most relaxing part of a fine repast.

tropiano biscotti with anisette flavoring

biscotti tropiano

This is my grandmother's recipe for biscotti—she taught my mother how to bake them and my mother taught me. They are wonderful with coffee or dipped in red wine.

2½ cups all-purpose flour

2 teaspoons baking power

¼ teaspoon kosher salt

2 tablespoons anise seeds

4 large eggs

1 cup sugar

¼ cup (½ stick) butter, melted and cooled

3 tablespoons pure anise extract or anisette
  liqueur

1. Preheat oven to 350° F. Grease and flour two baking sheets or line them with parchment paper, and set aside.

2. In a medium-size bowl, sift the flour, baking powder, and salt. Stir in the anise seeds. Set aside.

3. Place the eggs in a large bowl and beat with an electric mixer on high speed until foamy. Add the sugar and beat until smooth, about 1 minute. Beat in the melted butter and anise extract. Reduce the speed to low and beat in the dry ingredients just until incorporated.

4. With a rubber spatula, scoop one quarter of the dough out onto one of the prepared baking sheets. Use the spatula to shape the dough into a log about 10 inches long by 2 inches wide by ¾ inch thick. Repeat this procedure with the other three quarters of the dough. Place two logs 2 inches apart on each prepared baking sheet.

5. Bake until the logs are light golden brown and firm to the touch, about 25 minutes. Remove from the oven and allow the logs to cool slightly on the baking sheets.

6. Reduce the oven temperature to 325° F.

7. Lift each log off the baking sheet and transfer to a cutting board. Use a serrated knife to cut each log on the bias at 1-inch intervals. Lay the cookies, cut side down, on the baking sheets.

8. Return the biscotti to the oven and bake until lightly browned and dry, about 5 minutes. Turn them over and continue baking to dry and lightly brown the other side, another 5 minutes. Transfer to a wire rack to cool completely. Store in an airtight container for up to 1 week or in the freezer for up to 1 month.

— MAKES ABOUT 36 COOKIES —

VARIATION: Almonds make a nice addition to these cookies—stir ½ cup coarsely chopped almonds into the batter along with the dry ingredients.

tuscan biscotti

cantucci toscani

Gianni created this variation on the classic Italian cookie. "I wanted to produce a cookie with a wonderful anise-nut flavor," says Gianni, "and with a less tooth-breaking bite than I usually found when I sampled biscotti at American bars and cafes."

As my mother suggests in her recipe for biscotti, these cookies are delicious served with red wine. Sauternes, Moscato, and Vin Santo are all very good dessert wines that pair well with biscotti—which are also very good to eat in the morning with coffee!

3¼ cups all-purpose flour	2 large egg yolks
2½ teaspoons baking powder	¼ cup honey
½ teaspoon kosher salt	½ teaspoon pure vanilla extract
½ cup (1 stick) butter, softened	¼ teaspoon pure almond extract
1¼ cups sugar	¼ teaspoon pure anise extract
2 large eggs	1 cup unblanched whole almonds

1. In a medium-size bowl, mix the flour, baking powder, and salt. Set aside.

2. In a large bowl, with an electric mixer on high speed, cream the butter and sugar until light and fluffy, about 5 minutes. Add the whole eggs and yolks, one at a time, beating after each addition. Beat in the honey. Add the extracts and mix well. Reduce the speed to low and gradually beat in the dry ingredients. Stir in the almonds, mixing until they are well dispersed.

3. Turn the dough out onto a sheet of plastic wrap. Form the dough into a ball and flatten it slightly. Wrap and refrigerate until firm, about 30 minutes.

4. Preheat the oven to 350° F. Grease two baking sheets or line them with parchment paper, and set aside.

5. Remove the dough from the plastic wrap and divide it in half. On a lightly floured work surface, roll half the dough into a baguette-shaped log about 2 inches wide by 13 inches long, and transfer it to one of the prepared baking sheets. Repeat with the other half of the dough, transferring it to the other prepared baking sheet. Bake until firm and golden, about 30 minutes. Remove from the oven and allow to cool for 15 minutes.

6. Reduce the oven temperature to 250° F.

7. Transfer the cooled logs to a cutting board. Using a serrated knife, slice each log on the bias at ½-inch intervals. Place the slices on the baking sheet, cut side down. Bake until dry and lightly browned, about 10 minutes on each side. Transfer the biscotti to a wire rack and allow to cool completely. Store in an airtight container for up to 1 week.

—MAKES ABOUT 36 COOKIES—

ponticello's orange cookies

biscotti casarecci del ponticello

This recipe was given to Gianni by the proprietor of a bakery in his hometown in Italy. The bakery, called Ponticello—which means "little bridge"—has been run by one family for four generations, with each generation passing this recipe on to the next. They were originally cooked in the bakery's coal oven, just as the embers were dying. Gianni recommends serving these cookies for a sweet at breakfast or with coffee after dinner, or using them in place of the ladyfingers in tiramisu.

4 cups all-purpose flour	*1 cup sugar*
2 tablespoons baking powder	*½ cup (1 stick) butter, softened*
Pinch of kosher salt	*1 teaspoon pure orange extract*
2 large eggs	*½ cup milk*

1. Preheat the oven to 350° F. Line several baking sheets with parchment paper and set aside.

2. In a medium-size bowl, whisk the flour, baking powder, and salt.

3. In a large bowl, beat the eggs and sugar with an electric mixer. Add the butter and beat just to combine. Gradually beat the flour mixture into the egg mixture. Pour the orange extract into the milk, and with the mixer running, gradually add the milk to the batter. The dough will come together to form a ball.

4. Turn the dough out onto a work surface. Flatten it into a disk shape and cut into quarters. Roll each quarter into a log about 1 inch in diameter. Cut each log into ½-inch-thick slices, and place them 1 inch apart on the prepared baking sheets. Bake until lightly golden brown, about 18 minutes. Remove to a rack to cool completely. Store in an airtight container for up to 2 weeks.

— MAKES ABOUT 48 COOKIES —

fried cookies

regina

Regina means "queen" in Italian, and these cookies are crownlike in shape—thus the name. People used to ask my grandmother to prepare them for special occasions, such as weddings and christenings, and she was always happy to oblige. Now my mother makes them for her friends and family. She always laughs, recalling the first time she made them: "I cooked my first batch of these cookies as a young married woman to bring to a gathering at Stan's family's house, hoping to impress them," Joan says. "I watched with anticipation as the cookies were tasted and was surprised when no one said anything. When I sampled one myself, I realized why. I must have substituted salt for the sugar—the cookies tasted awful."

3 large eggs, at room temperature

¼ cup granulated sugar

4½ teaspoons solid vegetable shortening, melted

3 tablespoons milk

1 tablespoon whiskey

½ teaspoon kosher salt

3½ cups all-purpose flour

4 cups corn oil for frying

1 cup confectioners' sugar

1. In a large bowl, beat the eggs with an electric mixer until foamy. Add the granulated sugar and blend thoroughly. Beat in the melted shortening, milk, whiskey, and salt. Gradually add 2½ cups of the flour, ½ cup at a time, beating to form a firm dough. Turn the dough out onto a floured work surface. Knead, adding more flour, ¼ cup at a time, until the dough is no longer sticky. Tear the center of the dough by breaking it in half. The center should be almost as dry as the surface of the dough. If it is still sticky, add more flour and continue to knead. Set the dough aside to rest under a dish towel for 5 minutes.

recipe continued on next page

2. Cut off one third of the dough, leaving the rest under the dish towel. On a lightly floured work surface, roll the dough out into a large, evenly thin circle (the dough should be paper thin). Use a pastry wheel to cut the dough into long strips about ¾ inch wide. Separate three of the strips. Pinch the strips together at one end and then loosely braid them. Pinch the ends of the braided strips together. Pinch the top and bottom of the braid together to form a crown. Set it aside on a clean dish towel and continue to braid the remaining dough strips. Any scraps may be reserved and fried along with the crowns.

3. When the first third of the dough is finished, repeat the procedure with the remaining dough, one third at a time, braiding it into crowns.

4. Pour the corn oil into a small frying pan to a depth of 1 inch. (Reserve any remaining oil to add to the pan as needed. If you add oil to the pan, be sure to let it reheat before adding any dough.) Warm the oil over medium heat until it is hot but not smoking. Add one small scrap of rolled dough to the oil. If the oil bubbles and the dough rises to the surface, the oil is hot enough for cooking.

5. Line two baking sheets with paper towel. Set aside. Place ¼ cup of the confectioners' sugar in a fine-mesh sieve and set aside.

6. Add two braided crowns to the pan. Use a fork to lightly fluff each cookie so the braids open slightly as they begin to cook. Fry the cookies until lightly browned on both sides, bout 3 minutes. Remove from the oil to one of the paper-towel-lined baking sheets. Drain and transfer to the other paper-towel-lined baking sheet. Repeat with the remaining crowns, adding more oil to the pan as needed.

7. Shake the sieve with the confectioners' sugar over the warm cookies to lightly dust them, adding more confectioners' sugar to the sieve as necessary. When they have cooled, transfer the cookies to a serving dish. The cookies may be dusted with additional confectioners' sugar just before serving.

— MAKES ABOUT 12 COOKIES —

mamma's little fritters

castagnole o frittole della mamma bertilla

As we were preparing this cookbook, Gianni thought to include this recipe, which brings back great memories of the sights, flavors, and excitement of the festivals that are held in Italy, as in many other countries, before Lent. "My mother prepared these fritters for us only during that time of the year," says Gianni, explaining: "*Castagnole* are fried in batches and are similar to a doughnut without the hole." Note: They cook best in a cast-iron pan.

1¼ cups all-purpose flour

2 teaspoons cornstarch or potato starch

½ teaspoon baking soda

¼ teaspoon kosher salt

¼ cup raisins (optional)

1 tablespoon rum or grappa

¼ cup (½ stick) butter, softened

3 tablespoons plus 2 teaspoons granulated sugar

1 large egg

2 teaspoons lemon zest

¼ cup plus 1 tablespoon milk

½ teaspoon pure vanilla extract

Corn or canola oil for frying

Confectioners' sugar for dusting

1. Sift the flour, cornstarch, baking soda, and salt in a large bowl. Set aside. (If you are using the raisins, soak them in the rum for 5 minutes.)

2. In a small bowl, cream the butter and sugar until light and fluffy. Add the egg and beat until combined. Add the lemon zest, milk, vanilla, and rum. (Stir in the raisins if using.) Add to the dry ingredients and mix well to create a batter that is slightly thicker than pancake batter and can be pushed off the spoon with your finger. If it is too thin, stir in a small amount of additional sifted flour. Set aside.

3. Line a large plate with paper towels and set aside.

4. Fill a medium-size sauté pan with corn oil to a depth of 1 inch. Heat until almost smoking (about 425° F). Scoop out a generous tablespoon of batter and add it to the oil. It should bubble and float in the oil. Slowly add more batter, a generous tablespoon at a time. Cook in small batches, turning in the oil, until the castagnole are dark brown and cooked through, about 3 minutes. Remove from the oil with a slotted spoon, and drain on the paper-towel-lined plate. Allow to cool slightly, then transfer to a serving dish. Place the confectioners' sugar in a fine-mesh sieve and shake over the castagnole to lightly dust. Serve immediately.

— MAKES 6 TO 8 FRITTERS —

cream-filled cannoli

crema cannoli

This recipe for cream-filled cannoli, a classic Italian dessert, comes from my father's sister Dora and was handed down to my mother. "Dora prepares them during the Christmas holidays," says Joan, "making the cream several hours ahead of time and filling the cannoli shells just before serving. She prefers to use small shells, which may be purchased at Italian bakeries and gourmet shops. The cinnamon flavoring may be purchased at bakeries, supermarkets, or specialty food shops."

3 pounds ricotta cheese
½ pound confectioners' sugar, plus more for
  dusting
2 drops liquid cinnamon flavoring
⅛ teaspoon pure vanilla extract
48 small cannoli shells

Place the ricotta, sugar, cinnamon flavoring, and vanilla in a large bowl and stir to combine thoroughly. Cover and store in the refrigerator until ready to fill the shells, up to one day. Stir briskly, then using a small spoon, fill each shell with the cream. Arrange on a serving platter. Place some confectioners' sugar in a fine-mesh sieve and shake over the filled shells to lightly dust. Serve immediately.

—MAKES 48 CANNOLI—

italian cream

crema pasticcera

My father's family prepared cream puffs for dessert during the Christmas and Easter holidays or when special company was invited for dinner. Over the years they used different recipes for cream puffs from a variety of cookbooks, but the recipe for the cream filling always remained the same. The filling may be prepared two days in advance. Cover and refrigerate. Return to room temperature and stir briskly before filling the cream puffs. The filling may also be frozen for up to three months.

4 large eggs, lightly beaten

1½ cups granulated sugar

1½ cups cake flour (not self-rising)

4 cups milk

2 tablespoons finely grated lemon zest (from about 3 lemons)

1 teaspoon pure vanilla extract

1 cup (2 sticks) unsalted butter, softened

48 small or 28 large cream puffs

Confectioners' sugar for dusting

1. Place the eggs, granulated sugar, cake flour, milk, lemon zest, and vanilla in a large saucepan and beat with an electric mixer until smooth. Place the saucepan over low heat and cook, stirring, until thickened, about 5 minutes. Remove from the heat and set aside to cool slightly.

2. Stir the butter into the cream until it has melted completely.

3. Cut a ¾-inch-thick slice off the top of each cream puff and set aside. Remove any soft dough from inside the puff and discard. Generously fill each puff, capping it with the reserved top. Arrange on a serving platter. Place a few tablespoons of confectioners' sugar in a fine-mesh sieve. Shake over the filled cream puffs to dust lightly, and serve.

—MAKES ENOUGH FILLING FOR—

48 SMALL OR 28 LARGE CREAM PUFFS

plum and polenta cake
dolce di prugne e polenta

This is a family favorite, created by Gianni's aunt Angela. It's a great cake to make when summer fruit is abundant. It is delicious when made with the plums called for in this recipe, but you may also want to consider using figs—one of my favorite fruits—or pitted sweet cherries. You can substitute about 6 quartered figs or ½ cup of cherries in place of the plums.

½ cup plus 2 tablespoons finely ground
    cornmeal or semolina flour

1 cup all-purpose flour

1½ teaspoons baking powder

Pinch of kosher salt

13 tablespoons butter, softened

¾ cup granulated sugar

4 large egg yolks

2 large eggs

1 teaspoon grated lemon zest

1 teaspoon pure vanilla extract

4 plums, cut in half and pitted

2 tablespoons packed light brown sugar

1. Preheat the oven to 350° F. Grease and lightly flour an 8 x 2-inch round cake pan or an 8-inch springform pan, tapping out any excess flour. Set aside.

2. In a small bowl, toss the cornmeal, all-purpose flour, baking powder, and salt. Set aside.

3. In a large bowl, beat the butter and granulated sugar together with an electric mixer, until pale yellow and creamy, about 5 minutes. Scrape down the sides of the bowl with a rubber spatula and add the egg yolks, one at a time, beating after each addition. Scrape down the sides of the bowl and add the whole eggs, one at a time, beating after each addition. Mix in the lemon zest and vanilla. Add the dry ingredients and blend until just combined.

4. Spread the batter in the prepared pan. Place the plum halves, skin side down, at even intervals on top of the batter. Sprinkle the brown sugar on top of the fruit and batter. Bake until the cake is golden brown on top and a toothpick inserted in the center comes out clean, about 45 minutes.

— SERVES 6 —

traditional flaky cake
with mascarpone sauce

torta sabbiosa con salsa al mascarpone

This is a rather old-fashioned cake—one from Gianni's childhood—but its delicate texture and great flavor stand the test of time. Potato starch is one reason this cake is very flaky and light-tasting. It is available in health food stores and in some supermarkets. The cake may be stored in an airtight container for up to three days.

FOR THE CAKE:

14 tablespoons (1¾ sticks) butter, softened

¾ cup plus 2 tablespoons granulated sugar

1 teaspoon pure vanilla extract

1½ cups potato starch

½ teaspoon kosher salt

3 large eggs

1 tablespoon baking powder

1 tablespoon cognac or dark rum (such as Myers's)

FOR THE MASCARPONE SAUCE:

8 ounces mascarpone cheese, at room temperature

2 tablespoons confectioners' sugar

1 tablespoon Grand Marnier, brandy, or grappa

1. Preheat the oven to 300° F. Grease the bottom and sides of a loaf pan with butter or cooking spray. Line the bottom and sides of the pan with parchment paper. Lightly grease the parchment paper with butter or cooking spray, and set aside.

2. In a large bowl, with an electric mixer, cream the butter with the granulated sugar and vanilla until very creamy, about 5 minutes. Mix in the potato starch and salt. Add the eggs, one at a time, beating after each addition. In a small bowl, whisk the baking powder and cognac. Beat this mixture into the cake batter.

recipe continued on next page

3. Pour the batter into the prepared loaf pan. Bake until it is lightly browned and a cake tester comes out clean, about 1 hour. (Do not open the oven during the first 40 minutes of baking or the cake may fall.) Remove the cake from the oven and allow it to cool in the pan. When it has cooled gently remove it from the pan and peel away the parchment paper.

4. When ready to serve, place the mascarpone cheese, confectioners' sugar, and Grand Marnier in a small bowl and whisk together. Cut the cake into 1-inch-thick slices and top with a dollop of mascarpone sauce.

— SERVES 8 TO 10 —

VARIATIONS: Whipped cream or zabaglione (see Poached Pears in Red Wine with Muscat Zabaglione, page 346) may be served in place of the mascarpone sauce. This cake also goes well with assorted fresh summer berries.

crumbly cake
torta fregolotta

Fregolotta, or crumbly cake, is typically served in the autumn during the first pressing of the grapes. The cake is placed in the center of the table and each person is poured a glass of *novella*, or new wine, which is comparable to the French Beaujolais nouveau. Small pieces of the cake are broken off and neatly dipped into the wine before eating. You may serve this dessert with any sweet wine or with a steaming cup of espresso. The batter for this cake is very dry and loose. It may look strange, but don't worry—it will come together in the heat of the oven and turn out just fine.

½ cup plus 2 tablespoons finely ground
  blanched almonds

½ cup finely ground cornmeal

½ cup plus 2 tablespoons sugar

2 cups plus 2 tablespoons cake flour

2 large egg yolks

1 teaspoon pure vanilla extract

1 teaspoon grated lemon zest

1 teaspoon grated orange zest

10 tablespoons (1¼ sticks) butter, softened

1. Preheat the oven to 375° F. Grease a 9 x 15-inch baking sheet and set aside.

2. In a large bowl, toss together the almonds, cornmeal, sugar, and cake flour. Make a well in the center of these dry ingredients and add the egg yolks, vanilla, and lemon and orange zests. Use a fork to incorporate the wet ingredients into the dry ingredients. With your hands, rub the butter into the dry mixture to form a crumbly dough.

3. Shake the dough out onto the prepared baking sheet, spreading to distribute it evenly. Pat it down. Bake until golden brown and firm, about 25 minutes. Allow to cool, and serve. Or break into small pieces and store in an airtight container for up to 1 week.

—SERVES 8—

warm individual chocolate soufflé

tortine di cioccolato caldo

These individual chocolate soufflés, or tortes, were a favorite among the patrons of Le Madri, the restaurant where I cooked with Gianni while researching *Big Night*. He devised this recipe so the soufflés could be prepared in advance and frozen. Just pop the frozen soufflés into the oven twenty minutes before serving.

It is important that the chocolate used to prepare these soufflés contain a high percentage of cocoa butter—at least 52 percent. Bittersweet chocolate produced by Lindt, Valrhona, Callebaut, or Ghirardelli, all widely available in grocery stores, is recommended.

10 ounces bittersweet chocolate

1½ cups (3 sticks) butter

7 large eggs, separated

1 teaspoon pure vanilla extract

1 teaspoon all-purpose flour

3 tablespoons sugar

1. Grease 8 individual disposable aluminum tart pans (about 4 inches in diameter, 1⅜ inches deep, capable of holding 1 cup of liquid) with canola oil. Set aside.

2. Fill the bottom of a double boiler with water to a depth just below but not touching the bottom of the insert. Bring the water to a boil over medium-high heat. Place the chocolate in the top of the double broiler and fit the top into the bottom of the pot. Melt the chocolate, stirring frequently. Add the butter, stirring it into the chocolate as it melts. Remove from the heat and transfer to a large bowl. Allow to cool almost to room temperature, about 15 minutes.

3. Preheat the oven to 400° F.

4. Whisk the egg yolks, one at a time, into the chocolate mixture. Whisk in the vanilla, then the flour. Set aside.

5. In a large bowl, beat the egg whites with an electric mixer on high speed until stiff peaks form. With the mixer set on low, gradually blend in the sugar, 1 tablespoon at a time.

6. Use a rubber spatula to fold half of the egg white mixture into the chocolate mixture. When they are fully incorporated, fold in the remaining egg whites.

7. Divide the batter evenly among the prepared aluminum pans, filling each one to within ¼ inch of the top. Bake immediately, until a slight crack appears in the top of each soufflé, 10 to 12 minutes.

8. After a small crack has appeared on top, remove one soufflé from the oven. Gently run a thin, sharp knife around the edge of the soufflé. Turn the soufflé upside down over a plate. A fully cooked soufflé will come out easily. If it does not come out easily, return the pans to the oven and let them bake for an additional 2 minutes. Allow the soufflés to rest for 1 minute before serving.

— MAKES 8 SOUFFLÉS —

VARIATIONS: Greasing the tart pans with walnut oil (or any nut oil of your choice) before baking or freezing will subtly change the flavor of the soufflés. Chocolate soufflés are delicious served alone, accompanied by a dollop of whipped cream or a small portion of raspberry or strawberry sorbet. In summer, decorate each plate with a few fresh berries and a sprig of mint.

NOTE: To freeze the soufflés for baking at a later time, place the unbaked soufflé-filled tart pans on a baking sheet. Freeze until firm, about 1 hour. Cover the firm soufflés in plastic wrap and transfer to an airtight container and store in the freezer for up to 1 month. When ready to bake, preheat the oven to 350°F. Bake until a slight crack appears in the top of each soufflé, 20 to 25 minutes, and unmold as described above.

livia's tiramisu
tiramisu della livia

Gianni's sister Livia perfected this recipe for tiramisu. "I prefer my sister Livia's tiramisu to all others I've tried," claims Gianni. "Having tasted her share of tiramisu at the homes of friends and relatives, Livia took the elements that she liked best about each recipe (not too sweet, not too heavy, etc.) and incorporated them into a recipe of her own." Her secret? A well-beaten egg-and-sugar mixture to minimize the "eggy" flavor.

It is best to make this dish the day before serving so that the tiramisu has ample time to set. It also freezes well. You can extend the recipe to provide more servings by folding whipped cream into the mascarpone along with the egg whites. The width and length of ladyfinger cookies can vary from brand to brand, though generally a 7-ounce package will fill the rectangular dish recommended here.

4 large eggs, separated

½ cup sugar

1 pound mascarpone cheese

1 cup crushed amaretti cookies (optional)

2 cups brewed espresso coffee

1 tablespoon dark rum (such as Myers's), Grand Marnier, or Cointreau

One 7-ounce package ladyfinger cookies

2 tablespoons unsweetened cocoa powder

1. In a medium-size bowl, beat the egg yolks with 6 tablespoons of the sugar until foamy and pale. Beat in the mascarpone until smooth. Set aside.

2. In a large bowl, whip the egg whites with an electric mixer. When they are frothy, add the remaining 2 tablespoons of sugar. Continue beating until they hold stiff peaks. Fold the egg whites into the mascarpone mixture, then fold in the crushed amaretti cookies, if using. Set aside.

3. Mix the espresso with the rum in a shallow bowl. Soak each ladyfinger, one at a time, in this mixture until it has softened slightly and absorbed some of the liquid. (The cook-

ies should not be mushy, but your fingers should be able to make a light indentation in them.) Arrange the cookies in an 11 x 7 x 2-inch baking dish to form a tightly packed single layer. Use pieces of broken cookies to fill in any gaps. (If the cookies seem dry, a small amount of the coffee mixture may be spooned on top.)

4. Spread the mascarpone cream mixture evenly over the cookies. Shake the cocoa through a fine-mesh sieve to evenly coat the top. Refrigerate to set for at least 2 hours before serving.

— SERVES 10 TO 12 —

VARIATIONS: Instant or decaffeinated espresso may be used in place of brewed coffee.

And Ponticello's Orange Cookies (page 328) may be substituted for the ladyfingers.

poached pears in red wine
with muscat zabaglione

pere al vino rosso con zabaglione al moscato

Few children I know grow up routinely eating such delicacies as poached pears for dessert. But for Gianni's aunt Angela, making this warm, colorful dish was just the trick to keep him and his siblings occupied, especially on dark winter evenings while their parents were working at the family trattoria. "Aunt Angela would poach pears or apples on the wood-burning stove," recalls Gianni. "Some nights, for a special treat, she would whip up a *zabaglione* because she knew we loved this sweet sauce almost more than the fruit."

These pears may be poached one day in advance. Cool, cover, and refrigerate in their poaching liquid. Return the pears to room temperature and reduce the sauce just before serving. I find using a vegetable peeler the easiest way to peel the pears and avoid gouging into the flesh of the fruit.

FOR THE PEARS:

4 firm ripe Bosc pears, peeled, stems left
*   intact*

¾ cup sugar

3 cups fruity red wine, such as Beaujolais,
*   Merlot, or Dolcetto d'Alba*

2 cloves

One 2-inch cinnamon stick

1 tablespoon loosely packed long thin strips
*   lemon zest (from about ½ lemon)*

FOR THE ZABAGLIONE:

2 large egg yolks

2 tablespoons plus 1 teaspoon sugar

¼ cup muscat wine or other sparkling wine

2 tablespoons Marsala wine

1. Trim the base of the pears so they will stand upright on a plate. Place the pears in a small saucepan; they should fit snugly. Sprinkle the sugar over the pears, then pour the wine over to cover (water may be added if necessary). Add the cloves, cinnamon stick,

and lemon zest. Bring to a boil over medium-high heat. Cover, and reduce the heat to a low simmer. Cook until the pears are still firm but tender when pierced with a knife, about 10 minutes. Remove from the heat and allow the pears to cool in the wine mixture.

2. Use a slotted spoon to transfer the pears to a plate and set aside, reserving the wine in the saucepan. Over high heat, boil the wine, reducing the liquid to a thick syrup measuring about ¾ cup, 6 to 8 minutes. Strain through a fine mesh sieve and set aside.

3. Fill the bottom of a double boiler with water to a depth just below but not touching the bottom of the insert. Bring the water to a boil over medium-high heat. In the top of the double boiler, whisk the egg yolks, sugar, muscat, and Marsala. Reduce the heat to medium to simmer the water. Fit the top of the double boiler into the bottom of the pot and cook the mixture, whisking constantly, until it thickens and becomes frothy and light, about 2 minutes. Remove from the heat immediately.

4. Distribute the zabaglione equally among four dessert plates or shallow bowls. Brush each pear with some of the syrup and place in the center of the zabaglione. Extra syrup may be drizzled on the rims of the plates or bowls. Serve immediately.

— S E R V E S   4 —

VARIATION: This zabaglione may be served as a dessert on its own, garnished with fresh berries, or topped with sweet chocolate shavings. Prepare the zabaglione sauce as described in the recipe. Remove from the heat and cool by placing the pan in a large bowl filled with ice water. With an electric mixer, whip 1 cup heavy cream until stiff peaks form. Fold the whipped cream into the chilled zabaglione. Pour into individual glasses or bowls and refrigerate for at least 1 hour before serving, or prepare one day in advance.

recipe pictured on page 322

simple ricotta cake
dolce di ricotta semplice

This cake is best made one day before you plan to serve it. The cake is very moist and tender, so be careful when removing it from the pan. If you like, it may be served with the sauce described in the recipe for Ricotta Cheese with Fresh Fruit (page 349), using either raspberries or strawberries for the sauce.

2 cups ricotta cheese

1½ tablespoons butter, softened

5 large eggs

3 tablespoons all-purpose flour

1¼ cups confectioners' sugar

2 tablespoons pure vanilla extract

1 tablespoon dark rum (such as Myers's)
  (optional)

2 cups heavy cream

½ teaspoon grated lemon or orange zest

1. If the ricotta cheese is very wet, place it in a fine-mesh sieve lined with cheesecloth. Place the sieve over a bowl, refrigerate, and drain the ricotta for 2 hours.

2. Preheat the oven to 325° F. Completely line an 8-inch springform pan with two overlapping layers of aluminum foil. Grease the foil with the softened butter and dust lightly with flour, set aside.

3. Place the eggs in a large bowl. With an electric mixer set on high speed, beat the eggs just to combine, about 10 seconds. Add the ricotta, flour, sugar, vanilla, and rum, if using, and beat just to combine. Reduce the mixer speed to low and gradually add the cream. Stir in the zest.

4. Pour the mixture into the prepared springform pan, and bake until the edges of the cake are firm and the top is golden brown, about 1 hour. (If the top begins to brown too quickly, cover the pan with aluminum foil and continue to bake.) Remove the pan from the oven, set it on a wire rack, and allow to cool for 3 to 4 hours. Remove the outer ring of the pan and cut away the foil. Cover and refrigerate the cake for at least 3 hours before serving.

— SERVES 8 —

ricotta cheese with fresh fruit

cremino di ricotta con frutta stagionale

This dessert is similar to ice cream and may be prepared without using a machine. It is delicious topped with fresh berries or sliced soft fruits such as peaches and nectarines.

3 pints fresh raspberries

1⅓ cups sugar

1 tablespoon freshly squeezed lemon juice

1 vanilla bean or 1 teaspoon pure vanilla
*   extract*

¾ cup milk

2½ cups ricotta cheese

1. Place the raspberries in a blender or food processor. Add ⅓ cup of the sugar and the lemon juice, and process until smooth. Pass the mixture through a fine-mesh sieve and discard the seeds. Set aside.

2. Soak the vanilla bean in the milk for 1 hour, or stir the extract into the milk. Place the ricotta in a medium-size bowl. Stir in the milk and remaining 1 cup sugar. Mix until the ingredients are fully combined and smooth. Divide equally among six serving plates. Top with the raspberry sauce and serve.

— SERVES 6 —

VARIATION: This dessert may also be topped with chocolate sauce, chopped nuts, or semisweet chocolate chips.

peaches and wine
pesche al vino

My mother likes to serve this simple and wonderful summer dessert in glass goblets with biscotti on the side. "Whenever I serve this dessert it reminds me of Compare Pullano, a neighbor and good friend of my father's," recalls Joan. "They had an ongoing competition over who could raise the best chickens or make the finest wine. They also loved to show off to each other with examples of their successful gardening, although neither of them would ever admit the success of the other.

"One afternoon Compare arrived with a beautiful peach from his garden. Although the peach was bigger than any my father had grown, he was only willing to admit that it was okay. They decided to have a glass of wine and share this peach. My father cut it into several slices and they soaked the slices in their wine for several minutes before eating them. It is an exceptional dessert."

8 medium-size ripe peaches, peeled and pitted

3 cups dry red wine

1 tablespoon plus 1 teaspoon sugar

Slice the peaches into bite-size wedges (you should have about 4 cups). Place in a large bowl and cover with the wine. Sprinkle the sugar on top and gently stir. Cover and leave at room temperature for 3 to 4 hours before serving.

— SERVES 4 —

acknowledgments

I would like to thank all those who helped in bringing this book to fruition for a second time. My indefatigable, creative, and devoted parents, Joan and Stan; the talented Gianni Scappin; and the diligent and patient Mimi Taft. They are the real authors here. I would also like to thank Francesco Tonelli and his team for the stunning photos, and the folks at Simon & Schuster—Trish Boczkowski, Jennifer Bergstrom, Louise Burke, Jennifer Robinson, Alexandra Lewis, Lisa Litwack, and Jaime Putorti—for producing and publishing a book that means so much to us with such care and attention. I am most grateful to Deborah Schneider of Gelfman Schneider for introducing us. In particular, I would like to thank the lovely and tenacious Felicity Blunt of Curtis Brown (my fiancée, so there is a bit of a bias), for leading the charge and putting the pieces and people together that allowed us to create a book that we could all be proud of.

index